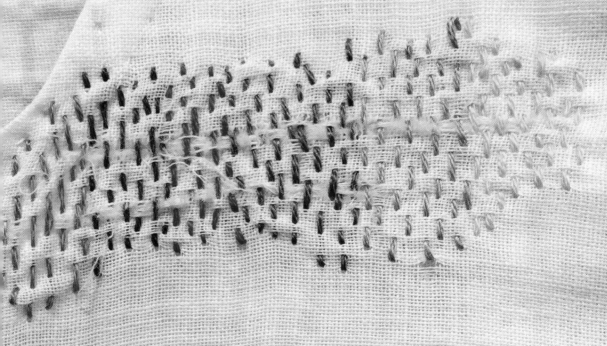

mend!

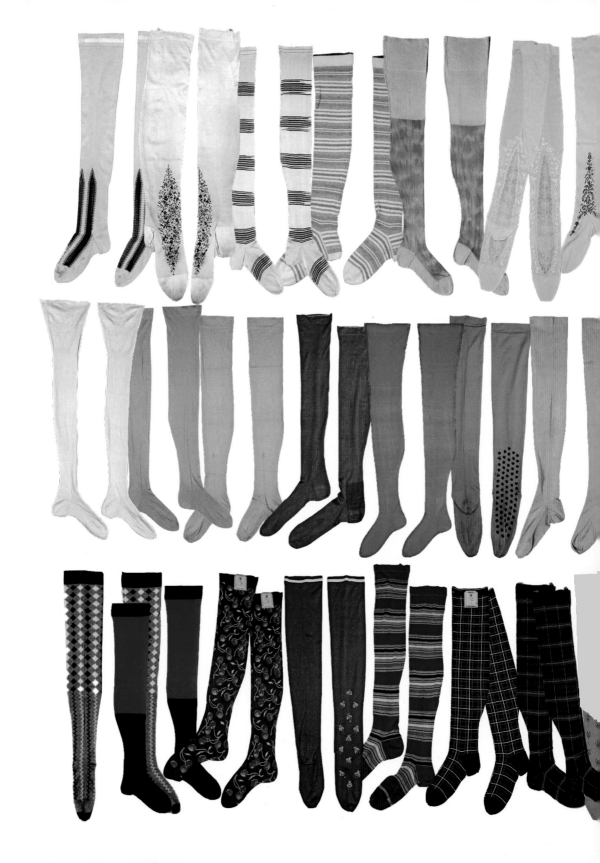

A Refashioning Manual and Manifesto

mend!

Kate Sekules

penguin books

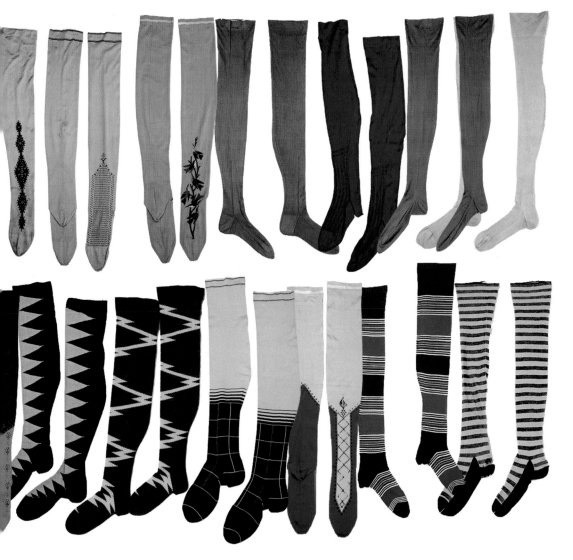

PENGUIN BOOKS
An imprint of Penguin Random House LLC
penguinrandomhouse.com

"Vogue's Eye View of the Menders" by Jessica Davies
from *Vogue*, March 15, 1953. Copyright © Condé Nast.
Used by permission of Condé Nast.

All photos by Kate Sekules unless otherwise noted.

Image credits appear on page 227

LIBRARY OF CONGRESS CATALOGING-IN-
PUBLICATION DATA
Names: Sekules, Kate, author.
Title: Mend! : a refashioning manual and manifesto /
Kate Sekules.
Description: New York : Penguin Books, 2020.
Identifiers: LCCN 2020024522 (print) | LCCN 2020024523
(ebook) | ISBN 9780143135005 (trade paperback) |
ISBN 9780525506669 (ebook)
Subjects: LCSH: Clothing and dress—Repairing. |
Clothing and dress—Remaking.
Classification: LCC TT550 .S45 2020 (print) | LCC TT550
(ebook) | DDC 646/.3—dc23
LC record available at https://lccn.loc.gov/2020024522
LC ebook record available at https://lccn.loc.gov/2020024523

Printed in Malaysia
2nd Printing

Set in Bau Pro, ITC Clearface and Adobe Garamond
Book design by Shubhani Sarkar, sarkardesignstudio.com

for bea

cont

introduction

ix

Chapter One
what
1

Chapter Two
why
5

Chaper Five
where
91

Chapter Six
how
121

ents

Chapter Three

when

19

Chapter Four

who

53

Chapter Seven

which

161

Postscript

whether

213

acknowledgments

218

notes

219

credits

227

introduction

Mending has baggage. Patched clothing speaks of shame and poverty and drudgery, even of slavery. But mending is a big word. It's about repairing more than clothes. History, for example, which must be unpicked and remade, healing systemic injustice, making reparations, exposing scars. Clothes historians do this via what we wear, which turns out to be more important than we realized. Visible menders do it literally, by stitching new stories onto the worn fabric of our lives. They're just clothes, but if enough people adopted more creative ways of sourcing, tending, and mending them, we'd fix much that's wrong with the world.

Take visible mending (VM) first. This is more than darning a hole. It's a protest movement and an art form and a fashion statement. To stitch or sport a VM is to declare independence from the sickness of consumer culture with a beautiful scar and a badge of honor: "Look! I kept this out of the landfill." Also, in-your-face embellishment is impossible to achieve without a smile—both while you're applying it and when you're wearing it. A colorful new layer applied to an old garment can be elegant and arty, or sassy and silly, but it's always got insouciance and effortless style. So, yes, mending isn't what it used to be. And stitching statements is only the outer layer of a deeper, more expressive relationship with style.

For me, it all started with vintage, or that's what we call it now. In the dark era of the 1970s, when as a preteen in London I discovered the nirvana of Portobello Market, vintage was just old clothes. Hippies had liked them,

and punks were about to adopt them, but the collecting of other (probably dead) people's castoffs was very much thought a bad idea, including by my mother, who was all tearful and "Oh, Kate, do you know where it's been, does it have fleas?" Nevertheless, I, starting at age twelve, religiously scoured the stalls under the Westway twice a week, collecting armfuls of Edwardian taffeta and Indian prints and 1960s ski pants and old tailcoats. Everything was 20p. Maybe a pound for a Mary Quant or some slightly mangy Victorian lace. Nowadays, of course, old clothes are mainstream—especially since the trade has been brought to scale in Silicon Valley—and provides a decent living (or side hustle) to untold thousands of clothes flippers. But secondhand always has been a major business. For a couple of centuries, it's been taking place in the shadows, a messy, unseemly gray market, unfolding, slightly shamefully, behind fashion. And for way more centuries before that, clothes were bank: liquid investments providing insurance for an uncertain future. The story of second-hand is huge, encompassing, as it does, all clothes that exist. And all clothes, sooner or later, need mending. Our relationship to them needs mending, too. To say these two things are linked is an understatement.

One of the most common terms for resold clothing is *pre-owned*. This is nonsense. All clothing is owned. A shirt belongs to someone until it changes hands, then it belongs to someone else. I feel, ideally, the changing of hands should happen in a more personal way than is currently usual, because clothes are personal. That's why I prefer them older, because then they have more stories under their belt, more charisma and substance. I see acquiring a garment not so much as a transaction, but more akin to pet adoption—and I adopt a *lot*. In 2009, wanting a more efficient way of rehoming part of my herd, I made a Petfinder for clothes called Refashioner—though it was much snobbier than that because only the best clothes were allowed in. At its height, a few thousand members were uploading their underworn couture, complete with obligatory story, stalking each other's closets, and selling—or swapping—merrily among themselves. Long story short, I learned I don't like business (it's fairly mutual), so Refashioner simply evolved into some epic collections of clothes, people, and stories, and now lives on as remnants in the underbelly of my website visiblemending.com.

It is encouraging that more and more people are noticing how the narratives we collect in our closets affect how we feel about—and in—our clothes. There are a few books about this, an academic strand that's often called wardrobe studies, and exhibitions on the subject. This wardrobe narrative is what visible mending builds on. Once you've taken the time and trouble to fix something, carefully pondering the design and utility of your overlay, you've bonded with it. This speaks to a general craving for the handmade and unusual that's growing in our Western culture. A similar syndrome happened a century and more ago as dissatisfaction with increasing industrialization gave rise to the Arts and Crafts movement and American Craftsman style. Perhaps we're experiencing the digital version of this, in which peak industrialization plus ultracommunication enables a nonhuman scale of mass production, and the creators and designers behind the product can't keep up. They get fed up. (Also laid off.) So do the consumers. As new factory-made clothes become more and more—oh, what's the word? *Boring*—increasing numbers of people are looking to the old stuff, just as fashion designers have done for decades, drawing inspiration from the archives. In today's sped-up mass market there's an industry term for the ubiquitous borrowing from vintage designs. It's called *shop and copy* because that's what they do: buy interesting pieces and recut them in cheap. Well, I don't want the poly-Lycra abomination churned out by fossil fuel and indentured slaves. I want the original. Sooner or later, the original goes holey. So, calling on my ancestral sewing skills—I'm the child of austerity-era make-do-and-mend, of domestic science lessons, of a dressmaking mother, and the grandchild of Viennese milliners (men) and whitework embroiderers (women)—I mend.

It is the most vicious of ironies that mending, because it takes time, is now the luxury. Throughout history mending has simply been a necessity, because, as I said, clothes were worth serious money. In fact, for most of recorded time, textiles were as valuable as gold, or more so. It's barely been a century since fabric has ceased to be inventoried in wills and tended by teams of servants, or preserved for generations by stitchery upon stitchery. Of course, only the rich could afford invisible mending and skilled remodeling of faded silk gowns or well-worn waistcoats; most folks were poor and quite ashamed of their overstitched and patched outfits. But ending a worn garment's life by discarding it, as we are now trained to do, doesn't vaporize it; it only displaces it. And the recent decluttering craze didn't help. (My *set point of stuff* theory states that decluttering must inevitably lead to recluttering until a comfortable possession level is recreated; see page 225, Chapter 5, endnote 4.) Simultaneously, we fetishize wornness in certain areas, especially jeans—a $56 billion industry that is among our most ecologically horrendous with its synthetic indigo dyes and chemical distressing processes. None of this makes sense.

Every swapping or (re)making session or community consignment store or clothes library collection redresses the madness we accept as normal. Every visible mend is a flag that points to it. These radical ways of getting dressed are intrinsically political. But, as everyone who tries them quickly discovers, they're also creative and interesting and more fun than sleepwalking the mall like zombies (though retail itself is the walking dead) or click-shopping in your pajamas. How we tend our textiles is as intimate and important as what we feed ourselves, and the industry that produces them—including all its tentacles (shipping, buildings, packaging, washing, etc.)—is even more damaging than food production, and may even prove to have as much planetary impact as fossil fuel. Renovating the way we dress is easier and cheaper than adopting an artisanal diet: buying less and better, vintage curation, and the practices of community wardrobe are within everyone's reach, not just elitist city dwellers. And mending! Mending is the missing link, the key to it all, especially *visible* mending, because of its sheer usefulness, high style quotient, and the way it casually flips the bird at the white cis male overlords of industry.

What those overlords don't want you to know is how much fun it is to mend, tend, and lend. But I want you to know. This book is a manual with a message. It will help you get better clothes for less. It will help you reclaim not only your broken garment but also your joy in getting dressed, and, by extension, your joy. It's a true style revolution. It's the future.

Chapter One

what

I did not invent visible mending—nobody did. For goodness' sake, it's been around forever. There's been so much mending, always, throughout history, it is bound to show occasionally. When fabrics were costly and clothes were handmade, we all preserved them for years, even generations; we had no choice. Until the nineteenth century fabrics were handwoven, too—that is, after seed was planted and grown (or flock tended), harvested, processed and spun, maybe all by the same person. The linen cloth (see page 2) came into my possession complete with handwritten provenance that tells how Marie Elizabeth Damier grew the flax in Tiège, near Baden, in the late eighteenth century and how Irene Marie Vedder, fresh off the boat on Ellis Island, sewed it in 1918. This still happens routinely in remote, poor, or destabilized regions, and many a back-to-the-land textile artisan these days is experimenting with the old ways by choice. *Farm to table* isn't only a food term.

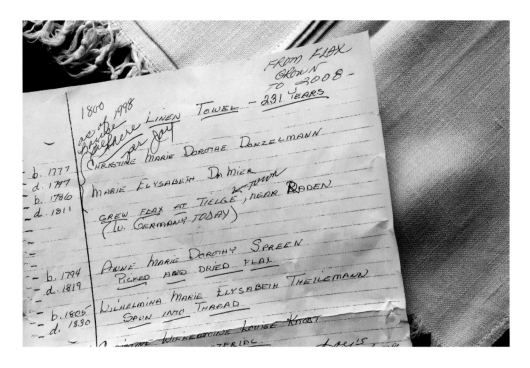

During the centuries when mending was not an aesthetic choice but a necessity, obvious repair was despised as a marker of poverty rather than valued and collected as artifact or fashion inspiration. These days, fashion is quite in love with imperfection and deconstruction and patching. It has loved them at least since the 1970s, which happens to be when most home mending faded away. From the abomination that is mass-distressed denim at the low end, to the likes of Alessandro Michele's embellished Gucci gear in *haute*, fashion likes the look, but it can only sell us brand-new perfect imperfection; it can never produce true mending. That is one of the best things about VM. Decorative repair is intensely personal and artisanal. It is done by hand, ideally by you, or at least someone you know. It is not outsourced to factories. And the skills are easy to acquire: visible mending is for everyone, including the nonvisual and the all-thumbs and the sewing novice. It's experimental stitchery, mending improv, fun with thread, arty and exuberant and colorful and silly. The only way to go wrong is to say, "I can't." It's a craft, but of a modern cast, more art than Etsy. There are infinite ways to execute a VM, and there will never be another one like yours. And though you will never sew two mends the same, you will evolve a style of your own—it's as inevitable as handwriting (if you can remember how to do that).

Generally, visible mending encompasses a rebellion against the fashion status quo, a refusal to dress correctly, and thus a refusal to further line the pockets of a few overrich, white male, conscience-free titans of industry.

Personally, I prefer VM militantly unpretty

Karen Nicol

and I often build in deliberate mess. If a mend ends up too professional, it simply looks shop-bought—and shop-bought usually means produced in titanic factories in China, or, worse, in semiregulated probably dangerous smaller ones in Myanmar or Djibouti (or wherever labor is currently even cheaper than in notorious Bangladesh). But there is no rule that a VM must be a statement or a mess. It truly is for everyone, and you will even find hearts and flowers in these pages. Also plenty of rainbows; no unicorns though. As the movement grows, there are menders of all stripes including stripes.

No matter how you do it, VM comes with myriad unsuspected side benefits. So, to sum up the "What" of visible mending, see the list on the right. *Mend*itation, which happens when you apply attention and mindfulness, or *mend*fulness, thus manipulating time, is my favorite, though the feeling of security that ensues when your elbow no longer protrudes from your old faithful sweater is not to be understated. I promise you will deeply understand and appreciate all ten by page 226.

Top 10 Reasons to Mend

Time	Sewing slows it
Earth	Every mend helps
Money	Costs little, is priceless
Fashion	Mending is truly trending
Respect	Honor the clothes makers
History	Domestic drudgery reborn
Security	The pleasant feeling of fixed
Uniqueness	Makes every garment special
Connection	Mending with friends is bonding
Mendfulness	Out of your mind, into your hands

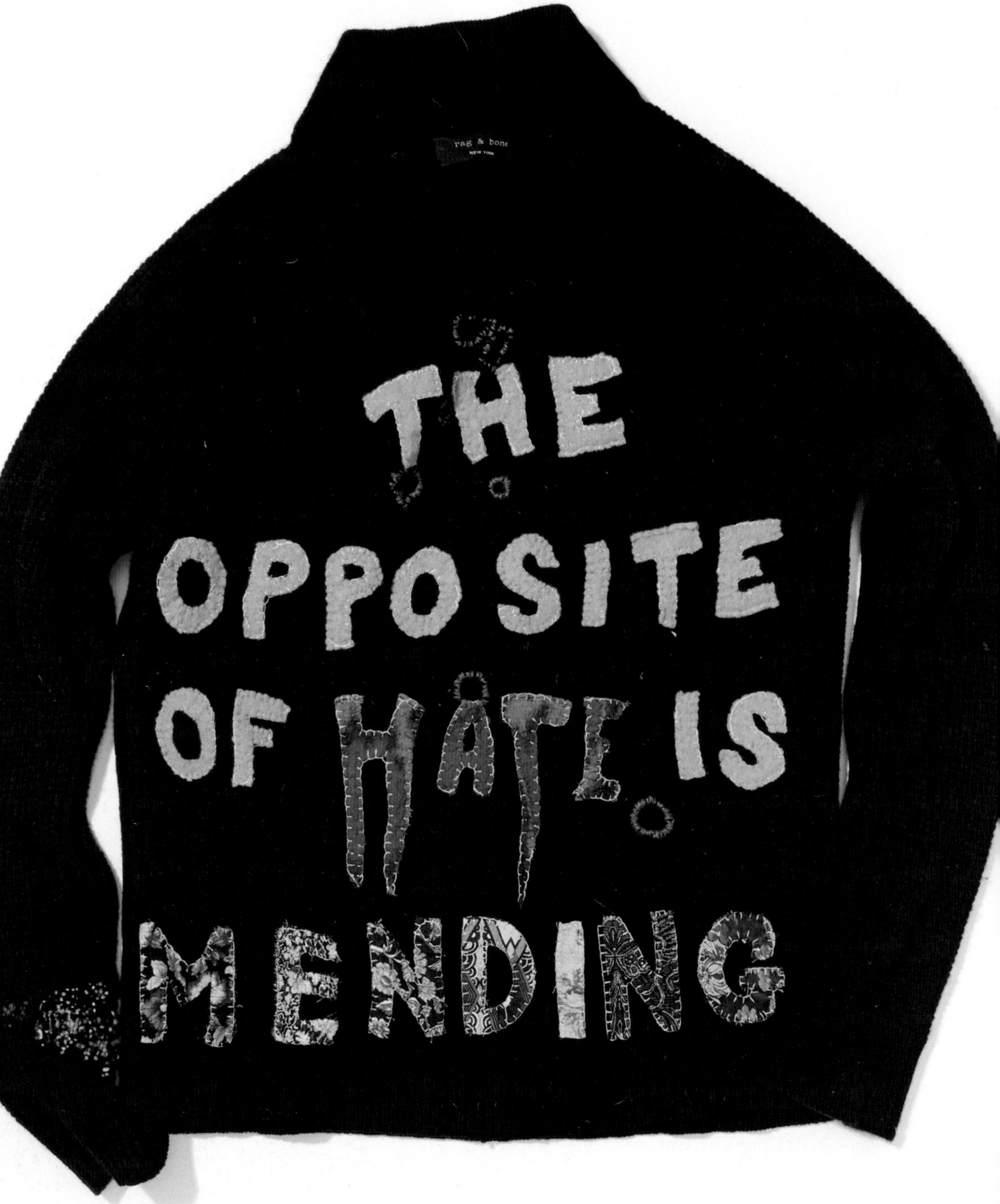
rag & bone
NEW YORK
THE
OPPOSITE
OF HATE IS
MENDING

Chapter Two

why

Clearly, visible mending isn't happening
in a vacuum. Those who practice it tend
to be evangelists for a world outside the
fashion-industrial complex, advocates of civil
disobedience, feminists, antiracists—in short,
humanists. If you lavish time and attention on
nonessential embellishment, adding extra layers
to a task that wouldn't occur to most people to
attempt in the first place, you are not doing it
just for eco-warrior cred—the more likely reason
than frugality when replacing the thing costs
less than breakfast—but as an opportunity. We
personalize, extend the story, flag the beloved
oldness, and render the item priceless—though
not literally, because well-VM-ed garments can
fetch a good resale price in my experience, and
many modern menders who take commissions
are quite unable to keep up with the demand.

You love clothes, or you wouldn't be reading, but do you know where yours came from? I don't mean Uniqlo or "stolen from my sister," but their fundamental origins and what it all means. Clothes can be complicated creatures. They are not inert, but become unique with wear, even from the first time we take them for a ride, and then they gain in individuality with each outing. Our collections become extensions of us ("That dress is so you!"), combining in their own special, comforting ways and routinely performing magic tricks. One of my favorite T-shirts, for example, a 1990s Loomstate with angel wings on the back (and an extensive greasytee mend—see page 190—on the front) has an identical twin that rarely leaves the shelf: it inexplicably leaves me cold. Many of us own a results dress or lucky

socks for sports, or a coat that's gorgeous on the hanger but ghastly when worn. Clothes "change our view of the world and the world's view of us," wrote Virginia Woolf. The "Why" of visible mending is all about that personal nature of clothes—oh, let's not mince words, the souls of clothes. And, while extending their lives, it also acknowledges their origins.

The first thing the organization Fashion Revolution did when it formed, after more than a thousand garment workers were crushed to death in the Rana Plaza factory collapse, was ask the simple question: "Who made my clothes?" As well as a handy slogan, this question is a deceptively profound thought experiment. In my two decades as a food and travel journalist I reported on the dawning and spread of consciousness about what we put in our stomachs. It was not so long ago that terms such as *farm to table*, *clean eating*, *locavore*, and *market driven* were coined and we could no longer automatically detach the product from its origin.

We need to do this with clothes. The term *fast fashion* was first used in print by *The New York Times* in December 1989,[1] evoking its food corollary to report on the new stores in town, including The Limited and Zara. I use the more sinister *Big Fashion*.[2] Though there is a burgeoning *slow fashion* movement, the US fashion revolution was a bit muted at first. Partly this is because (a) much "eco-fashion" produced in response to the issues of the industry is not tasty—it's really expensive and just not sexy, and (b) nobody likes to be scolded.

It's all too human to shy away from apparently insoluble problems. The Gordian knot of issues in the fashion system is simply too depressing. We glance at the horrifying story of some industry abuse—children employed by Nike,[3] microfiber ocean pollution—then look down at our performance fiber leggings and the swoosh on our new sneakers, feel a stab of guilt, and head to the gym. Who can afford to dress correctly? Where do you even get those clothes? How can you tell what's been made ethically? What difference does it make anyway? Just this little $12.99 sequined top.

Neither are you off the hook if you're a designer dresser, not once you've heard the industry's not-so-secret that most luxury-label clothes are produced in the exact same factories as their cheaper sisters, and those factories are trashing the planet about as much as your car is. It's all enough to make you run the other way—straight to your phone for some comfort shopping. Fashion isn't meant to make us feel guilty, confused, and angry. We need fashion to make us feel *good*.

A Disclaimer

I wrote this chapter in early 2019, when the fashion industry was already troubled. By November, one *State of Fashion* report opened with the words "Fashion leaders are not looking forward to 2020." They were, it said, in "a state of high nervousness and uncertainty."[4] Then the pandemic hit. Now (early April 2020) I'm trying to future-proof a chapter about what's wrong with fashion, when fashion may by now (your "now") have already expired.[5] It won't have been a peaceful death. There was a lot of talk in 2019 from those nervous fashion leaders about becoming more "sustainable"—but they didn't mean by the crash and burn method, where less is produced because few can afford it and fewer desire it, and therefore companies go under. Tragically, the kind of independent fashion leaders who truly do lead by design, creativity, and innovation are going to struggle even harder to survive, and the prognosis is . . . desperate. I'm hoping for miracles. Meanwhile, back in the fashion-industrial complex, nobody wanted to lose their ludicrous profits (detailed on page 15), but I'm guessing one of the better side effects of the pandemic will be that the entire world will begin functioning more like the global system it is, and that we can therefore regard this chapter as a snapshot of the dying days of late-stage capitalism and rampant overconsumption, and a warning to not go back there.

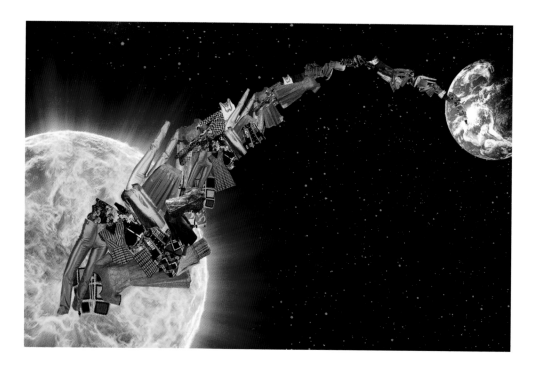

Do We Need Fashion?

Getting dressed is a thing every person on the planet does—and we aren't only doing it on the planet, we're doing it *to* the planet. It's not so much the megillions of clothes that already exist; the problem is the roughly fifty billion new garments made and sold each year. We don't need them. Well, we do. We need fashion. Kind of.

To examine our need for this sort of uber-clothing, let's utilize that famous chart of human motivation, Abraham Maslow's 1943 Hierarchy of Needs, a classification system expressed as a pyramid with society's most universal primary requirements at the base, and self-actualization at the top: the pinnacle of fulfillment we can only pursue once we've taken care of all other necessities. Where does fashion, traditionally deemed unnecessary, really belong on the pyramid?

At the base? Clearly, garments belong here to keep us warm and not arrested, but if we define fashion as clothing acquired for reasons other than protection, then that is not a fundamental need. Second tier? Wearing clothes that are apt for our circumstances can indeed be an aspect of personal safety, but it's hard to argue that anyone is put in peril by dressing ugly or unhip. But at the third level we are already in fashion territory. The pursuit of love definitely requires a level of dress beyond the basic (need I explain?). And, as tribal creatures, we signal our allegiances via careful adornment, whether blatantly with a uniform or more subtly with the latest Yeezys, a Chanel 2.55, or a pink pussy hat. By the time we reach *esteem*, well, we all need more than basic coverage to rise in the world, selecting looks to get noticed, get ahead, and get respect. Therefore fashion—or clothes we don't need but we really want—is not some peripheral luxury, surplus to requirements; it's merely one or two small necessities above the bare.

In other words, the solution to our overwhelming overconsumption is not to deprive ourselves of our fundamental desire for new clothes—that would be going against nature. We simply have to acquire at least some of them in other ways and from other places than we currently do. Let's look at what we currently do.

What's Wrong with Fashion

You already know apparel is among the most polluting[6] and exploitative of all industries, but what does that really mean? How can we visualize such an amorphous, overwhelming idea? Because I wanted to be able to do this for my own peace of mind, I crunched the numbers myself into concepts I could understand in a flash.[7] So here is an unpretentious, unsubtle, uncompromised rundown of the state of clothes production today.

Quantity . . .
If, instead of dumping it, we pegged all the textiles we discard out on a clothesline, after fifteen months at our current burn rate, that line would reach the sun.

Toxicity, Oceans . . .
The poisonous marine plastic waste derived from textiles that we dump every year weighs

the same as the Eiffel Tower, the Statue of Liberty, the London Eye, one hundred jumbo jets, one hundred London Routemaster buses, two large submarines, and a space shuttle combined—93.7 million pounds.

Rivers . . .
Hazardous chemicals are choking our rivers as major brands continue to source from manufacturers who dump vile, synthetic dyes into the water. See Greenpeace's *Detox My Fashion* campaign for many pictures of attractive but evil colors.

Water Consumption . . .
It takes thirty baths full of water to produce one T-shirt. In the US alone, we buy two billion T-shirts each year. That's 1.5 trillion gallons, or enough water to drown Manhattan.

Size

Here is the global fashion monolith expressed in terms of countries and continents

Money . . .
What the world spends on clothes every year is the same as the combined annual income of the entire continent of (Sub-Saharan) Africa, plus (Big Fashion hub) Myanmar, $1.78 trillion.[8]

People . . .
Just as fashion's environmental impact is not fully measurable, its people power can only be approximated. There's an endemic lack of transparency around employment, and it's just about

Triangle Shirtwaist Factory manager in suit made of money locks door
on burning workers when a lethal fire broke out on March 25, 1911

impossible to draw a line around an industry that involves bits of so many others: think dockworkers; truck drivers; call centers; image processing teams; warehouse workers; makers of tissue paper, plastic bags, sewing machine parts, shipping containers; etc. So always add "at least" to any estimate of the size of the fashion worker ranks.

The number of people who work in fashion is (at least) equal to the entire population of the United States and Northern Europe. Of these, (at least) 40 percent have no job security, no rights or contracts, and certainly no benefits. (Health insurance! Are you crazy?) That's about equal to all the people in Bangladesh, the world's second largest apparel manufacturer, plus Cambodia with its 600-odd fast fashion factories.

Worst of all, those who don't even earn enough to live on number about the same as the populations of Zambia, Somalia, or Zimbabwe—or two times that of New York City.

But it gets even worse. This isn't only about money.

Treating People Poorly

The worst clothing sector industrial accident in the United States was the 1911 Triangle Shirtwaist Factory fire, in which 146 women perished by being roasted alive or jumping to their deaths from the ninth and tenth floor windows. They had been locked in by the owners of the Washington Square–adjacent, blouse-producing sweatshop. Great public outrage and protests ensued.

The reason there hasn't been a worse (or, really, any) clothing factory accident in this country in over a hundred years is twofold: (a) the Triangle Shirtwaist catastrophe led to the implementation of safety standards and strengthened the International Ladies' Garment Workers' Union (ILGWU), leading to lasting improvements in working conditions and pay. And therefore (b) we now outsource those horrible sweatshop working conditions. In 1911, 95 percent of clothes bought in the US were made here. Today that figure is 2 percent. The domestic garment industry died largely on account of unionization and improved industrial standards that raised production prices. Then the expiration of trade quotas with China set off an avalanche of cheap clothes imports and a continuing race to the bottom to seek out the least-expensive, least-regulated manufacturing centers.[9] China, which has produced roughly one in three of all new garments for most of this century, is now a mature center of production. Factories there are soulless, gargantuan pollution monsters, but they're relatively safe and sophisticated, and tend to pay over minimum wage.

So, Big Fashion moved on to countries with more lax attitudes to safety and human rights, and settled on Bangladesh as the most competitive market, promoting it to the second-largest clothing exporter, right behind China (check your labels). *Competitive* means a minimum wage of around six dollars a day, 10 percent of the US's minimum wage, but most of Bangladesh's twenty million plus garment workers are paid considerably less than that. You know what's coming next.

In April 2013, a factory in Dhaka collapsed on top of 3,600 workers. That morning, seeing huge cracks in the walls, many of them had refused to go in, so the owner, Sohel Rana, threatened to sack them and hired thugs to force them inside. More than 1,100 people were crushed to death; nearly 2,500 were injured, many grievously.

There was some outrage. Fashion Revolution was founded in London. Shamed CEOs made some panicky promises.[10] But five years on, nothing substantial had changed.[11] It's easy to believe otherwise, because we want good news—and we seem to be getting it. Big Fashion wishes very urgently that we continue to look the other way, so it has bigged up its corporate social responsibility (CSR) departments. CSR was invented by George Orwell in *1984*. He called it doublethink.[12]

The Math of Greenwashing

CSR departments are fashionable. Everyone's wearing them. Their typical tone is oxymoronically shrill and feel-good. In luxury, the loudest include Kering (Gucci, Saint Laurent, McQueen . . .), and in Big Fashion, H&M. Any CSR is infinitely better than no CSR, but significant change coming from something beginning with *c*—for *corporate*—is impossible. This is elementary mathematics. No massive fashion company can make both clothes and profit at scale. So of course they talk in doublespeak, offering, as LVMH did, "solutions that could enable economic growth while tackling the challenges of global warming." Translation: "increasing profits while pondering the weird weather."[13]

Ploys for reeling in the concerned consumer include:

- Carbon offsets. Not reducing their own emissions but paying to plant a tree someplace else.[14]

- Take-back schemes. Time needed to recycle a year's taken-back clothes: 234 years. Time taken to remanufacture the same amount back again: 39 days.[15]

- Pledging a thing by a date, then changing the thing's rules on that date. H&M promised to pay all workers a "fair living wage by 2018." In 2018, having totally failed, this pledge changed to installing "improved wage management systems."[16]

- Pledging a thing in the future to get a PR hit now, regardless of success. François-Henri Pinault,

CEO of Kering, setting a "science-based target," promised to reduce its greenhouse gases (GHG) emissions by 50 percent by 2025, for example. Good luck, Kering![17]

- Sponsoring sustainable fashion conferences and circular design prizes. And getting shouty about them at the annual "Davos of sustainable fashion," the Copenhagen Fashion Summit.

- Massaging numbers, the basic method. For example, Gucci's eco-success rose 80 percent from 2015 to 2018. But factor in the brand's growth and this becomes a 32 percent bigger *cost* to the planet.[18]

To revisit Orwell's *1984*, "If you want a picture of the future, imagine a boot stamping on a human face—forever." Only the boot is the colossal carbon footprint of fashion. Okay, stop! This is the maximally cynical version of affairs. There is definitely genuine change percolating and greater awareness—shout-out to certain visionary designers and companies: Stella McCartney, of course; Vivienne Westwood, who told us to "buy less, choose well, make it last";[19] and outdoors outfitter Patagonia, which does free repairs and whose CEO, Rose Marcario, said, "Doing good work for the planet creates new markets and makes [us] more money."[20] And that's okay. Solutions have to rise from the bottom line, it's how business works. Profit is king, the shareholders must

feed. Big Fashion, however, goes too far. In order to prove this, I made a graph. I charted the 2019 revenues of ten brands with the personal net worth of their top man or men (none are female), and the GDP of entire countries.

Here we see how LVMH boss Bernard Arnault, who competes with Jeff Bezos and Bill Gates as the richest man in the world, had a 2019 net worth greater than the amount Puerto Rico earned that year—greater, in fact, than the GDP of 131 entire nations. Amancio Ortega, who owns Zara, had a fortune that exceeded the earnings of 123 whole countries, or about $13 billion more than the entire population of fashion-producing Myanmar made in 2019. In fact, the combined fortunes of the twenty richest men in fashion is the same as the total GDP of the seventy-three poorest countries. Or, to put it another way, of the wealthiest countries in the world, only twenty-nine earned more than these twenty individuals' combined net worth in that single year.[21] This is not apples to apples, but it makes you think. It makes me think the moneygrubbing is obscene.

Yes, this is how business has always worked. But it needn't. Those profits are bought at the expense of the earth, and definitely of the workers. Cheap materials, toxic dyes, cut corners, superlow wages, no security—it all comes from the same corporate social irresponsibility department of lazy, greedy, old-world thinking. The usual justification for using cheap foreign labor is that you can't simply shut the machine down. It may be in unregulated, dangerous, violent, below-subsistence wage sweatshops, but hey, at least it's work! This

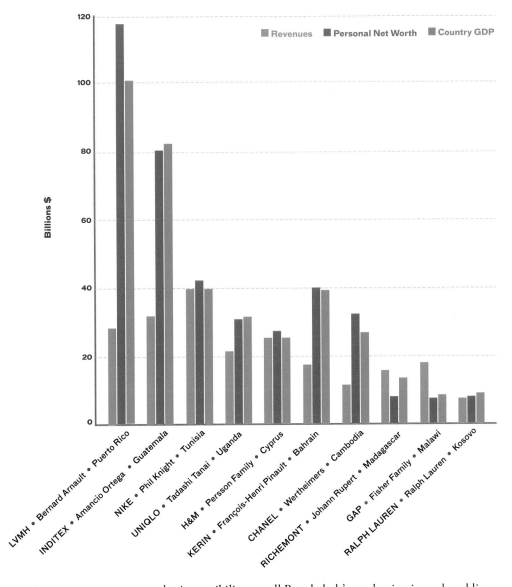

Billions $

Legend: Revenues · Personal Net Worth · Country GDP

Categories:
LVMH • Bernard Arnault • Puerto Rico
INDITEX • Amancio Ortega • Guatemala
NIKE • Phil Knight • Tunisia
UNIQLO • Tadashi Tanai • Uganda
H&M • Persson Family • Cyprus
KERIN • François-Henri Pinault • Bahrain
CHANEL • Wertheimers • Cambodia
RICHEMONT • Johann Rupert • Madagascar
GAP • Fisher Family • Malawi
RALPH LAUREN • Ralph Lauren • Kosovo

specious argument assumes the impossibility of replacing the malignant supply machine. There is nothing to prevent "fringe" economic ideas such as debt cancellation, basic income, and microfinance—which has solidly proven effectiveness—from being instituted. Nobel laureate and Grameen Bank founder Muhammad Yunus has calculated that we could solve all Bangladesh's production issues by adding a set amount to each garment's retail price. That amount is . . . fifty cents.[22] I bet we'd all pay two quarters quite happily, but we can't because the board took that option off the table before we even had the chance.

That idiotic, toxic, me-first thinking is finally fading. Eileen Fisher, Mara Hoffman,

Reformation, Nudie Jeans, People Tree, and Allbirds are among the pioneers of total transparency, responsible sourcing, and fair labor practices, and there are hundreds of smaller brands, too. Iteration—or the existence of many more, smaller companies—is one model that looks attractive when staring down the barrel of everything being owned by Jeff Bezos. In short, it's time for humanity to update our business plan, because scaling "make more money" has been a disaster.

These gargantuan issues are insoluble by the likes of you and me. I'm just tired of fueling them, so I make tiny votes with my wallet. I haven't bought a new garment (aside from underwear) in well over ten years.[23] Okay, I'm peculiarly in love with old clothes (did you notice?), but every time we resist auto-buying the temptingly cheap trend popping up on our feed, we are being a minor, but important, activist. Scale *that* up, and the Ortegas, Perssons, Arnaults, and Pinaults will notice in their bottom-line area.[24]

A Clothes Playbook

I realize converting everyone to a strict *owned clothes* diet is unlikely—and it's also undesirable. Let's dismantle and rebuild the fashion-industrial complex, but let's please have thousands more new wave, right-thinking, gorgeous-clothes companies to replace the monoliths as they drop dead from our neglect. The aim, in tandem with the mending to which you will soon be addicted, is to buy a little bit better, selecting with more knowledge,

because, as with food diets, the more rigid you are, the more likely you are to fail. Me, I haven't gone completely cold turkey on Big Fashion product (check my confession hidden in endnote 23), I just find I don't like it very often. So here follow some tried and trusted checklists and gentle rules to keep on your phone.

The Seven Magic Shopping Questions

Never buy another mistake!

1. Do I want to wear it out of the store? Would I buy it without one-day shipping? (No? Then leave it on the rack or in the cart.)

2. Do I already have it? (I have two dozen black pants.)

3. Do I have occasion to wear it? (Cocktail frocks are of limited use.)

4. Do I only want this for my alternate personality? (Mine is attracted to Hermès-style prints, chain loafers, and ladysuits.)

5. Do I want it at twice the price? (An unworn bargain is pricey.)

6. Does it fit me right now? (You won't lose the ten pounds, and, honey, you don't need to.)

7. Do I think it's useful? (It's not useful, it's just boring.)

Shopping Rules

Food for thought:[25]

1. Does the fabric end in –ene, –on, or –ester? It's poisoning something, perhaps you?[26]

2. Are there more than ten branches of this store? It's too big.

3. Have you seen this brand advertised on television? It's too big.

4. Can you believe how cheap this is? Someone else has paid full price, with sweat.

5. Remember "your personal stylist" is in fact a robot and you are its algorithm.

6. If it's new it should not need mending; premade holes and rips are abominations.

7. Is it very stretchy? It probably can't rot and it will definitely wear out fast.

8. The whiter the shirt, the filthier the dirt. Bleach kills the earth.[27]

9. Dress more like the French. Or the Japanese. Or the Italians. They invest in quality.[28]

10. Are you a sheep? So don't shop like one.

11. Are you trash? So don't dress in it.

12. Don't trash it. Mend it, lend it, swap it, sell it, gift it.

13. Pay more, buy less.[29]

14. Buy less.

15. Unless it's secondhand, in which case, go wild.

16. Treat. Yo. Self.[30]

17. Shop slowly. Think twice. Consult your gut.[31]

18. Take care on the way in. Once you own it, you owe it a nice life.

19. Your click-shopping finger turns evil after midnight.

20. Don't worry. Nobody's perfect.

DE FIL EN AIGUILLE

Dessin de A. Vallée.

— Une robe c'est comme l'amour : plus ça se raccommode plus ça vous tient chaud.

DARN IT! I PLUM FORGOT TO WRITE!

—AND THAT'S MY YARN!

when

Search for mending in history books and you'll search in vain, but seek a bit deeper and around corners, and mending in the human story, as in the human closet, is everywhere. I hated history in school. Wars, kings, land grabs, pestilence, famine, but mostly wars; it was unspeakably boring. Historiography has moved beyond the military now, but not enough to completely redress the standard notion that humanity evolved from slaughter, whereas the truth is the opposite. Civilization grew from the mending of damage. And now here, finally visible, is some history of *clothes*-damage mending.

Mending is ancient history, as old as clothes themselves. And how old is that? Well, to be sort of precise, at least a hundred millennia old. We know this not from having seen any actual clothes—the oldest surviving garment is around ninety-seven thousand years younger—but from sequencing the DNA of obligate human ectoparasites, a.k.a. lice.[1] In the Upper Pleistocene era, the louse that lives in clothing and feeds on the body diverged from the sort that finds only the scalp delicious, thereby proving we first got dressed around the time we spread out from Africa and colonized more of the planet. These things are intimately linked: clothes made living at higher latitudes and in colder climates bearable, and, though there's no evidence, bug or textile, there's also no doubt that these earliest clothes were mended—because they were valuable. In fact, until a few short decades ago, garments were by far the most valuable commodities most people possessed, and they were treated accordingly. So the story of mending is really about how we value our stuff—*stuff* in the old sense, of material.

Firms

The first fun fact about clothes history: it's all news.[2] Because in history, battles and rulers were all that counted, nobody bothered to look at the humble everyday business until recently, when it dawned on historians that they weren't Augustus Caesar or Napoleon in a previous life, but some plebeian bathhouse attendant or a starving farmer of the ancient régime Third Estate. It occurred to other historians that not only were they not Cleopatra, but they weren't even mentioned because they were women. Clothes very much belong in the category of things that seemed too ordinary to matter but turned out to matter the most. So, whereas everything has already been said about the first Roman emperor, discoveries are still being made about his togas— for instance, there was a lively trade in used ones (well, not Caesar's). Scrutari (in ancient Greece, κρυτοπωλω῀ν, *grutopólai*) were dealers in secondhand goods, with a hot trade in fabrics.[3] The more we probe the material worlds of the mighty ancient civilizations, the more downright cloth obsessed they appear, however inconveniently ignoble that is. They draped everything in sight. Their monumental stone edifices were made cozy and domestic by curtains and screens and hangings and veils. The Roman toga—and the female peplos, chiton, and stola—was a cherished personal fashion item, signaling status like a designer label, and susceptible to looting. Most of the Roman Bath curse tablets[4]—think of these defixiones as engraved lead tweets calling out misdeeds—excavated at the famous sacred spring in Roman Britain rail against clothing thieves, and the better-off patricians would pay someone to watch their precious linens while they bathed. *Sarcinatores* were the clothiers of ancient Rome, but because sewing and tailoring were moot when clothes were draped cloth, they were really darners and patchwork makers. There were even the collegia centonariorum, guilds of specialists who manufactured, but mostly collected, repaired, reused,

The Egtved Girl

Ötzi's patchwork pants

and resold, wool textiles.[5] All these clothiers were menders.

The First Clothes

The earliest clothes we know of feature hauntingly familiar silhouettes you can imagine wearing, and were probably sewn with the likes of the earliest needle we know of, a still usable fifty-thousand-year-old Denisovan bone awl from the Altai Mountains of Siberia,[6] and the first thread, thirty-four-thousand-year-old twisted flax fiber discovered in Dzudzuana Cave in Georgia in 2009.[7]

For about fifty years, beginning in 1921, the oldest ever outfit of woven cloth belonged to a 1360s BC Danish teenager known as the Egtved Girl, named after the burial place that had miraculously conserved all her clothes but none of her. Then in 1977, a pair of (female,

duh) conservationists at the Victoria and Albert Museum finally bothered to examine a grubby bundle of First Dynasty Egyptian linens that had been lying around since 1913. They found an astonishingly complete V-neck shirt. Now known as the Tarkhan dress, it was confirmed in 2016 as the earliest garment we'd ever seen, over 5,000 years old.[8]

The First Mends

It's tempting to spot mends all over the Egtved shirt and Tarkhan dress; and though mends are entirely likely, the material evidence is admittedly inconclusive. Then there's Ötzi. Ötzi the Iceman, over 5,300 years old, was found mummified in the Ötzal region of the Tyrolean Alps in 1991. He immediately won the oldest clothes contest, although what remained of them was extremely shabby—and they were not woven

when

Tutankhamun's 3,350-year-old VM-ed kerchief

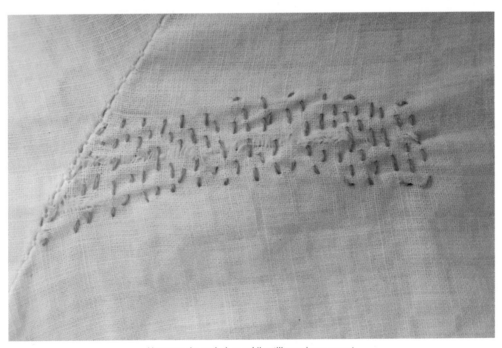

Hasty road mend, done while still wearing garment

but pieced. So, if patchwork can be accepted as a form of mending, we can definitely call the shreds of Ötzi's ensemble the earliest surviving mends. Made from five different animal species—goat, sheep, cow, roe deer, and bear—and reconstructed by the museum that houses them, the leggings of the iceman are indisputably made of patches upon patches upon patches. This would be the mending method of everyday folks' clothing and work wear for the next fifty-two and a half centuries. It will be how clothes are preserved and, therefore, honored, right up until the dawn of designer labels and super mass production in the mid-to-late 1980s, and even to this day, communities living at a less than digital pace or lacking the overdeveloped world's full slate of privileges use patchwork.

But don't go thinking only primitive Copper Age dwellers (we used to call them cavemen) and the working poor sported patched and mended wardrobes through the ages. Virtually everyone did, because—say it with me—*textile was very, very valuable.* Ancient Egyptians (whose civilization, let's remember, lasted twenty-seven centuries—about five times longer than Rome or Greece) would mend a textile three or four times, then make it into something else, ending its life, aptly, in the tomb, as embalming cloth. You had to be a pharaoh not to wear mended clothing, though (as far as I can tell, and I don't think anyone else has even looked) the oldest surviving *visible* mend belongs to the most celebrated Egyptian king of them all: Tutankhamun.

Admittedly the small blue headcloth darned with white thread probably hadn't been worn by the king since childhood, but still it sports a typical mend of the day. Using needles of pierced fish bone kept in the hollow leg bones of birds or rolled up papyrus, ancient Egyptians would work darns away from the body using isolated lines of elongated twisted chain stitch, beginning with a backstitch and ending with a knot. (See Chapter Six to decode all these stitches.) Simpler darns—like King Tut's kerchief—were executed with a simple running stitch, and the most complex used the techniques we now know as Swiss darning or stocking web darns. Frayed edges were dealt with by rolling and overcasting.[9] Aside from the unusual chain stitch lines, remarkably little has changed in the mending universe. The tiny three-thousand-year-old white pickstitch darns from the tomb of Tutankhamun are completely familiar and all the more charming for it. I couldn't help thinking of a hasty road mend I'd recently done on a sleeve, in the reverse colorway of blue thread on a white Edwardian cotton petticoat.

So modern do ancient clothes and their mends appear, it's hard to grasp how staggering it is that they've survived. Any cotton is particularly incredible, because that fabric is not long-term durable, being a short staple cellulosic (plant) fiber, spun into thread that breaks down with age—if you've washed and washed a bedsheet till it tears like pastry, or put your fingers straight through a vintage frock (see hasty road mend), you know what I mean. Wool is just as vulnerable, if not more so, because the protein fibers are—as anyone who's ever owned a sweater can tell you—magnetic to certain small flying bastards. (See Chapter Six for tips on moth survival.)

Lasting Value

The most durable natural textile by far is woven from bast fibers—plant stems—as evidenced by the quantity of surviving ancient Egyptian linens and the oldest European textile remains, fragments of five-thousand-year-old Alpine pile dwellers' fishing nets.[10] Linen is made from the principal bast fiber, flax, whose botanical name *Linum usitatissimum* translates, appropriately, to "most useful," partly, presumably, because it requires less mending. It's so durable because it's essentially pre-rotted. Preparing flax (and hemp and ramie and jute) involves retting: soaking the stalks to strip the lignin and pectin from the stem. Linsey-woolsey, one of the great fabric names, was cloth with a linen warp and a wool weft to improve the durability and make the precious wool stretch further; fustian was a similarly stout cloth, originally linen with cotton. (Food for thought now that our main fabric blend is cotton contaminated with polyester, the petroleum-based filament fiber that does not rot, ever.) You know how textile was *very, very valuable*? In Middle to New Kingdom Egypt, linen was literally money—fabric was the principal currency, right until the dawn of coinage.[11] In northernmost Europe so was the heavy napped wool fabric called vaðmál,[12] and, for centuries in China, silk, both in skeins and woven pieces.[13]

How on earth someone in China, some five thousand years ago, thought to boil *Bombyx* moth cocoons (they're not worms) in the first place is a mystery wrapped in a legend.[14] Early Europeans, thoroughly hooked on silk, were similarly baffled—it was two millennia before they caught on that the fabulous fabric from the Far East didn't grow on trees.[15] Until we reach the heyday of the stocking, silk is but a side note in mending history, though it has immense overall importance because of its sheer value: its cost could exceed that of a house. Indeed, this fabric affected everything, everywhere, its trade advancing exploration, invention, and cultural exchange—in a word, civilization.

The (Not) Dark Ages

Civilized is not the word most associated with the age formerly known as Dark. This is wrong. Please now banish any vestige of prejudice that medieval people were barbaric, ignorant, illiterate, or whatever adjective may cling vaguely to your nether thoughts regarding the period from the fall of Rome to the Rennaissance. Ten centuries! It's a long time. Uncountable discrete worlds unfolded east, west, up, and down. In textiles, the Islamic world was ascendant, Constantinople and the Byzantine Empire illustrious. China continued to flower and Western Europeans collected all of it while making their own fabulous fabrics. Medievalists are dependent on art-historical and manuscript sources for dress clues—so few garments survived from that time that they all take the definite article: *the* pourpoint of Charles de Blois, *the* Cologne alb, *the* underpants from Lengberg. Still, mining all the data, some forensic reconstruction of mending practice and technique has been possible.[16]

These underpants and not-matching bra upended underwear theory when archeologist Beatrix Nutz unearthed them beneath the floorboards in Lengberg Castle, Austria, in 2012, and had them carbon-14 dated to the mid-to-late fifteenth century.[17] The (in the vernacular) breast bags predate the invention of the bra by four hundred years and had lingerie obsessives and dress reconstructors in a tizzy. More interesting to the obsessive *mend* reconstructor are the equally modern-looking tie-side underpants, their stitching and patching, and the general medieval recycle-reuse picture. Though long-legged braies are more familiar to historians, and though these look so bikini, this is masculine underwear—women wore no drawers till at least the late 1700s. Pictorial evidence of the late-medieval minimalist underwear style is scant: hence this gruesome image, which is not some elaborate tong-based valet ritual, but St. George being martytred with red-hot chain mail.

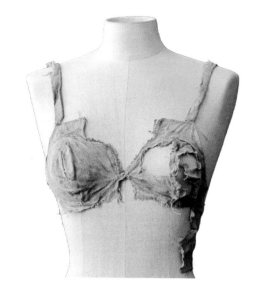

The briefs were sewn after 1440, in-castle, skillfully (it took six and a half hours to make a modern reconstruction) with imported linen, and were eventually passed down to a lesser member of the household, who applied—less skillfully—three successive patches to the outside crotchal area, one atop the other, thus keeping these in service a long time, probably over forty years. The patches were hemmed with an overcast stitch and applied with straight and zigzag running stitch. Other scraps in the Lengberg haul showed back- and stem stitches and whipstitch. Altogether the late-medieval Tyroleans tell a similar story to the ancient Egyptians—that needlework is

universal and timeless. They sewed the same stitches, with varying degrees of neatness and skill, just like us.

The Golden Age

Well, I say that, but in fact, the most celebrated medieval stitchery is the very opposite of "just like us," because this was the golden age of embroidery—or the age of golden embroidery. If textile was valuable, Opus Anglicanum, or English work, was priceless: dazzling masterpieces, or mistresspieces, produced for (and usually by) the church, in silk and precious metal threads. This is what you expected in the medieval section, not grubby underpants.

Two embroidery techniques are particularly characteristic of Opus Anglicanum—a fine split stitch and underside couching, which maximized glittering effects by catching the laid thread, often made of precious gold or silver, by pulling it through with linen worked from the back. Both have a reputation for technical difficulty, but split stitch is easy and all over visible mending. Underside couching a little less so.

"To know the history of embroidery is to know the history of women," Rozsika Parker memorably stated in her seminal 1984 book, *The Subversive Stitch*.[18] Her book corrected many misconceptions about this art, including that men took over the sewing once worldwide demand for the luxury English

work grew overwhelming around the mid-thirteenth century. But in an era when church law stated verbatim that "woman's authority is nil," there was obviously a gulf between maker and wearer of cope, dalmatic, and chasuble.[19] Unsurprisingly, ecclesiastical vestments were probably *mended* exclusively by women, because mending is humble. The *Ancrene Wisse*, a guide originally written for anchoresses (women who sequestered themselves and devoted their lives to prayer) around 1230 that remained popular for centuries, taught that the coarser the sewing, the finer the soul, and that the highest-lowest form of needlework was the mending of church vestments and poor people's clothes.

The champion of the poor (and animals) was, and still is in certain circles, St. Francis of Assisi. Above is the cowl that he wore and sewed with his own saintly hands, one of three surviving. I declare it (forgive me, Catholics) the second-oldest visible mending icon. "All the brothers are to wear inexpensive clothing, and they can use sackcloth and other material to mend it with God's blessing" was the rule St. Francis himself wrote, and, true to his word, he applied several rounds of assorted patches in five fabrics to this tunic of coarse wool twill. A sixth type of patch was cut from fellow saint and follower St. Clare's cloak, and apparently attached by her, because the accuracy and quality of the overcast stitching is noticeably finer.[20] Quite separately from any religious significance, I find this evidence of the hand—four hands—of downright legendary historical personages more moving and miraculous than the most ravishingly jaw-dropping embroidered golden copes of popes.

The First Fashion

St. Francis, the son of a wealthy silk merchant, was particularly attuned to the symbolism of clothes and cost, but in fact, everyone was. Dressing correctly marked your place in society, especially from the mid-fourteenth century on when sumptuary laws began to proliferate and styles changed to more fitted silhouettes. Scholars often cite the notorious circa 1470 pourpoint of Charles de Blois, a padded, silk lampas doublet with an arresting overabundance of buttons, as the first garment made purely for style, that is, the birth of Fashion.

More interesting from a mending standpoint is its rarely glimpsed interior, a palimpsest of linen dings and mends that show the wear and tear—though it's supposed not to have been worn much by its namesake owner, the sainted Duke of Brittany. Better still for

mending is another, slightly younger pourpoint, belonging to the hapless Valois King Charles VI, known as the Well-Loved when crowned at age eleven, but subsequently the Mad owing to his forty-four bouts of serious crazy. What is touching about this crimson twenty-seven-button coat made to wear over a mail shirt is its child's size and the makeshift belt holder for the young prince to hang his sword and scabbard: a collection of slits too botched (wrong word: see below) to have been made by the *pourpointier*, outlined in terrible buttonhole stitch: the first porthole mend. Young Charles's was utility slashing, but in this heyday of the opposite of mending, everyone was shredding their clothes on purpose. Surcoats, hoods, gowns, doublets: all were decorated with elaborate cutting, slitting, and, especially, dagging—geometric edging patterns made possible by advances in fulling: nonfraying wool. Dagging was a guy thing, as fashion, then, generally was.

Slashers and Botchers

Moralists railed against shredded garments—it was a "wast of clooth in vanitee" scolded Chaucer's Parson. Yet cutting remained all the rage for centuries, growing out of the fetishization of knightly attire slashed in battle or even of Christ's wounds, but oddly never symbolic of the abject rags of poverty. Au contraire, this was luxury attire.[21] A tailor was not a stitcher of clothes but a *cutter*. A clothes mender was a *botcher*.[22] Botchers also made linen armor—pourpoints—and both

trades together were given their first royal charter in 1326 as the Company of Taylors and Linen-Armourers, which evolved into one of the "great twelve" livery companies of London, and remains today the very snob Worshipful Company of Merchant Taylors. So mender-makers—botchers—along with tailor-slashers—cutters—sit at the very foundation of fashion as the most important anchors of dress history. Botching, that indispensible VM technique, is a noble tradition indeed.

Botchers were also vital to the secondhand trade, which grew only more widespread, the Roman and Greek *scrutari* and *grutopólai* continuing uninterrupted. One Victorian chronicler of London's infamous Rag Fair wrote: "that it [secondhand trade] has existed for centuries is beyond question." Indeed, the antecedent of London's Petticoat Lane Market (now all florists and beard barbers) extended at least a mile every weekday, featuring, he noted, "the worn-out apparel of the whole population of London . . . [in] mountains of old clo'."[23] Accounts also exist of the secondhand merchants

of Italy with stock far more glamorous than mountains of clo, notably the silk-recirculating *strazzaroli* of Tuscany, Genoa, Venice, and Bologna, and the Florentine *Arte dei rigattieri*, a guild formed in 1266 that organized the first ready-to-wear marketplace—thus placing secondhand, along with mending, at the very root of fashion.[24]

In fact, non-new clothes practices abounded throughout history, too commonplace to record. It was less about fashion than value: clothes were money in the bank, proof against future penury. As well as repairing and reselling, there was *re*-everything—remaking, recycling, recutting, and rental. When fabric was grown, tended, harvested, processed, spun, and woven even before it became clothes, of *course* those clothes would recirculate. Wearable garments became donations, gifts, rentals, and bequests (wills listed linens first for centuries). Big bits were remade into other clothes; good trim cut off and saved; scraps recycled as bandages, cleaning rags, paper. Rag pickings fed the papermaking industry, right down to textile

Mountains of old clo: Thomas Rowlandson, *Rag Fair*, ca. 1800

toilet tissue.[25] In one tenth-century tale, a dying matron is mended by miraculous trim after St. Dunstan tells her in a dream she'll recover if she sews "the golden embroidery, which you keep hidden away in your money chest" onto his chasuble. The writer notes it was incredible how the embroidery fit the chasuble without alteration. A mending miracle.[26]

What the Poor Wore

The story continues in a similar vein, with old clothes repurposed, rehomed, and mended many times over. The poorest populations often had only one set of clothes, which they were obliged to patch and darn continually. To see these kinds of clothes we turn to art.

Art is an unreliable witness. Some artists were chroniclers of reality—Pieter Jansz Quast, Jacques Callot, and Rembrandt (overleaf) appear to have faithfully recorded professional beggars of the seventeenth century—but many more genre artists painted picturesque poverty for patrons to ogle, or hid morals in the shabby garb.

For scraps of truth about scraps, we can also scour contemporary accounts, such as these late eighteenth-century writers. One recorded "trowsers . . . torn from the bottom quite up to the thigh. I fastened several parts together as well as I could with some thorns

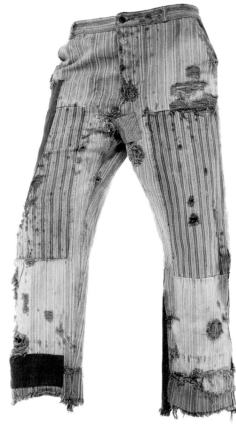

from the hedges"; another wrote of a visibly mended "'church suit' . . . of very coarse cloth, containing a number of patches of almost every colour but that of which it was originally made."[27] Why we should care about horrible garments torn, patched, motley, and stinky (only the linen inner layer was washed; outerwear was worn continuously till stiff and reeking and even rotten) is because it might have been us. It's a lost history of hidden ordinary things, the opposite of the court dress and couture we see in museums. It's more real.

That explains why I've been obsessed with this pair of much-patched farm laborer's pants for years. Incredibly, they date from around 1730; it is utterly implausible that they survived at all, let alone in this condition—and, don't they look modern? I'd wear them. They were found stuffed up a Norfolk, UK, chimney and acquired by Pamela Clabburn, a visionary costume scholar and museum curator who "championed the study and collection of rural dress, and that of provincial middle and lower classes," something that nobody understood then and few do now.[28] But they will. There are signs.

Your reading this book is a sign, as are the ever higher prices fetched by young brethren of the Norfolk trousers, including the much-patched French work pants from the 1930s on the previous page: "condition is worse than a wash rag and that is what makes them cool," explained their sellers. Slowly, museums are doing a Clabburn and collecting ordinary dress alongside the usual finery, and increased attention is being paid to the stories of clothes, because this is what the people want.

Stitched Stories

Few textiles tell a clearer story than the sampler. They speak through the words sewn into them about the life of the girl—it's always a girl—who labored over them, and of their own evolution.[29] They first appeared in Elizabethan England as *examplers*, sewn guides to the multiple and proliferating stitch types—because embroidery—but the more familiar kind were worked during the seventeenth to nineteenth centuries by *all* European girls aged five to fifteen for learning stitchwork, whether they wanted to or not. Samplers display changes in sewing as it became increasingly associated with the woman's province of the home, denigrated as not-work, and split into fancy and plain—decorative and functional. The English, Dutch, and German darning sampler (like Rindeltie Brougers's Dutch one here) is plain sewing on steroids, virtuoso darns bearing little relation to regular mending.

Early colonial American samplers are said to be "primitive" compared with their flashier European and English counterparts, or you could say they're more vigorous and moving.

Imagine being twelve years old and stitching, "This work in hand my friends may have / When I am dead and in my grave," or "Mother dear weep not for me / When in this yard my grave you see," as did Ellen Caufield and Margaret Barnholt, respectively (overleaf). Life was hard when the clock was reset to medieval; clothes were as precious as they'd ever been. All womenfolk could spin, weave, and sew; everyone grew and processed flax or hemp, kept sheep—for wool, not meat—and repairing was continuous. Compare old and new world mending in these English and American 1630 verses:

"In Praise of the Needle"

JOHN TAYLOR

A Needle (though it be but small and slender)
Yet is it both a maker and a mender;
A grave Reformer of old Rents decayde,
Stops holes and seames; and desperate cuts displayde.
[. . .]
And for my Countries quiet, I should like,
That Women-kinde should use no other Pike.
It will increase their peace, enlarge their store,
To use their tongues lesse, and their Needles more.

"Forefathers' Song"

ANONYMOUS

And now our garments begin to grow thin,
And wool is much wanted to card and to spin;
If we can get a garment to cover without
Our other in-garments are clout * upon clout:
Our clothes we brought with us are apt to be torn,
They need to be clouted soon after they're worn,
But clouting our garments they hinder us nothing,
Clouts double are warmer than single whole clothing.

———

*clout = patch

This work in hand my friends may have
When i am dead and in my grave
And when my work each time you see
With fond rememberance think on me

Ellen   ulfield work'd in the 12ᵗʰ year of her age—1831
C.W.T.   Wheeling -Va.
teacher

By the 1790s, rural life was still arduous. Elizabeth Fuller, fifteen, of Princeton, Massachusetts, outlined the schedule for making "Pa's surtout": Picking wool: three days; breaking the wool: three days; spinning: twenty-four days (by Ma). Then it was sent out to be dyed blue. A woman came in to warp the loom (everyone had one). Elizabeth wove it: two weeks. Then "Mr Deadman" fulled the cloth and Ma cut out and sewed the coat. It took from February to June.[30]

The Hand That Holds the Needle

Calamanco, paduasoy, bengaline, bagheera, nainsook, ducape, dimity, pongee, surah, coutil—I love the litany of fabrics our eighteenth- and nineteenth-century sisters knew, even those for whom the luxury stuffs were out of reach. To a woman, they could sew. If rich, they hired seamstresses, but they still had the knowledge. This was true in Europe and England, but especially in America, where the image of the hardworking needle-wielding pioneer woman persisted. As a point of honor, a bride would stitch a dowry of men's shirts and knit her own stockings, even if she could afford ready-mades. Stockings alone can stand for the story of mending over the long nineteenth century. They were the first mass-produced garment, starting with Englishman William Lee's 1589 frame.* The original Luddites were handloom stockingers and textile artisans, whose smashing of industrial equipment was made a capital offense in 1812 (never enforced) and whose violent objection to being "thrown out of employment" by the inferior "spider-work" of the wide frames was audaciously defended in Parliament by the poet Lord Byron, but who inevitably lost the war against industrialization.[31] Innovation, as it must, accelerated, building on the spinning jenny (1764), Arkwright's water frame (1769), the spinning mule (1779), and the cotton gin (1793), with the 1864 circular knitting machine turbocharging stocking production.

The mid-nineteenth-century spike in textile demand and production was horrible for the workers, and the most downtrodden were, of course, women. Proliferating fabric mills furnished hellish, hot, noisy, dangerous, backbreaking employment, but garment sewing was often menial home-based or tenement sweatshop "slop work" for a pathetic pittance.

---

*Which took a couple of centuries to catch on, but that's another long story

With fingers weary and worn,
With eyelids heavy and red,
A woman sat, in unwomanly rags,
Plying her needle and thread—
Stitch! Stitch! Stitch!
In poverty, hunger, and dirt,
And still with a voice of dolorous pitch
She sang the "Song of the Shirt."

"Cheap Clothing: The Slaves of the 'Sweaters'," *Harper's Weekly*, April 26, 1890

Everyone could recite "The Song of the Shirt" by Thomas Hood, first published in *Punch* in 1843—especially the lurid part where the woman was "Sewing at once, with a double thread / A Shroud as well as a Shirt"—yet this destitute labor force grew to at least 35 percent of the entire female population of New York City. "The sewing-women are paid next to nothing for their toil. Their starvation wages fill the counters with the cheapest of cheap goods," wrote the reformer Helen Campbell in 1887.[32] This is related to mending in the same way it is today—exploitation of labor lowers prices; cheap clothes aren't mended. It's just that now we outsource the misery to far-off countries, so we don't have to look at it.

Darn Darning

But back to the stockings—and darning. This centers on New York but stands for most everywhere. Over the last quarter of the nineteenth century, the growing middle classes, including the new breed of workingwoman, needed the cheap stuff, and they needed stockings, lots of stockings. Everyone did, men and children included, but especially women, who would never, *ever* appear without being properly shod (as they would say: stockings were footwear!). And stockings needed darning, all the time, all the family's, repeatedly. The task was beyond relentless and it was loaded: "There is nothing in the whole range of feminine economy on which personal and domestic happiness is more dependent," as fashion oracle *Godey's Lady's Book* put it.[33]

Trouble was, not only did nobody knit their own hose now, the skill to mend them was disappearing, along with the desire to

when

39

Annie Ware Winsor Allen
darning a stocking, 1884

Mending is literally in *Vogue*:
the NYC Mind-Your-Mending shop, 1915

darn. "What an awful waste of time," declared "a girl of the period" in a *Harper's Bazar* story. "I should think it was a sin. I couldn't do such work as that, and I'd be ashamed to if I could."[34] As darning was dropped, so were stocking prices, and hosiery fashion exploded into mad flamboyance. A typical wardrobe consisted of dozens, even hundreds, of pairs in rainbow colors to match every dress. They were bejeweled and beaded, with embroidered clocks and lace insets, stripes, lozenges, plaids, trompe l'oeil boots, among many other wild designs. And there were newfangled dress reform bifurcated tights and combinations, and even—*scandale!*—socks. This is where the story of silk becomes everyone's business, because even a humble amanuensis or school-teacher would own a pair, or three, of silk stockings, along with her everyday black lisle and winter balbriggans.

The medieval notion (remember the *Ancrene Wisse*) that mending is humble and righteous had by no means dispersed; quite the opposite. Badly done darns corresponded to badly made characters, and women were judged by their shabby hose. Attempts were made to shame girls into re-darning with morality tales, such as one summarized as (and often titled) "He Married the Girl Who Could Darn," in which stockinged feet are accidentally exposed and a dear old lady tells her granddaughter, "The slattern's stocking cured his love. He married your cousin Mary. She had the cleanest of stockings with the daintiest of little darns. He could resist no longer."[35] It didn't work. Darning needle sales dropped 95 percent from 1850 to 1870.[36]

But it turned out darning hadn't disappeared; it just skipped a generation. The terrible plight of the sewing woman met a swelling female workforce, including newspaperwomen, suffragists, and philanthropists with social consciences, and the result was a darning rennaissance. Young women raised not on compulsory mending and sampler stitching but on

Darning class at Waverly Massachusetts School for the Feeble-Minded, 1903

fashionable fancywork from the Kensington School in London noted how the lost skills of plain sewing could help their less fortunate sisters. Students formed darning clubs, hired darning teachers, mended bachelors' socks out of the kindness (and hopefulness) of their hearts, darned for pin money, and—"the latest fad in society"—threw darning parties, even *men's* darning parties.[37] Then they grew up and founded the academic discipline of home economics, with darning and mending prominent in the curriculum.

In their didactic Victorian way, they were mending the people. There were plain sewing classes for the poor, the feebleminded, the kids of sewing women, and for all children: from nine elementary schools in 1888, darning and mending were in every public school in all New York by 1900. Mending became a profession with new mending bureaus established, a sensible idea that

spread wide, lasted long, and I wish would be reestablished right now. "Professional mending is not a luxury, but a necessary economy," wrote *Vogue* in 1915 about the Mind-Your-Mending Shop, a "sanatorium for worn clothes and worn souls" on East Thirtieth Street. The article featured "a roomful of girls who need refurbishing so that they, too, can go out into the world as good as new and reinforced in the many worn places."[38]

War Patching

Note the date of that article: the Great War cast mending in a new light. There was no shame in patches now, said *Vogue*; they were "a proclamation of generosity toward a suffering Europe." In New York great menda-thons were organized for European refugees,

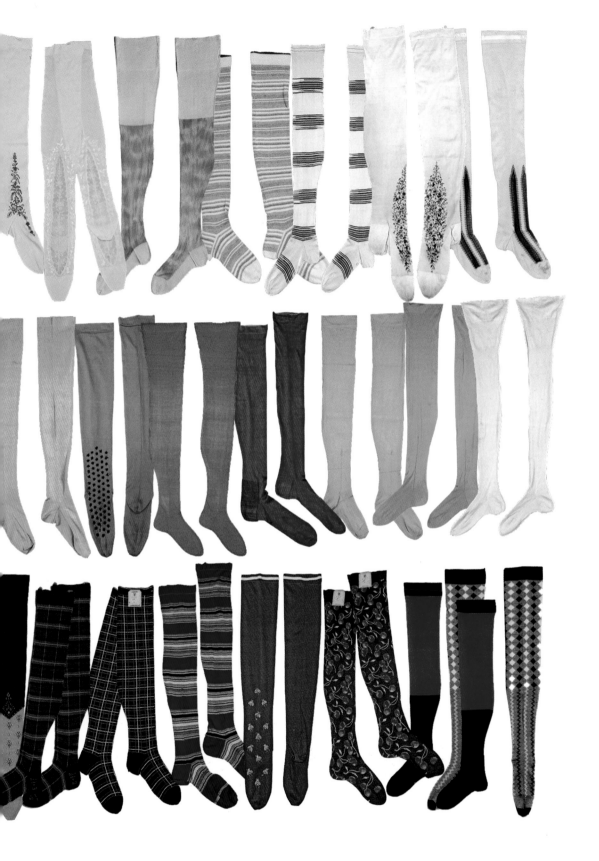

department store girls mingling with socialites to repair a quarter million garments a week. This was "most perplexing to American needlewomen," reported *The New York Times*, "but the task was presented as a patriotic duty."[39] World War I is altogether too huge a subject, so I'm representing its spirit with a single object of mending: Gabrielle de Montgeon's exquisite patchwork dressing gown. De Montgeon served as assistant director with Toupie Lowther in the all-female Hacket-Lowther Ambulance Unit near the Compiegne front lines. A close mutual friend was Radclyffe Hall, who wrote part of *The Well of Loneliness* while staying with de Montgeon, and who based its protagonist, Stephen Gordon, on Toupie Lowther—thus making this hand-patched coat, rather delightfully, an emblem not just of the Great War, but also of lesbian history.[40]

The war also meant that—in the words of *Vogue*—"fashion sanctions economy these days." Magazines and papers ran tons of articles about secondhand, thrift, and making do, like one in *The New York Times* that listed specialists—reweavers and lace replacers, lost-shoe pairers and sourcers of special buttons—to augment "the familiar old-clothes men in every city."[41] How countryfolk would scoff though. In rural America the thread of dressmaking-patching-mending-thrift ran unbroken from the early settlers—and survives still in 4-H clubs, county fair contests, and, especially, in the great tradition of quilting, another vast subject I'll distill into one picture.

Older than World War I: crazy quilting with decorative feather stitch joins was a Victorian fad

Austerity Dressing

I was going to say something about the Great Depression being great for mending but thought better of it. Times were terrible. I'll mention but one cunning and famous austerity fashion work-around: the seed sack dress, which was born well before the 1929 crash.

Ever since grain, meal, seeds, and flour were sold in sacks, country women had repurposed them as yardage, using lye and kerosene to extremely dangerously remove the labeling. Manufacturers spied a marketing opportunity (or, for the uncynical, wanted to help), switching to paper labels on plain cotton, then, starting with gingham flour sacks in 1924, progressed to pastels in 1936 (Tint-sax), and finally in the '40s, full-blown florals on quality percale.

Mamie Sweetnam and her seven siblings,
all in home-sewn seed sack dresses, ca. 1942

Quilt of vintage feed sacks

Make. Do. Mend.

Meanwhile across the Atlantic, flour sacks were just one item in a vast battery of work-arounds. England during World War II has to be the best-known era in mending history, thanks to the Board of Trade's slogan "Make Do and Mend," which launched with clothes rationing in June 1941. The campaign starred the nightmarish doll Mrs. Sew-and-Sew who featured in ads and booklets, the first of which sold (yes, you had to pay for it!) half a million copies in two weeks.

But restrictions and shortages—and general interwar cultural thriftiness—meant the Englishwoman had probably been making do and mending all her life and had many a trick up her patched sleeve. She might turn (resew, inside out) not just shirt collars, but entire shirts; boil ink and paper off cambric-backed architectural drawings for handkerchiefs; fashion bras from net curtains or even (probably apocryphal, but such fun) from parachute silk picked off downed enemy pilots. Then there was the infamous painting a line down the back of the leg with gravy browning to simulate stocking seams.[42] Nylons had no sooner come into being (May 1940) than they were wrested away, contraband smuggled in by American GIs, because DuPont's wonder fabric (see page 139) was restricted to war uses. So in these dying days of compulsory legwear, the old Victorian-style upkeep issues still pertained, only without the infinite supplies. Anyway, it was wrong to buy stockings even if you could, because wasting money on fashion was exactly what the evil Nazi "Squander Bug" wanted—he was a pear-shaped swastika-covered devil with a Hitler hairdo dreamed up by the National Savings Committee. This

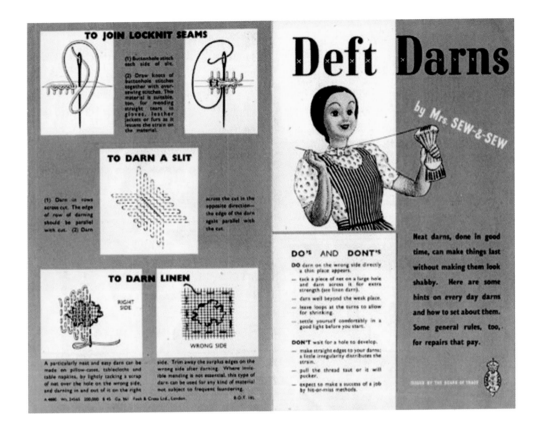

resulted in a revival of the mending bureau: socks and stockings darned and refooted, no rationing coupons required. I can't help coveting the return of such sensible arrangements—only with the Squander Bug covered in $ £ ¥ € instead of swastikas. And with no war, please.

Clothes weren't rationed in the US, but millions had been so poor for so long there was no need. In fact, the war effort boosted the flailing economy, which was still suffering Depression-era unemployment. Franklin D. Roosevelt established his Works Progress Administration in 1935 to assuage the misery, including sewing rooms that went on to employ almost 180,000 women, who ultimately stitched some half a billion items.[43] Mending projects were certainly among them, and, though we don't know the proportion, there was a dire need for garment life-extension services. The 650 women of the Fort Worth sewing rooms liked to say WPA stood not for Works Progress Administration but for We Patch Anything.[44]

Salvage Sewing

For the better off, patching was their fun new hobby for the war effort. "Thousands of US women are experiencing for the first time the practical value of the adage 'waste not, want not,'" reported *Life* in 1942.[45] In another article it advised readers, "As war progresses and the cry for conservation grows, patches will become increasingly popular" (conservation, disappointingly, of war matériel, not the earth). Patches, said *Life*, have "deep soul-satisfying qualities" and "are of two kinds: the hidden, secret ones which create a deep bond between wearer and garment, and the rakish, flamboyant ones which proudly display their

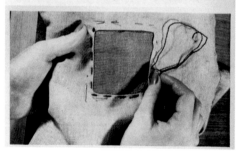

Leather elbow patches may be bought for 50¢, are here used on man's jacket, girl's coat. Note patches around the man's pockets, purposely done in contrasting material.

PATCHES ARE POPULAR

War and conservation bring them into the open

THE PATCH THAT DOES NOT MATCH IS BOLD

function."[46] Yes, that would be full visible mending, about eighty years ago.

Then there was Bundles for America to supply the armed forces with knitted garments, and salvage sewing workrooms collecting scraps, mill ends, and even car upholstery to make into clothes "for the needy" and as war reserves. None of this lasted. A year after V-E Day *Life* reported, with glee, on the $2 billion (equivalent to about $13 billion today) the US was spending on fashions as part of "its great spring splurge."[47] In some ways the Squander Bug had won.

Revolt against Bigness

The postwar boom generation went right on spending for a couple of decades, until the late 1960s, when a small but influential band of "freaks" put sewing and crafting, patching and mending firmly back on the map. The "Craft Comeback," said *The New York Times*, was "a revolt against technology and bigness," caused

by these counterculture hippies, whose style was all vintage bricolage, patchwork, and embroidery borrowed from the backpacking trail: in short, the homemade and mended look.[48]

"Patchwork is fashion news . . . It's A Quilting Be-In!" cried industry bible *Women's Wear Daily* in 1969. In 1971 in the US, home sewing boomed to a $3 billion industry (about $20 billion today), plus a further $115 million worth of premade embroidered trimmings, 80 percent of teenage girls were sewing, and the entire July 1971 *Vogue* was a "Make-It-Yourself" issue. As for what they sewed, sadly, I've found scant evidence of mending and making do outside the fringe economies of hippiedom. Mostly, they made precut clothes. Ready-to-wear was phenomenally expensive (remember the Triangle Shirtwaist fire and the strengthened unions?) resulting in companies called Mr. Most Pre-Cut Originals,

I Did It Myself Mother, and Apaches Do It, Ltd. stocking whole departments at Macy's and Bergdorf's (which called its department "Bigi Does It" for some reason).[49] A little left of the mainstream, a boatload of embroidery and embellishment was happening, lots with the look of visible mending, but not actually performed on holey clothes. A 1974 American Crafts Council and Levi's Denim Art Contest gives an idea of the skill level.

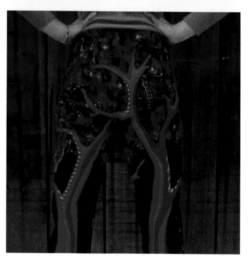

This was hippie-*ish*—the winner was Bill Shires's studded denim jacket with a naughty built-in ashtray (top right, above)—but the cooperative, anti-bigness impulse to preserve and conserve was really not the point. Mending was at the very root of the movement that birthed eco-everything, including the slow fashion branch, but by 1974 the radical part was done. And along with the hippie went the

sewing, and with the sewing, the mending. The 1970s turned out to be the last gasp of universal needlework. And what made it fade? Well, the hippie look was tortured into a twee, trying-too-hard style that nobody could get behind, and it was decades before you could say the word *craft* with a straight face.

I have always suspected it was craft that killed mending in the end.

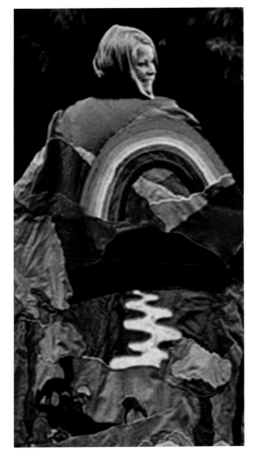

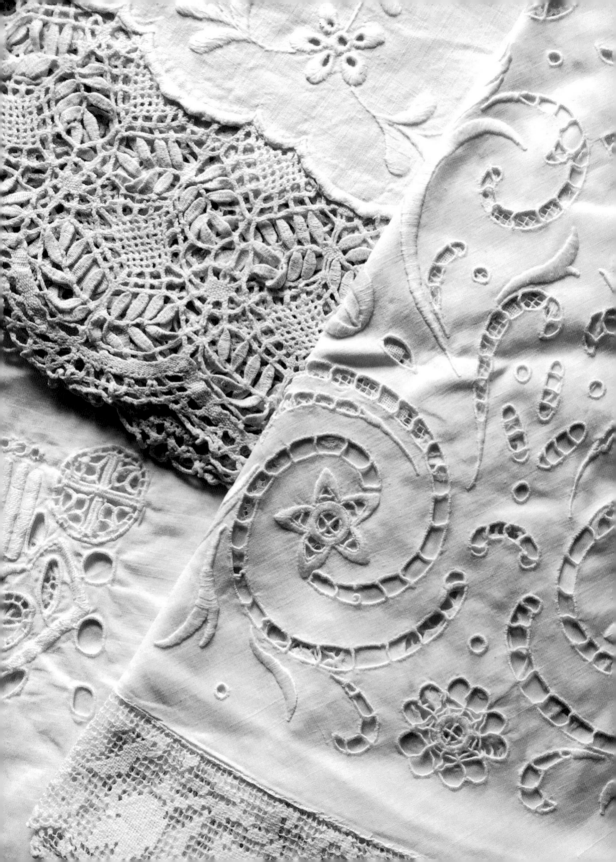

Chapter Four

who

The contemporary mending world is expanding exponentially with only one downside: this chapter will inevitably go immediately out of date. So I'll present this who's who in mending as a highly subjective introduction of various founder-menders, personages, and traditions, and—because I do go on so about clothes and mending being personal—a highly selective intro of me.

Grandmother Rosa, sewing, ca. 1914

My mother, mending, ca. 1990

Me(nd)

My textile gene is Viennese, down the paternal line. Great-grandfather Siegfried Engl founded his *Stroh und Filzhut Fabrik* (straw and felt hat factory) in 1882, and his fifth child, Rosa, married Siegfried Sekules, scion of a Budapest hat trimmings firm. Hat manufacture eventually continued in London,[1] where I had a continuous supply of hoods (unformed felt hat forms)

as a child milliner, plus an exciting selection of Weimar fur coats. We also had tons of drawn-work embroidery that Rosa and her mother and aunts and sisters and cousins had made as girls, which I now see is stunning, but was just our tablecloth. They stitched their last untroubled months into this whitework, thousands of hours of peace and safety, all that good time sewn up.

Then they escaped with it. This is why I'm devoted to hand-embroidered table linens. I

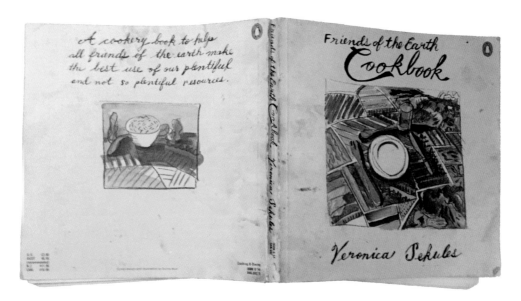

didn't know my family was Jewish till I was twenty-two. Missed some clues there.[2]

My father didn't sew. His sister did; she mended (I still use the ancestral haberdashery; see pages 104–5). But it was my German mother who taught me and my sister, Veronica, to sew.

Refugee and rationing memories still fresh, we were make-do-and-menders, investment spenders (his Gieves suits, her shantung blouses), and dressmakers—my sister and mother very expert ones. Veron, eleven years older, had a hippie-Victorian vibe; a marvelous, pungent

Portobello's North End today: much the same

"Our" rag-and-bone man's horse and cart, 1965

Afghan coat; and a wardrobe of early Laura Ashley, army surplus, and Biba.[3] She bought me my first fashion (elephant cord flares from Kids in Gear, Carnaby Street, which I wore to pieces, not a mender yet at eight). She left home and, while becoming Dr. Sekules the medieval art historian, worked at Friends of the Earth (FoE). Later she would write their zero-waste cookbook. My first job was at FoE, summer of eighth grade. Not to boast, but we were green before they invented green.

Rag and Bone

Even if green had been a thing, the idea that it was noble to buy secondhand was absurd to my mother, who was raised in couture silk dresses for *Tanzschule*, then lost everything, and was a bit nervous ever since.[4] The term *flea market* did nothing to ease her fears, but *flea market* definitely applied to my first clothes playground, my church, my happy place: Portobello Market. Forget Alice's Antiques and Rellik where Kate Moss goes, this was the slummy North End, under the Westway, where the old clothes were.[5]

I went alone every Friday and most Saturdays from age twelve. It was a wonderland and a history education, populated by fringe elements—eccentric costume collectors, weed dealers, hippies, Rastafarians, and, presently, punks, which, presently, was me. The stalls under the Westway were not "vintage"; they were the direct descendents of the Rag Fair. We still had a rag-and-bone man, too, one of the last in London, collecting scrap metal and textile waste house to house, clip-clopping past on his cart, crying, "*Raaaag* and bone! *Aaaany* old iron!"

And so I fell in love with rag. It was excitingly uncharted, almost illicit, and dirt cheap. A misfit teen, I mismatched 1920s tailcoats with '60s stirrup ski pants; crimplene old-lady tops with Edwardian taffeta mourning skirts. I altered and mended it all as a matter of course. Also I botched (not medievally dagged, just made up as I went along) strange trousers from old curtains. Cocktail frocks circa 1965 that I bought in quantity for 20p were my uniform for my first job after Friends of the Earth: frontman in a punk–new wave band.[6]

I was hardly alone in dressing like this; I was just part of the counterculture. Then in the 1980s a whole generation of designers came of age who were part of the same tribe, my people—rag people! Capital-*F* Fashion got great: Ann Demeulemeester, Dries van Noten,

and Martin Margiela from Antwerp; Yohji Yamamoto, Issey Miyake, and (the founding goddess) Rei Kawakubo from Japan; and, from down the street, hordes of them—English Eccentrics; Workers for Freedom; Helen Storey; Wendy Dagworthy; Vivienne Westwood, of course; and John Galliano, maker of my first designer investment.[7]

The world was all power shoulders and *Dallas* and Princess Di and this new fetish, the luxury label, but these iconoclasts channeled the ragpicker (so much nicer in French: *chiffonier*) with a holes-and-safety-pins, cut-up, dress-up, punk aesthetic. They were very *mendy*, Comme des Garçons and Maison Martin Margiela especially. Kawakubo did punk holes and body-deforming lumps; in his Artisanal line, Margiela pieced fabulous garments from all kinds of junk—gloves,

Comme des Garçons jumper, 1982

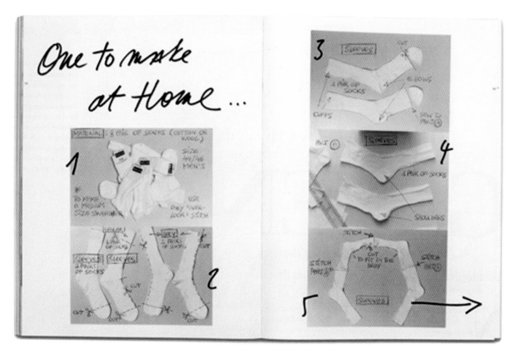

Martin Margiela's instructions for making a sock jumper

hats, plastic bags—and told you how to sew your old gym socks into a sweater. They were, and still are, major influences on everyone— their importance only increases with time, but mostly in theory now that it's all about money. The final genius graduated in 1992: Alexander McQueen. Rest in peace.

And that's when I became a fashion authority. Kind of. I was a columnist for *Clothes Show* magazine, banging on about, well, about this exact same stuff.[8] I wrote about the fashion industry's vintage appropriation, went undercover at Fashion Week and Bond Street boutiques ("Kate Sekules Shops with the Super Rich") and with wardrobe consultants ("Can You Buy Style?" No). I promised in print to invest in quality ("though I'm too cheap to spend £X on one garment I love when I can have four garments I hate for the same money") and— not really a thing yet—to *dress green*. I had the worst profile picture ever.

I started redistributing my too-vast Portobello (and designer) collection by organizing swaps and becoming a vintage dealer with my own stall at Camden Market. I still mourn those lost pieces. I did my first visible mend, a blanket stitch closely related to the felt rabbit I made at age five. It was atrocious. Nonlinearly, I moved to New York and, while working as a food and travel editor, fought professionally as a boxer: tasting menus and press trips versus damage and hand wraps. It was unusual at the time.[9] Then, the moment I reached great-job nirvana as editor in chief of *Culture+Travel*, magazines started dropping dead, including my own. I went into old clothes full time.

Fields of green. Increasing awareness of the environment has resulted in a wide range of eco-friendly products filling our cupboards. But what of our wardrobes? The Nineties dream may be of running through the fields dressed by Mother Nature but the practical reality is rather different

THE DILEMMA OF DRESSING
GREEN

It can be hard to find clothes that are ecologically sound, as Kate Sekules discovered

Now that we're allowed to eat Cape fruit and there aren't any furs about to jeer at (it is after all the middle of summer), I'm feeling the lack of a good cause to pursue while shopping.

How is it that I know I should buy recycled loo paper and eco-friendly washing-up liquid, but I don't know whether the process to produce a pair of tights is burning a hole in the ozone layer? Perhaps there's a scandalous cover-up afoot (pun intended). Perhaps I should start asking questions.

I did. Now I still don't know what to buy when I shop, but I do know a bit more about doing it sensitively. Here's one suggestion to start you off.

You know the back of the cupboard where you shove expensive mistakes that make you feel guilty? Well, apparently, if you joined the backs of Britain's closets together, you'd be looking at a collective credit card statement of £30 billion. As I've always suspected, and the Women's Environment Network suggests, we should be recycling the stuff. Buy long-lasting clothes, they say, give to Oxfam, buy from Oxfam, wash them less and iron only when strictly necessary. I like that part.

The other day I plunged into the rear of my wardrobe, filled a few bin liners for Oxfam, then retrieved what I felt sure were superior mistakes and hauled them to a swanky local dress exchange.

I don't recommend this latter method. 'That's a no', madame dress exchanger kept saying, aiming a scarlet talon at some pinhead of antique soup on my Donna Karan. Sadly, at that point I didn't yet know how un-green (positively purple, in fact) are trichloroethylene, formaldehyde and the other substances used to keep madame's finery immaculate.

I would like to stick my neck out here and guess that, sooner or later, looking 'immaculate' will mean looking very unfashionable indeed. This is not to say that the staff of *Vogue* will be seen in jerkins made of potato sack hessian, but rather that an unbleached organic cotton shirt will become a more desirable item than a pristine snow white Lagerfeld number. At least for a season.

If the shirt was made in Hong Kong, South Korea or India, though, you've got to worry about human rights, since there's a thing called the Multi Fibre Arrangements which forbids the poor Bangladeshis from expanding their shirt industry, while those newly industrialised countries, relatively speaking, rake it in.

So a hand-woven, vegetable dyed and co-operatively produced Thai silk skirt is okay to wear, right? Wrong. As it turns out, you have to worry about silkworms since, to keep the cocoons intact, silk moth pupae genocide is committed daily with boiling water, acid and gas.

Mind you, it's no good replacing silk with something synthetic unless you're happy to extract a teacupful from the 25,000 barrels of oil used every day to manufacture it.

Last August, the anti-fur group, Lynx, cremated about 5,000 fur coats which newly disgusted fur owners had given to a Fur Amnesty. Now all we need is a nylon, silk, rayon, acrylic, bleached cotton and dry-clean-only garment amnesty.

Oh my goodness me, I haven't a *thing* to wear.

PHOTOGRAPH: TRANSWORLD FEATURES

MY NEW YEAR'S RESOLUTIONS FOR 1993

Kate Sekules flings open her groaning closet to share some Great Fashion Disasters of 1992 and vows to take stock for New Year

Feel sorry for me if you l please, if you happen to riffing through racks of ballgowns, drooling ov blue brocade and peac Empire lines, come and yourself. Say you read t then drag me out of the of us has our little vice, other people's old ballg mine. For 1993, though to stop taking them hor In fact, it isn't only ballg Anything glittery seems my name and, judging amount of sequined an numbers in the shops b Christmas, I'm not alon infantile taste. Maybe w flock of magpies togeth former life.

I wouldn't need to m Year's Resolution if I w

KATE SEKULES

SHOPS WITH THE SUPER RICH

If the rich are different what are their favourite shops like? Kate Sekules enters the world of serious designer dressing

I f my clothes were people, they wouldn't throw catered dinner parties or go to balls at the Dorchester. Clothes like that probably wouldn't get us

£11,000. I had to breathe in sharply, completely blowing my cool. "So, what kind of person buys this?" I asked. "Someone who likes it," said the assistant.

Opposite: *Clothes Show* magazine, "Dressing Green," 1991.
Above, left: fashion resolutions and secret shopper, 1992.
Above, right: April 1992 cover with my
Confessions of a Fashion Junkie.
Below, left: shadow boxing, Gleason's Gym, 1999.
Below, right: great job nirvana:
May/June 2008 *Culture+Travel* cover.

who

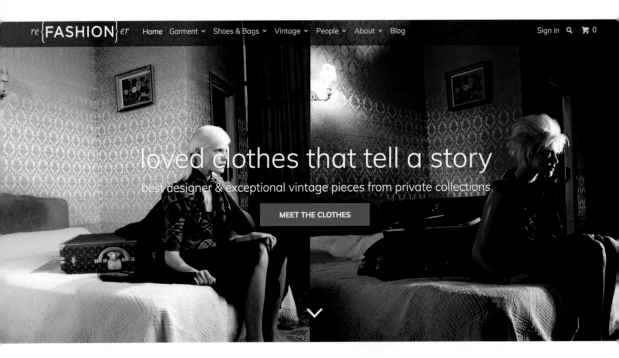

Refashioner: top, v. 3.0 homepage; below, screenshots of members' closets, 2012

Refashioning

I wanted to switch out my fancy-designer-editor gear but, unable to get the girls together for a swap, I figured I'd put it online. Simple! It wasn't. Refashioner, I called it, spelled re{FASHION}er. The idea was to release old clothes—the ones you don't wear but hang on to because they cost an arm and leg, or love but they hate you, or were Grandma's—from the backs of closets and trade them among peers. We'd curate like crazy, only the best, and you'd upload it *complete with its story*, and then you would stalk each other's closets. It launched (beta) in 2009. (thredUP also launched in 2009 as a men's shirt swap, but that was it for curated online resale.) Refashioner got press, won awards, broke the ten-thousand- member mark, and then I killed it. (A slightly tragic story about the site being hijacked by the developer. Ask me sometime.)

Mending

I made bad decisions, but Refashioner was really doomed all along. Silicon Valley exists to disrupt, monetize, and scale, and I'm only into the first of those. What I most loved was permission to wallow in rabbit holes of research—garment histories and industry horrors—and to mend vintage things. Therefore, another pivot: visibly mending mending historian! Hello.

Visibly

I thought I invented the term *visible mending*, but once I'd bought the URL in 2013, I found,

nope. There was already a scene in England, and it was named by one Tom van Deijnen, who goes by Tom of Holland, because he is Dutch and because he has a sense of humor.[10] Tom was mender in residence at the inaugural Mend*rs Research Symposium in Cumbria, July 2012. I expect the legendary status of this foundational event to grow, because it has been the only Mend*rs symposium to date. But there will be more: watch this space. Now let's meet some founder-menders.

Visible Mending Now: Ten Menders

Having related my own automendography, I'm honored to introduce a few of my favorite pioneers interfering in the death cycle of garments. Each mender's approach is different, mixing up art, craft, and intellect in various combinations, but always with the conscious intention to mend more than clothes. Repair, wrote information scientist Steven J. Jackson, "is the secret history . . . that has always sustained (but invisibly) the higher profile stories of exploration, empire, and globalization." His handy phrase "broken world thinking" suggests an upending of our tired old idea that production and innovation are the be-all and end-all. Instead we could conceive of society as a lot of stuff continuously in flux, being broken down and reconstituted, because, as Jackson says, "the world is always breaking; it's in its nature to break."[11] The fixer knows this. These visible menders live it.

Tom of Holland

Tom of Holland models the Six-Year Sweater

Aleatoric Fair Isle Swatch #1

I call Tom van Deijnen, who lives in the southern English coastal bohemia of Brighton, the Godfather of VM, whether he likes it or not—and he doesn't really, because "it kind of makes it sound like I'm the first one to do visible mending." But Tom was indeed the first to capture the spirit, tag it, and send it out in his Visible Mending Programme (est. 2010).[12] And, in my book, he also earned the title by being generous—an exemplary mending mendsch, as I discovered when I stole his domain name. Well, to be fair, he didn't want visiblemending.com because it doesn't encompass all the kinds of work he does. "I feel making and repairing are all part of the same thing and I don't want to create a separation," he says.

Tom's making is knit based. He has a deep love of a yarn in every sense. He often uses wool from around the UK with a tale behind it (resisting Bo Peep pun), mines historical techniques from his library of vintage knitting books, and invents entire new genres, such as (with fellow knit-head Felicity Ford) Aleatoric Fair Isle, in

Amazing Jumper, 2015. A wearable darning sampler

which the music of John Cage meets the traditional pattern knitting of the Shetland Isles meets a throw of the dice (full story on his blog; it's worth the read). It was knitting that begat mending, when Tom's proudly sported, first homemade socks ran to holes. "Wanting to repair these 'properly,'" he says, "started me off on the journey I still find myself on now." Visibility quickly followed, partly inspired by the multicolors in antique darning samplers (see pages 34–37). "I like how [VM] highlights the fact the item has been repaired, adding to the history of it. It allows you to be creative," he says.

All Tom of Holland mends get a serial number and are recorded in the Visible Mending Programme logbook, but none wins. "I have a fair few favorites, all for different reasons. It might be the background story, technique used, or simply because I was particularly happy with the end result." Here, his 2013 *Amazing Jumper* has to qualify: operated on with multiple patterns of fancy darning—several herringbone variations, a Prince of Wales–Sanquhar tweed pattern, a simple houndstooth. "A darning sampler gone slightly out of hand," he calls it. Another is the *Six-Year Sweater*, begun at the Mend*rs Symposium, finished in 2018, and one of his toughest challenges "because it felt never-ending." Tom has shared his formidable expertise in workshops from Australia to Finland, and is represented by the New Craftsmen, a gallery of elite British makers, but also volunteers at Brighton's monthly Repair Café, whose mission statement reads, "We bring people together to give the objects we share our world with a second lease of life and to chat

and have a cuppa whilst we're at it." Like I said, humble. "I have learnt so much about repairing textiles, and yet I feel I have only just scratched the surface of what is possible," Tom wrote about the Six Years of the Sweater, which, in retrospect, was the gestation period of visible mending itself. In 2012 mending felt fringe; now Tom sees growing awareness of the underlying issues, and says, "I'm just hoping that repair will become the norm again, just like it used to be in earlier times." If anyone can make that happen, it's the Godfather.

Bridget Harvey

The single most recognizable emblem of the VM movement is the *MEND MORE Jumper*. The backstory of this iconic piece is as political, thoughtful, and multilayered as you'd expect from its maker, Londoner Bridget Harvey, who is quite literally the Doctor of Mending, thanks to her doctoral dissertation, titled "Repair-Making: Craft, Narratives, Activism." But this dynamic activist-scholar-teacher-feminist-artist

Bridget Harvey's iconic MEND MORE jumper

Dr. Bridget Harvey mending, April 2020

calls herself simply *maker*. Like Tom, she volunteers at public mending sessions. In short, she lives her principles with every pore.

The jumper, which featured in the 2018–19 *Fashioned from Nature* exhibition at the Victoria and Albert Museum, where Bridget was an artist in residence, was born as a 2015 London climate march placard (opposite). The jumper is made of "scraps dug out from my stash" hand stitched onto a large suffragette-purple acrylic sweater. "Its material supports its message," says Bridget. "With its humanlike form, it speaks about clothes and people. It's saying, 'We mend, join us!'"

As with many (all?) of these menders, Bridget has always repaired. "I didn't recognize it as a skill; it was just a way of caring for my possessions and understanding how things worked. If I couldn't mend it, maybe I didn't want to own it." Amen to that.

Then over that same six years surrounding the Mend*rs Research Symposium ("It was quite rainy, which sorta brought everyone together," she remembers), her ideas of repair blossomed. The central revelation was that "repair-making needs to be a first thought that's designed and legislated for, rather than an afterthought. It's a method, involving stories, communities, and politics." Now, from where she's standing, dead center of the movement, she sees mending evolving fast, politically, personally, and communally. "It's actually very exciting," she says with a smile. And amen also to *that*.

Amy Twigger Holroyd

Amy Twigger Holroyd stitch hacking

Her reknitting sampler

If Bridget Harvey is the Doctor of Mending, Amy Twigger Holroyd is the Knit Doctor, after her dissertation, "Folk Fashion: Amateur Re-Knitting as a Strategy for Sustainability." There's a lot behind that title. Amy coins terms and leads yarn-based movements apparently by the dozen, including the Reknit Revolution, where people are encouraged to alter their jumpers at the stitch level, like molecular biologists of wool, stitch hacking and cardiganizing with the help of her Reknit Revolution. (Find it on page 136. Amy brilliantly slapped a Creative Commons license on this work, which she's been developing for over a decade. You knitters, whom I neglect, are welcome.) And what is folk fashion, you ask? This Twigger Holroydism (and title of her 2017 book) describes the territory we're in right now, making or mending our own clothes. "I hear more and more people enthusing about mending," Amy says. And she is listening closely, creating the Stitching Together network with other make-and-mend researchers specially for the purpose. "It's amazing how the experience of making together can lead to really open, revealing conversations," she says. "It really is going from strength to strength." The multitasking, stitch-hacking Knit Doctor is certainly one reason why.

Karen Nicol

It's hard to resist filling several pages with Karen Nicol's staggering, ravishing embroidery, but we'll make do for now with a small javelina. An Honorary Fellow of the Royal College of Art, elite Royal Designer for Industry, veteran of countless solo exhibitions, and commissioned to do work for everyone from Alexander McQueen to the actual Pope, Karen is perched at the very top of the tree where this art form lives. Her style is elemental, using materials from antique lace to found trash with free-form precision and controlled exuberance, and she's long worked in fashion, Chanel couture and Anthropologie designs alike. So imagine my delight when this major artist unhesitatingly agreed when I asked if she might try a visible mend or two. "I revere the human aspect of a mend and the uniqueness it gives to a piece," she said. "One's interaction creating a piece of cloth, which previously had been one of many, suddenly becoming a thing with a personal signature, history, and story." Exactly! So I picked my best holes: a mid-1960s windowpane check wool shift dress, courtesy of my friend Tina's late mother, and a valuable collector's item, a 1981 Vivienne Westwood Worlds End pirate pant. "I decided to use the damage placement to just add to the design process and show that mending could be any form of mark making," said Karen—as if this were easy. Well, she does make it *look* easy.

When I picked up the pieces at her south London home studio, Karen sat at her charismatic antique Irish Singer, with its single

A small javelina

free needle, no presser foot or feeder teeth, to demonstrate the flower technique. She uses "thread" of torn-up old chiffon scarves "to emulate a painterly brush stroke. With the slightest twist it can change from a fat, flat mark to a tight, taut one, giving transparency one minute, intense color the next." It was astonishing to watch. The machine was like a third hand. "One can draw very freely with it," said Karen,

At the charismatic Irish Singer

"Drawn" with old chiffon scarves

The 1981 Worlds End pant, bird-mended

"but one is moving the 'paper' rather than the 'pencil.'" She draws freely when stitching by hand also. "I like to try to use hand stitch in a gestural, uneven way," she says. Lately she's been drawn to darning, finding "the quirky, slightly eccentric addition of a woven lattice on top of a different weave simply wonderful." One of Karen's favorite possessions is an Edwardian work overall that's practically all darn, evoking the entire life story of a "fragile yet resilient young woman." A poem in stitch, she calls it. Which is coincidentally what I call Karen Nicol's mending.

Margreet Sweerts
and Saskia van Drimmelen

Golden Joiners Margreet (left) and Saskia

Playing clothes doctor at Droog Design, Amsterdam

The game in action

Next we head to Amsterdam for a spot of Golden Joinery. Around 2013, theater director Margreet Sweerts and fashion designer Saskia van Drimmelen began a project that united their handwork-heavy, Big Fashion–disrupting line Painted Series with kintsugi, the ancient Japanese art of visibly mending porcelain with gold. It all started with a workshop. "It's playful and a bit performative," says Margreet. "We do musical chairs. Saskia and I are dressed like first aid doctors." Because it was impractical to perform all over the world, they decided the next best thing was to translate the gist of it into a parlor game to spread the word.

Now, I'd heard of the Golden Joinery game, but I wasn't prepared for how literal is the word *game*, nor how fun it is, till I played a round. It's a real board game created with

Result

the help of artist friends, complete with gorgeous cards, golden supplies, and rules. I won't spoil the surprises, but it does exactly what it says on the box, viz: "through playful interventions, this workshop will lead you out of your mind and into your hands." Eight of us, four fashion historians, a museum curator, two lecturers, and a designer, that is, blasé been-there-done-that types, were enchanted. "*Gold* refers to value, to treasure, to alchemical processes; engagement and care, not exploitation of the material world," says Margreet. "We think healing something in *togetherness* is the core of the experience. Therefore the game, with only winners!" I don't care if I sound like an advert, but now all my friends know what they're getting for their birthdays.

Ruth Katzenstein Souza

In America the mending scene has been unfolding in disparate pockets for decades, so it seems apt to visit first with LA artist Ruth Katzenstein Souza, a mending lifer dedicated to spreading the word through workshops and teachings under the umbrella Mending as Metaphor. Ruth learned from her grandmother, "laying out pretend landscapes with the scraps in the bottom drawer of her chiffonier" as a small child; marveling at her ability to fix everything with her mending kit, "a small plaid case she made, lined with felt"; learning "the sacredness of textiles."

Her mending circle was birthed in 2012, while resurrecting her granny's final quilt alongside "a very special young woman" she was mentoring—and the talking-sewing-talking wove the same magic it always has

Top: Ruth's embroidered faces; bottom: Ruth patching

Mending as Metaphor as reality: the LA mending circle in action

throughout history. Ruth wants this phenomenon back. "At one point, mending was part of the culture; clothing and linens were valued," she says. The metaphor of mending is, of course, about healing, individual to societal. "At every turn we are confronted with cracks in our world that are so deep that many of us despair. Where do we begin?" she wonders, answering with the route her own mending circles take, "Identify the crack near you." Partnering with Textile Arts Los Angeles, Ruth designated 2019 A Year of Mindful Mending: "A laboratory for trying lots of different ways to think about meditative stitching," with Golden Joinery–ish games, plenty of conversation, and some silence. "I'm interested in people finding a personal voice with their mending," says Ruth. "It's about process, community, storytelling." And, above all, the wisdom of a lifetime's mending.

Jessica Marquez

Jessica at work.
Opposite: precision mends and dogs

Going by Miniature Rhino after her young cousin's imaginary friend, a dentist called Dr. Rhino (an emblem of pure creativity, obviously), Cali-born Brooklynite Jessica Marquez rocks Etsy, is an Instagram ninja, and garners hordes for her online classes, but what sets her apart among the new generation of visible menders is a dedication and depth I can only describe as *mendy*.

Jessica lives for "getting people excited about making with their hands and rethinking their relationship to their textiles," which she also does in sold out IRL classes and through her book *Make and Mend*, a primer in and love letter to the Japanese art of sashiko. "Sashiko just ticks all the boxes in my brain. I happen to geek out on drawing my own patterns and creating crisp, complex designs, but also it combines my love of history and textiles, hand embroidery, and resourcefulness in a way that speaks to my environmental concerns," she explains.

The latter go deep in this animal-batty vegan from a sewing family—"my grandmother had nine children and sewed, altered, and repaired much of their clothing"—who connects past with present through her very stitches. "I always ground my practice and teaching with the history of sashiko," she says. "Through contemporary eyes these layers of stitching, pattern, and patches can seem purely aesthetic, but the reality was that often these mends were made out of need and meant to be hidden." (See page 80 for more on sashiko.) So, along with deep stitchery, Jessica teaches the joys of "repair, reuse, and living with less, because our modern-day abundance is a bit shocking." Dr. Rhino the dentist would be proud.

Miriam Dym

Nobody visibly mends like Miriam Dym. This LA-based systems artist mixes design, engineering, and business into her work, and has done exactly that with the Logo Removal Service (LRS), est. 2006, which I have to admit is about my favorite ever mend-based ruse. "At Logo Removal Services," goes the pitch, "we renew any and all soft goods through special transformation methods . . ." LRS was born as a rescue for a gifted T-shirt "that fit well and that I wanted

Miriam Servicing logos
Left: results and rules

to wear, but I wasn't going to help advertise the company, whose logo was suddenly ubiquitous. So I spontaneously hacked a solution." And thus the eponymous service was conceived, a "reverse appliqué with stitching that riffed off, without slavishly following, the logo's outline. I didn't want a logo ghost, I wanted a brand new, never-before-seen shape!"

This soon became "a small, to-me-delightful, performative gesture against mass production" that debuted at a Berkeley Center for New Media conference with a live excision and display of a de-logoed T-shirt ("Yes, they clapped!") Now LRS is a business (a suboptimal one, as Miriam points out) that does a thing loathsome to business, presented live in museums and conferences, or, in the artist-CEO's words, "a ritual performance that questions supply chain, material reality, and corporate branding." I admit, at the risk of losing friends and readers, I never did get why people like branding themselves—it is, as Miriam points out, "a word with a spectacularly ugly origin." So, in my opinion, Dym's Logo Removal, or visible mending of branding, is a service the world urgently needs.

Anne Graham

Now we go behind the scenes in a rare righteous corner of corporate America: Patagonia Worn Wear, whose—literal!—wagon Anne Graham, of Los Osos, California, has been riding since it launched. The customized, salvaged-redwood-clad, biodiesel-burning '91 Dodge Cummins set off in 2015 on its mission to mend. It was a driveable mini version of the company's Reno repair center (which mends customers' clothes), where Anne worked for three years, scaling up her skills—though "my first mending teacher," she says, "was motherhood."[13]

The invitation to operate the truck's industrial Juki machine came "at a time of life when it was most enjoyed," says Anne, a semiretired grandmother (twenty-five years working for California State Parks) or, as she puts it, "a simple person with a sewing machine affliction." The machine that started this addiction was a thrifted "cool-looking Art Deco desk" that turned out to conceal a 1930s Eldredge Rotary, and now . . . "Honestly I don't know how many [I own]. Maybe fifty? Vintage sewing machines are design history. I took them in as one would an orphan, out of love." But neither vintage orphans, nor experience—she

Anne doing in-truck mending

Adopting a few vintage sewing machines

was a sewing child—prepared Anne for pro mending. "I thought it would be no big deal, but oh man, was I in for it!" Still, with the help of Reno's "very international team," she soon learned the industrial machines' ways, and so began "a deep sense of satisfaction when I was able to finally make a living from the work of my hands."

Reno is all speed and efficiency, but Worn Wear, Anne found, is personal, artisanal. *Visible*. "The garment's owner is standing right there so can request what they want. When people would ask me to use a print for a patch or different thread for darning I would get a little anxiety. I am kind of old school and was a bit resistant to the visible mend. You know what would happen? It would come out *great*. I mean, these look fantastic. Fun to do as well. I get it!" Mending is more important now than ever, believes Anne, so it's nice to show it off. "Our clothing can say so much with no words. Why not make it say what we want?"

Michael Swaine

"The conversation always starts with the sewing machine and the holes and tears," says Michael Swaine, our final mender, and also the first: the first to make mending into living artwork, the first public mender, the first and only mending *librarian*. Every fifteenth of the month for the first fifteen years of this century, rain or shine, Michael trundled his salvaged treadle machine on a repurposed ice cream cart to an abandoned alley in San Francisco's Tenderloin with a mission: to mend.

"It started in a simple, romantic way, like 'I want to do something for the city I live

Michael Swaine, mending librarian of the Tenderloin National Forest. That's Veronica in the stripey sweater.

too, right by what a 2018 *New York Times* article called "the Dirtiest Block in San Francisco" ("developing-world squalor . . . open-air narcotics market . . . street crime . . . human waste," etc.).[14] Michael calls it "a diverse neighborhood, with more holes per capita than other parts of the Bay Area." Most of his clients lived in low-income housing, if they were housed at all—and *client* is too transactional. Mendees wanted to give Michael things, gifts of PB&Js or clothes. His most regular regular, Veronica, told him "You are the only one who listens to me." "People helped strangers in ways that felt so much larger than my few minutes of sewing," says Michael, attributing the "moments of amazing humanity" to quietly putting this private inside act out on the street.

In the end, says Michael, it wasn't even about the mending. "I know the mending was in the middle, so I am not wanting to erase its power, but it felt like all the other things surrounding it that made the city slow down, made me remember things about this life we live. This project changed who I am. It was an honor for me to sit there."

Now, still at Cohen Alley, 509 Ellis (which has been officially renamed the Tenderloin National Forest by the adjacent, always supportive Luggage Store Gallery), there is a new head librarian, friend and longtime collaborator Laurie Moyer. As Michael told me in an email, "The Free Mending Library is still going every 15th (WOW!!!!!)."

WOW!!!!! is definitely the word.

(But I do think it's about the mending.)

in and I could mend clothes for free,' and it became more and more un-simple," says Michael; "un-simple" meaning deep, not complex. The idea of the Free Mending Library is easy to grasp—I remember hearing about it and being delighted and dazzled (also wishing I'd thought of it and had the guts)—but what it actually did was different from its raison d'être. "The Free Mending Library is a place to mend holes in our life" was how Michael described it at the time. Now looking back, he says, "An empty chair and an invitation to talk and just listen was so much more important than I thought." The location was important,

Mendspiration/ Appropriation

Mending and sashiko, mending and boro— the Japanese textile traditions are easily the most utilized in visible mending, and are sometimes the most misunderstood. To go purely by hashtag is to risk playing the popular sport of cultural appropriation. When applied to your jeans, Japanese-style sewing is unlikely to be sashiko; it's probably just running stitch in patterns. "Borrowing" traditions that evolved over centuries in very specific circumstances is offensive if you're, say, Levi's, and using it to look cool so you can sell more product.[15] Curator and scholar Glenn Adamson called this "the 'hit-and-run' tactics of Western designers when they parachute into craft cultures, extract ideas and feel-good symbolism, and then move on."[16] For most of us, if you're not blatantly mining ideas for profit, it's fine to look to other people's traditions as inspiration, but let's please take the time and trouble to know where they came from and proceed with sensitivity. In addition to the historical examples in the previous chapter, there are certain artifacts, artists, and traditions I revere, even though their culture doesn't belong to me. My intention is to honor them through this display of mendspirations, because it's the very depth of meaning, feeling, and history that makes me love them. The hand is everything.

Above: Meiji-era boro kimono
Below: My own prized boro fragment

Sashiko and Boro

The hashtag doesn't exactly lie: sashiko ("little stabs") is indeed the use of running stitch to form designs and actually was used, as

Above: Meiji-period sashiko jacket
Below: Detail of its shippō-tsunagi sashiko stitching

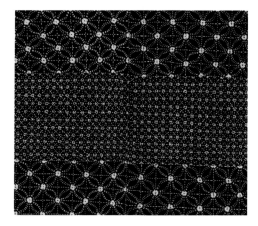

Wikipedia can tell you, to stitch together layers and pieces of fabric for reinforcement and warmth. Similarly, boro ("rags") does denote multipatched, sashiko-stitched textile. But here we've lost a thousand layers of meaning.

Sashiko developed during the Edo period (1603–1867) in the rural north of Japan to maximize the longevity and utility of a scarce resource—so far, so exactly like every culture everywhere. Then, basically, strict sumptuary laws forbidding the use of color or fine fabrics or patterns bigger than a grain of rice backfired into the ordinary people creating this universe of symbolically rich, ingenious designs in undyed thread on permissibly blue-indigo-dyed fabric. Local laws led to regional variations, such as *kogin*, the dense stitching on coarse single-layer hemp from Aomori Prefecture in the Tōhoku region.

This *hitomezashi* ("one stitch") sashiko is way beyond most people's skill level, as is the *shippō-tsunagi* (linked seven treasures) *moyozashi*, or pattern, sashiko to the left, but surely not the simpler, rustic boro, right? Wrong. Surviving examples were made and worn (and worn and worn and mended and mended) by farmers during the Meiji era, necessitated by great poverty and causing lasting shame. We can't make boro or even boro-style garments, because they were carefully and frugally constructed and preserved over lifetimes and generations; they belong to history, and, unless we're Japanese, not ours. Much boro was lost, discarded for its association with terrible times, or simply worn out, but it began to be valued as folk craft during the mingei movement of the 1920s, especially owing to the advocacy and personal collections of the folklorist and cultural anthropologist Chuzaburo Tanaka, and today, well, it's properly practically priceless.[17]

Japanese fabric reuse also has deep spiritual roots. The Buddhist vestment, the *kesa*, consists of pieces devotionally, symbolically patched by monks from discarded rags, or, often, fine silks donated by the lay community for religious merit.[18] Sashiko patterns are

also replete with meanings religious, secular, auspicious, protective, or personal, singly and in combinations. "The idea that you are constantly learning is part of Japanese craft culture," says Susan Briscoe, who, though author of (the highly recommended!) *The Ultimate Sashiko Sourcebook*, says she'd never call herself an authority ("how about 'sashiko enthusiast'?") and that she'll herself "be learning forever."

Kantha

As *boro* means "rags" in Japanese, so does *kantha* in Sanskrit, and it, too, names a fabric tradition used for centuries to utilize and preserve that most precious resource—this time in West Bengal, Bihar, and Bangladesh. Kantha refers to running stitch as well as to the quilts made by using the stitch to join layers of saris and dhotis (usually cotton, usually old). Nowadays it's so familiar, you'll hear kantha stitching cited as a technique by many a mender, when what they've made are rows and rows of not-completely-even stitching resulting in gentle puckering. That's fine, but original kantha are from a region once battered by British rule, a region that is now suffering in the name of fashion through low wages and underregulated factories—that are no doubt churning out "kantha throws" sold at T.J. Maxx with unintended gross irony. By contrast, this gent with the lovely darns above his fish is from a nineteenth-century Bengali kantha quilt embroidered with multicultural motifs at the RISD Museum. The quilt, say the curators, "symbolically repairs a politically and religiously divided place."[19] The other one here is from my own collection of undistinguished but special vintage kantha, sewn with marvelous randomness, which can't really be random, because it works so well.

Jogakbo

I love the ultrapatchwork of a type of bojagi—Korean wrapping cloth—called *jogakbo*.[20] Its rescuing of tinier scraps than any other traditional art of any other people tells quite a tale. It was an art of the gyubang culture—meaning "boudoir" or "women's quarters"—born of the usual preservation impulse, but also the conservative Joseon dynasty ideals of frugality and simplicity. Museum of Korean Embroidery director Huh Dong-hwa says a jogakbo was "a family portrait before photography," containing the life of the woman who stitched it, excluded from male society, and expressing all her creativity through this mistresspiece of patchworked cloth. Many are made of multihued scraps from family dressmaking, but this black hemp one showcases the exquisite flat triple-seam *gekki* stitching that makes for the characteristic windowpane effect.

Kuba Cloth

This extraordinary fifteen-foot-long wrap skirt made by the Kuba people of Zaire (now the Democratic Republic of the Congo) has mending in its very nature. The tricky fabric woven from the *Raphia vinifera* palm is pounded into pliability, leaving weak places that are then appliquéd, patched, and embroidered from a repertoire of two hundred shapes, which evolved and were passed down over the ages. Kuba cloth influenced a generation of important Western artists—see the motifs echoed in works by Paul Klee, Henri Matisse, Georges Braque—and is collected by every other museum. But one art history professor teaches quite a different lesson through this cloth, one about learning through looking and paying attention to the stitch: Which patches are intrinsic? Which are mends? Why? This professor is my brother-in-law, Sandy Heslop, which is how I was lucky enough to get close and personal with this particular piece from his own collection, and now so can you.

Bargello

Speaking of family, my mother, Marianne, taught me and Veronica to sew, but never like this. *Bargello* is named after some chairs in the eponymous Florentine palace that are adorned with a species of needlepoint, done vertically and precisely in a sort of flame arrangement and not at all to my taste. Not to my mother's, either, apparently, because she started this cushion cover in about 1985 and never did finish it. I include it here to show how not every sewing tradition is mendy (sorry, needlepoint, you're really not), and to get Ma into the "Who" technique section. I still mend with the leftover tapestry wools in those ghastly 1980s pastels, in a kind of posthumous darning collaboration. The yarn has acquired significance and value it lacked while stuffed in the back of her closet. My point is to illustrate the eternal truth that mending is personal, intimate, and sometimes sentimental.

Textile Tokens

▬▬▬

And to drive home that point with the opposite of a bullet, here are the most heartbreaking fabric scraps you will ever see. They represent the yearning of a mother for a lost child and also how important fabric used to be.[21]

For a destitute woman in mid-eighteenth-century London, to leave her baby at the new Foundling Hospital was to give it a chance in life. Thousands of mothers abandoned their infants with a token of identification, usually a scrap of material, precious and valuable to her, in the hope that she might be able to come back for the child someday. A heart cut from red wool and a morsel of paduasoy silk, or a yellow ribbon inscribed "My name is Andrews"—though foundling babies were assigned new identities—still transmit tenderness and sorrow down the centuries, such is the power of cloth and stitch. When you know that practically none of the abandoned babies were reclaimed, the intensity

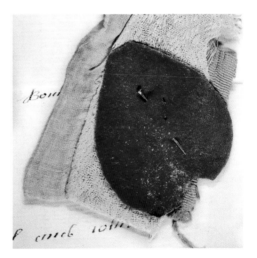

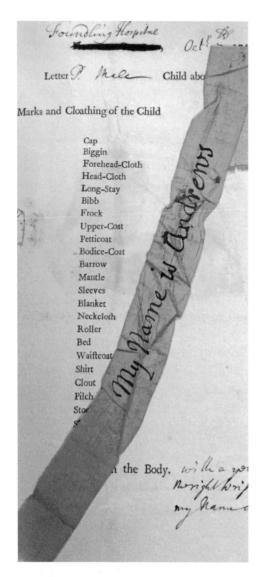

Mending Broken Lives

The following century, when unfortunate circumstances might put the woman herself, not just her infant, in an institution, she occasionally managed to stitch her plight into a textual textile. Rare examples have survived the asylum to form a small corpus of extraordinary muscular intensity, which are great inspirations to many a visible mender. Agnes Richter's jacket is the best known of such pieces, which are often mislabeled outsider art, though the makers were very much inside, and sewing not for art, but sanity.

contained in the scraps only grows.[22] At least this patchworked needle case embroidered with half a (broken) heart had a happy ending. Sarah Bender returned for her Charles in 1775 after he'd spent eight years as the foundling Benjamin Twirl. The token, abandoned, had done its work.

We know little of Richter. She was a German seamstress, committed at age forty-nine for paranoia when she said people were stealing from her. Only a few odd phrases from the dense deutsche Schrift she embroidered all over her regulation-issue (but altered by her) jacket have been deciphered: "I am not big" (true: this thing is child-sized), "I wish to read," and "I plunge headlong into disaster." The jacket is stained with sweat and very worn.

Less famous, but more legible, are the autobiographical embroideries of two Victorian Englishwomen committed for dubious reasons. Mary Frances Heaton suffered from delusions—specifically of a secret marriage to Lord Seymour, whose children she tutored. I feel we might unpick the threads of a cold case if we could read her entire oeuvre, so cogent is it, so detailed, so nicely punctuated. "The drunken wife of a ranter parson countenanced, as I have reason to suspect, by 'Sir Oracle de Twopenny,' takes it upon herself to dispose of the private affairs of a nobleman's governess," one concludes. Who can be sure her stitched name, "Mrs Seymour," wasn't the truth? Who knows if people actually were stealing from Agnes Richter?

Mending Minds

Fast-forward another hundred years, and the anguish and horror vacui expressed in mending-type stitchery in asylum-type institutions is replaced by exuberance and creativity in art studios. In the early 1970s two visionary facilities opened where people with developmental disabilities produced (still do today) the most staggering works of needle art. The Nui Project of Shobu Gakuen in Kagoshima City, Japan, houses twenty-five makers in its embroidery atelier, who are not taught to sew, but let loose to express what they call "power set free without imposed ideas" and "the strength of the accidental." The results are absolutely enviable as free-associative supermends (not to mention high fashion objects).

And who knows if Lorina Bulwer entered Great Yarmouth Workhouse around 1893 a "lunatic"? Her letters (one is fourteen feet long) stitched in unpunctuated apoplectic capitals are semicoherent, but wholly understandable. I imagine Lorina, the wrongly accused, stabbing and stabbing and stabbing her needle into scrounged scraps, accusing everyone with righteous indignation: "THE PEOPLE ARE REAL ENGLISH TRAMPS HAWKERS SHOW PEOPLE NOT ONE HERE HAVE ANYTHING TO DO WITH MY PARTY. . . ."[23] Is it wrong to love something so much if it came from so much anguish?

Then in 1974, Florence Ludins-Katz and Elias Katz took the dregs of the hippie craft movement and channeled it into the Creative Growth center for artists with disabilities in the Bay Area. As well as nurturing world-renowned artists who show at the Venice Biennale and are collected by MoMA (e.g., Judith Scott and Dan Miller), Creative Growth mounts the annual Beyond Trend runway event to showcase the artists' hand stitched clothes—my very prized pants patched with pants (and other clothes) are by Creative Growth artist Christine Szeto. It's all very punk, very personal—very, very *mendy*. And you know that's the highest praise I can give.

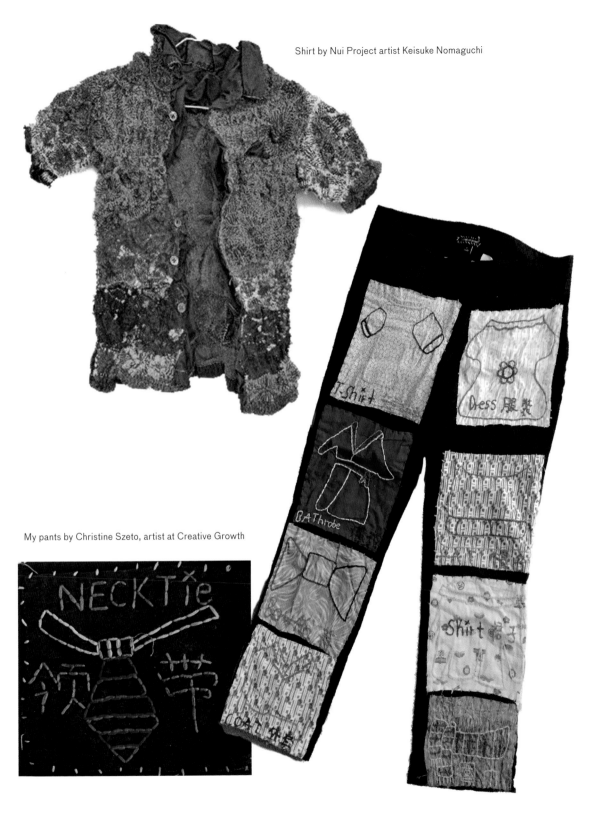

Shirt by Nui Project artist Keisuke Nomaguchi

My pants by Christine Szeto, artist at Creative Growth

NECKTie 领带

Chapter Five

where

Some adore stationery; many obsess
over makeup. Me, I could fill a book with
haberdashery* porn alone. New matériel from
the notions store is tasty (also pricey), but my
helpless passion for old garments extends to
their tiniest component parts; it's vintage stock
that slays me. With its bold, colorful graphics
and superior quality, it improves with age, like
wine. But whatever sort you're into, old or new,
haberdashery is the engine of mending and one of
its chief pleasures. Prepare for addiction.

---

* *Haberdashery* is *English*-English for "notions."
I insist on using it because it's just about my favorite word.

Microscopic

Mini

This chapter answers various mend-related "Where" questions, chiefly where to source and store supplies, and where to use them. Then we'll take a peek at where clothes live. Wardrobe organization is a very popular fetish, but the mending-tending part is less about eye candy than practical solutions for problems you don't even know you have.

Kitting Out

Who doesn't love a kit? The complete tools for the job all in good order. Things that come in kits are always obsessible (by me): hardware, art supplies, stationery. I'm even partial to a first aid kit. I confess to secreting sewing kits all over the place. In fact, I wager that in no time flat, your mending kit will breed little baby kits, because mending is portable and impulsive and supplies near every chair are such a boon to the lazy. Then again, it is

imperative that you keep tabs on your stash, otherwise it will take over. But never fear! All you need remember is the prime directive: *like with like*. This means keeping all your sewing things together in one place, or several places. And within each place, like with like: fabrics by weight or type, design or color; same with needles, pins, floss, yarn, thread, etc., each thing discrete. Simple. Here follows a breakdown of where to keep your supplies, in ascending size order, illustrated by some of mine.

Microscopic

Miniature things are adorable, and these teeny tiny kits—from my niece Clio, Tokyo, the 1960s, and a Christmas stocking—just slay me. Unfortunately, they are too adorable to actually use.

Traveling

Basket

Mini

Compact mending kits have been in production for at least a century, often as promotional giveaways, alongside needle books. In the realm of the hotel amenity, opinion is divided as to whether vacuuming all the shampoo bottles into your wheelie bag is stealing. All I can say is, half a lifetime as a travel journalist, no pre-threaded mending kit left behind, and I remain at large. Admittedly, about eighty-seven of mine now contain only pink and yellow thread and a plastic button, yet I adore them. Sorry not sorry. Irrationally I despise those modern kits from the drugstore, no doubt made in the same ecologically ruinous factory.

Traveling

Ah, the vital travel kit. Contrary to popular belief, sewing needles are TSA compliant. So are scissors smaller than four inches, but they often trigger extra inspection anyway, so I fly

with the blue plastic barely-a-scissor from a mini office kit. Crafters live to make patchwork sewing organizers, but mine is a lousy plastic zippy pouch I've had about twenty years. I also have my mother's superior red leather one, but haven't the heart to change her stuff out.

Wearable

Hardware store tool belts are an unexploited fashion statement without the retail markup. Repurpose the big drill pockets for fabrics, nail or fastener ones for notions. I have one, and admire its design, but am usually found in my dead stock waitress's mini apron with pockets, which is comfy and amusing.

Basket

I don't know why sewing and baskets belong together. Maybe it's because baskets are constructed like 3D darns. My main basket happened when I moved house and dumped some supplies temporarily in a seagrass bowl

from St. Lucia. Seventeen years ago. If you're deliberately making a sewing basket (recommended), easy access is key. So is neatness. I have four deputy baskets, and more are threatening to form any second if a basket is stupid enough to hang around empty.

Portable

While all the foregoing can be moved, the salient characteristic of this mending container is its handle. In this category belongs that icon, the metamorphic or concertina sewing box on little legs your grandma had. Magnificent as they are, I've never owned one, but if you're going to invest in a single vintage or antique kit holder, this is the one. I love my folding frame made by (guessing) a Depression-era Catskills farmer. Check out the mason jars screwed to the top. Heart. My supply satchel

hoards boxes and baggies of things: darning and tatting thread sets, mostly. But my favorite portable is the paisley stripe drawstring bag with pockets inside that my sister made me for my tenth birthday: still in use.

Furniture, Small

Easily scored online is the Martha Washington cabinet, a design dating from the early nineteenth century that was reproduced in quantity during the Depression. It has the great mending attribute of being half mess collector (outer yarn bins, bottom drawer floss dump), half neat freak filing cabinet. This is command central for my best and most used implements that always, without fail, get put away immediately. I also confess to further small drawer units, chests, etc. In fact, it's been scientifically proven that you cannot overdo containers.

Furniture, Large

Finally, if you become a true addict, you will need to reassign a place for the big stuff: your mending pile, your fabrics, your spare parts (clothes to be dismembered), and perhaps your iron, your granny tins, your *baskets*. It needs compartments is all. This Arts and Crafts beauty was my major score from AptDeco after years of searching. One furniture genre that works great and can be got for a song: the dodo that is the TV armoire with DVD storage.

Mending Nooks

So that's where to keep your stash; now a word about where to use it. This is about creating a haven, and a mend basket is as good as a sewing room—it's not the size of the place, it's the quality of its haberdashery. And organization is part of the pleasure. Clearly, where you site your nook, or nooks, depends on your home layout, but also on your body positions, which are personal and change according to which mend you're working. But whether you're doing an armchair darn, a tailor's cross-legged lap mend (my tendency), or a full table spread-out patchiko operation (see page 169), some general considerations always pertain.

Supplies

And what's in the kit? Suppose you're just starting out visibly mending: What do you need, and where do you get it? Nobody said you have to keep a menagerie of supplies; you can easily do some fun mending with the bare minimum. Then again, you have the opportunity to start all sorts of new collections, if that appeals. Here's all you need to know.

Optimal Mend Conditions

- Lighting. It's paramount. I read in crepuscular conditions but need klieg lights to mend.

- Comfort. It's easy to be so immersed you don't realize your leg's gone to sleep.

- Back support. A cushion rolled up in the lumbar region is nice.

- Mess. There will be it. If you don't have a designated spot you can leave in disarray, I recommend clearing the worst after each session. This can get out of hand very quickly.

- Accessible supplies. Bring the kit to you or set up next to it. You cannot overestimate the extent to which you will not want to move mid-mend.

- Farsighted? Plant drugstore glasses everywhere, as you probably already do.

- Aural pleasure. A great time to catch up with your podcast queue, or . . .

- Menditation. Revel in the most underrated, cheapest, rarest commodity: silence.

- Nature. Trees plus mending equals magic. Use whatever open-air space you can access.

Most Needed Needles

Buy lots. Though you buy lots, you'll keep using your one favorite. Using them is the only way to find out which needles suit you best. There are lots of types, which seems confusing, especially when you get into vintage stock, where all bets are off. But let's try to make it easy.

Remember

- Quality counts. Cheapo needles are snaggy or bendy or blunt or have half-closed eyes.

- Usual advice is to use the smallest viable needle so as not to over-perforate the cloth.

- But because visible mending uses thicker threads and yarn, you often need bigger needles.

- Once you've found your jam, stock up. Needles don't need haystacks to get lost.

Size

- They come in sizes 1–28, the higher the number the smaller the needle, just to confuse.

- Worse, they're sized within each type: a Chenille 22 is about the same length as a Between 3.

- If you must choose blind, size Embroidery 3 and Chenille 22 are common and good for VM.

- For darning, add the blunt-pointed, large-eyed Tapestry; size 18 or 22 is easily found.

- For sewing nonvisible parts, a Sharp size 4 or 8 is a standard-issue, general-purpose needle.

- I like the extrashort quilter's needle, the Between, for speed; 5 is a good medium size.

- I don't know what needle makers have against sizes 19, 21, 23, or 25, but I've never seen one.

- Hell, get a variety pack, or a vintage needle book, or "borrow" your mother's.*

---

* Does not apply to my daughter.

Types

- In order of mendiness, with alternate names: Embroidery (crewel), Chenille, Tapestry (cross-stitch), Darners (cotton, long, and yarn darners), Sharps, Betweens (quilting), Glovers (leather), Milliners (straw, beading), Self-threading (calyx eye).

- Embroidery, Chenille, Darners, and Tapestry have larger eyes; the former two long and narrow, the latter two big and fat. You need to balance easier threading with bigger punctures.

- Oddly, the blunt Tapestry is better than Darners for most darning, to prevent splitting yarn.

- Specialist needles—Sail, Carpet, Saddlers, Packing, Upholstery, Mattress—are good to have around for odd jobs and tough places. Especially the glover with its triangular point.

- Less common antique or specialist needles worth having include Double Eye (two threads at once!), Sashiko (long, strong; round, medium eye), and Bodkin (giant eye, very blunt ballpoint)

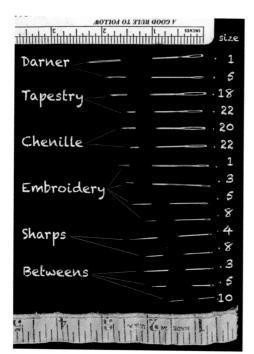

A GOOD RULE TO FOLLOW
INCHES 1 2 3

size
Darner — 1
— 5
Tapestry — 18
— 22
— 20
Chenille — 22
— 1
— 3
Embroidery — 5
— 8
Sharps — 4
— 8
— 3
Betweens — 5
— 10

MADE IN U.S.A.

Try Virginia Slims
Regular or Menthol

You've come
a long way, baby.

It used to be that men had
the problem of women's rights all
sewed up.

You've come a long way, baby.

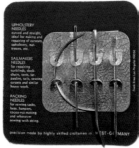

UPHOLSTERY NEEDLES
curved and straight,
ideal for making and
repairing of garments,
upholstery, mattresses, etc.

SAILMAKERS NEEDLES
For repairing
sunblinds, deck-
chairs, tents, tar-
paulins, sails, sewing
carpets and similar
heavy work.

PACKING NEEDLES
for sewing sacks,
bags, hampers,
cocoa-nut-matting
and whenever
sewing with string.

We hope you enjoy
this assortment of quality
all-purpose sewing needles
compliments of

Virginia Slims

precision made by highly skilled craftsmen in WEST-GERMANY

Need or Not?

ITEM	NOTES	ONE	MANY	MAYBE
Needles	Obviously, your most important thing. See page 98 for details.		✓	
Thread: embroidery floss	Obviously, your other most important thing. See overleaf for details.		✓	
Thread: cotton/poly	Obviously, also an important thing.		✓	
Thread: specialized	No need for metallics or silks or sashiko or variegated threads, but it's all nice.			✓
Yarn: thick wool/blend	If you're darning, it's a must; see section on following pages.		✓	
Yarn: thin wool/blend	Ditto.		✓	
Yarn: other fibers/fancy	Variegated wool is a great cheat. Fancy yarns to use for couching are also fun.			✓
Needle threader	No, you don't really need one. Really!			✓
Fabric scraps	Obviously, your other-other most important thing. See pages 110–11, 138–46.		✓	
Trim, lace, ribbon, etc.	No need, but you'll want some. Then you'll get hooked.			✓
Pins	Essential. The glass or plastic head kind is best. Also gather a few safety pins.		✓	
Pincushion	Mine look like Chia Pets stuck all over with pre-threaded needles.	✓		
Scissors	Do not be cheap. Get the best, and never lend them or use them for paper.	✓		
Small scissors/snips	Feel free to get cute bird-shaped ones. Don't bother with cheap snips.	✓		
Pinking shears	Not a must, but very handy to limit fraying; also to add a decorative element.			✓

ITEM	NOTES	ONE	MANY	MAYBE
Rotary cutter, mat	A cutter does bulk or multilayers. A self-healing mat is almost an essential.			✓
Seam ripper	A tiny thing that you'll find indispensable.			✓
Crochet hook	Multiple uses as well as crochet, e.g., catching threads through.	✓		
Bodkin	Like a giant blunt needle for threading, say, a drawstring through a pant.			✓
Snag needle	With a textured end to pull loose threads through. Handy.			✓
Thimble	Many swear by them. Personally, I use my oddly strong fingernails.			✓
Iron	Press early and often. Ironing boards are good but towel on floor will do.	✓		
Darning mushroom/egg	Only really needed for socks and socklike curves.			✓
Embroidery hoop	Good, essential, even, for intricate embroidered bits.	✓		
Fabric markers	Tailor's chalk, quilting pencil, soak/fadeaway pens . . . A must for many.	✓		
Thread wax	Beeswax or silicone to coat for smoothness. Use soap in a pinch.			✓
Fusible web/ iron-on patch	Good cheats, and reinforcers, but rarely actually needed.			✓
Cut/tearaway stabilizer	Made for embroidery and good for embellishmends on limp fabric.			✓
Hook and eyes, snaps	Not really visible mending supplies, but useful to have around.			✓
Buttons	Ditto. Though replacing them with more decorative ones is visible mending.			✓

Thread and Yarn

Though there are infinite varieties, you can get by quite well with only the basics. Who am I kidding? You will want all the colors in the paint box and all the shiny ones, too.

Remember

- Quality counts. Very much. Cheap cotton thread will snap and snag. Inferior yarns are eco-evi artificial fibers with ugly, poisonous dyes. Avoid the bulk craft packs of embroidery floss like the plague or you'll get all twisted and knotty in no time. So will the thread.

- To start, look for a range of thicknesses for all the mend jobs. Color up later.

- You may never need more than black or white regular thread for utility joins and basting.

Types

- Cotton thread. Mercerized has been treated to be smoother and glossier.[1] Cotton rots—better for the earth, but dangerous if you're collecting vintage spools: see box on page 113 for more on this.

- Polyester thread. Nowadays, this, and cotton-wrapped polyester, are the most commonly found kind. The latter is a fine all-purpose option. Favor pure poly for synthetics and stretch.

- Embroidery floss. You will use this (normally) cotton floss found in a billion colors for everything, including darns. This mercerized, lightly plied six-stranded thread is often split into two or three strands (or one or four), making for maximum versatility.

- Yarn, wool. If you're a knitter (or crocheter), well done you, you're set for life—and the rest of us can get by very well on your hank ends, thank you.

- Tapestry wool, Persian yarn. Three twisted strands of two-ply wool in handy miniskeins.

- Retors Mat. Nonmercerized, S-twisted soft cotton nondivisible thread made for tapestry. If you can find it, its chunky, matte look is great for darning cotton knits, and for accents.

- Pearl or Perle cotton, also sold as tatting or crochet thread, or coton à broder. A tight S-twisted two- to four-ply, nondivisible, mercerized thread in various weights; great for many VM applications.

- Floche. Similar, but obscurer: a five-ply nondivisible silky lustrous long-staple cotton.

- Sashiko thread. The (usually) three-ply cotton with a tight S-twist is used unsplit, even doubled. Traditionally white, now it comes in colours everywhere.[2] It has a matte finish.

- Darning cotton or wool. Found in the past. It's the packaging of this that distinguishes it.

- Silk. In clothes it's common, in thread it's still luxury. Nice for finer work on, well, silk.

- Linen. It's hard to find, but lovely to work, and is hard wearing.

- Metallics. Many sorts of which will drive you insane, because they twist like crazy. Hard to manipulate, but irresistible.

- Variegated. A color, not a thread type, but separately listed for its limitless VM usefulness.

- Fancy. Beware bouclé, fringed, sequined, etc. They're for knits. They dislike sewing needles.

- Invisible. Colorless nylon filament. I have no idea why you'd want this.

- Brands. High quality, easily found. DMC floss, A&E Gütermann, Coats & Clark.

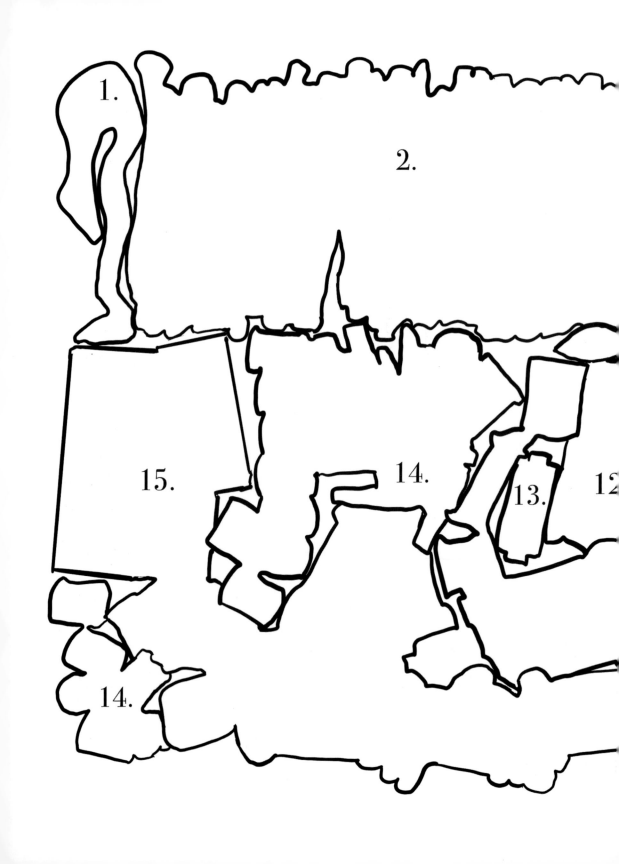

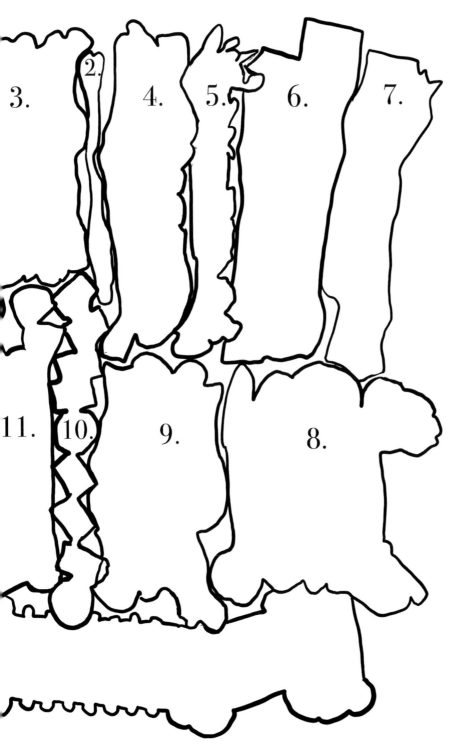

3.

2.

4.

5.

6.

7.

11.

10.

9.

8.

Key to the Threadscape

1. My favorite 1920s French floche

2. Embroidery floss, mostly DMC brand, mostly new

3. Variegated floss, DMC and Threadworx

4. Perle cotton, DMC, new

5. Rayon, "art silk" floss, Belding Bros., ca. 1915

6. Sashiko thread, Olympus brand, modern

7. Braid of mending wool strands, 1970s

8. Tapestry wool/Persian yarn, Anchor brand, 1980s

9. DMC Matania, 1940s: similar to Retors Mat, only four-ply not five

10. Pure silk thread, various, 1940s–1970s

11. A selection of metallics, 1950s–modern

12. Lovely glossy cotton thread from Japan that I can't read

13. Invisible nylon filament, in case of beading

14. A variety of mercerized cotton threads, Austrian and American, mostly 1940s

15. A grand array of mending yarns, English and American: Emaness, Coats Flosheen, Chadwicks, Peri-lusta, Star, etc., 1920s–1980s

The Rest of the Kit

You have the idea by now: sewing supplies are a classic case of "buy cheap, buy twice."

Pins

Fancier ones are sharper, stronger, cleaner, and worth it. I find those with a glass or plastic head 700 percent easier to use, and I like the flower-headed, thinner, longer ones best of all. If you see fine fabric in your future, get silk pins, which are long, extra sharp, and extra fine. Safety pins are useful for knitwear and marking holes. Insert pins perpendicularly, not along the line of work.

Pincushion

I do think this is an opportunity for novelty ware. Or make one! Fill it with ground walnut shells (*not* for the allergic—in case holding pins in mouth). That baby strawberry on a string on the tomato-shaped kind is an emery sack, filled with sand to polish and de-rust your needles.

Scissors

Invest. For accuracy, efficiency, balance, longevity. And never let anyone else use them. Shears are unnecessary, since they're shaped for cutting out patterns, which you're not doing. You'll need a tiny pair, too. Everyone's into the traditional Japanese nigiri-basami, a.k.a. snips, including me. (I once bought a twelve-pack online. They lasted one single project each.) My Gingher German-made 4" embroidery scissors changed my life: even the end of the tip cuts clean.

Special Cutters

Pinking shears are useful for limiting the fraying of patches and are the lazy person's serger for seam finishing. Seam rippers are great for unpicking mistakes as well as machine stitching. They're good at hiding, so I have several. The rotary cutter—you know, from *Project Runway*—is fantastic if you cut out a lot of things, or multiples in piles, or complicatedly. Do not use without its . . .

Self-Healing Mat

It doesn't lie—you cannot slice it. I find this indispensible. It measures everything, keeps lines straight, is support for lap mending, and usually gets inserted inside what I'm working on to help avoid my specialty of sewing the back to the front.

Thimble

I don't. You might. You will if you're mending leather or multilayers. A useful sort of pulling thimble: cut off fingers of old rubber dishwashing gloves for gripping the needle to pull through tough fabrics.

Holders

A darning egg or the flatter mushroom sound crucial, but they really aren't, unless you are very devoted to toe and heel mending. For anything else, it's too easy to end up with a bumpy or nipple darn, having stretched the hole over the device. The embroidery hoop—there's a clue in the name—if you're doing any kind of accurate embellishmend (as on the cover of this book), you need it, but it can cause tension issues: don't pull the fabric too tight.

Holders

Four old aids: the Imperial Patent Darning Machine, 1896; a Gilded Age sewing bird; my Mashina dlia Shtopki; and a bona fide Speedweve

Cheats and Aids

No such thing as cheating! Sewing replacement innovations are fine and handy, especially fusible web, which grips folds and hems when heat is applied. It's not visible but helps. Iron-on patches—okay, if you must. Marking pens, pencils, and chalk you'll need, especially for any word mends. I'm still seeking the one universal marker. So far, quilting pencils are winning. Stabilizers—I dislike the sticky ones, which leave gunk on the fabric and don't stay put, but try them for yourself. I like to add an ad hoc stabilizer for tricky darns, sewing through a layer of ordinary tissue paper, which you then tear away, or thin fabric, which stays in place.

Defunct Equipment

I have such a soft spot for vintage mending apparatus. These can be scored in the usual eBay manner, but I've been watching the prices creep up, sometimes with great drama.

Speedweve

"Lancashire's Smallest Loom," patented by E & A Chesstok, Ltd. of Rusholme, Manchester, in the late 1940s (which didn't stop my *Mashina dlia Shtopki*, the Soviet rip-off), does what it says, fashioning a teeny plain weave blanket over your hole. It is a complete cult item, and fetches a fine price. People have started putting these back in production, often in lovely handmade versions.

Darning Machines

Speedweve predecessors abounded in the late nineteenth century when maximum stocking ownership met minimum darn-ability (see page 39), but they were pretty useless on the whole. I am always on the lookout for them nevertheless. If anyone finds a Canfield darner-on-a-stick, please get in touch.

Sewing Bird

In the same era, every household owned this little guy, the sewing bird, who clamps your work to the table, while simultaneously offering pins and an emery ball. Ingenious and genius.[3]

Tiny Menders

In the mid-1980s Singer suddenly produced a range of very specific mending engines—mendgines—the Tiny Tailor, the Stitch-Me-Quick, and, best, the Match-a-Patch, which was basically a fabric hole punch. I'd like to try them, but they went extinct. I think we know why.

Zizzers

Also '80s. I found mine in one of my other-people's-sewing-baskets. Similar electric scissors are still in production, though not the Zizzers by Black & Decker, which is a shame. Much to my surprise, they're amazing! They cut intricate things in a ridiculously fun manner.

Fangnadel

Finally, a distinctly nonelectric doobrie that does the niche repair of zipping up stocking ladders. I inherited mine, along with its name (German for "fishing" or "catch needle"). It's most useful nowadays for things like catching pulled threads to the backs of knits. Going by the alias latch needle, it's what professional re-weavers use (all three of them) and any rug-makers among you will recognize their hook (thanks for all those half-used kits by the way), but I prefer to leave it as a mend enigma with an amusing name.

The Fabric of Our Lives

One of the most fun parts of visible mending is the selection of fabric from your collection. And where does your collection come from? This is a good question. Where it does *not* come from, *please*, is a craft chain. Sure, Michaels, Hobby Lobby, JOANN, and certain Walmart aisles are convenient, but sourcing bad factory textile to mend your bad factory (or even your vintage) textile is a Band-Aid on gangrene; it's baking a cake with maggoty flour and rancid butter. You can't do real quilting—the love child of austerity and community—with bundles of fat quarters from eQuilter.com. (Especially not when they cost $64.95 for twenty bits.) No, your mending patch stash will be infinitely more creative.

Remember

- You can't always tell which salvage will become the MVP of your stash. One trashy Topshop tank I never wore is the gift that keeps on giving. It gives my signature eye mends.

- A print or a hue you'd never *ever* wear can make a perfect patch, appliqué, or underpatch.

- Relax your ethical standards: any garment is fair game when you're going to slice it up.

- Break through your natural aversion to cutting clothes. It's now your most needed skill.

- Consider cutting pieces up immediately: less bulky and instantly available as material.

Where to Source Stuff*

- Your closet. Why not shop your closet for spare parts as well as whole clothes?

- Other people's closets. Let it be known you're in the market for "rag." The enterprising might even start a side hustle, cutting truly sustainable fat quarters for quilters and patchers.

- Thrift. The stores are now crammed with Big Fashion tat. Mine that tat for parts.

- Thrift on sale. My local does fifty-cent T-shirt specials; I now own a cotton jersey rainbow.

- Thrifted baggies of scraps rejected by quilters, ideally vintage, but may be from Michaels. I confess I weed out these rejects of theirs and toss my resulting rejects. See shopping rule 20 in Chapter 1.

- Thrifted baggies of yarn rejected by knitters. The same rule 20 applies for the nastier acrylics.

- Learn frogging. The knit-head's onomatopoeic term for unpicking: *ribbit = rip it.*

- Card, skein, or ball the unzipped sweater yarn immediately or you'll be buried in spaghetti.

- Another old-knits hack: boil it to shrink it for a supply of invaluable cuttable, wool felt fabric. This only works with pure wool and not when it's washable, preshrunk, coated, etc.

- Online. Proliferating quilters have caused a surge of vintage fabric dealers who sell scraps.

- Auctions, online or IRL, often have fabric lots in bolts, scraps, and everything in between.

- Hoard any little baggies of spare cloth (thread, buttons) that come with fancy new clothes.

- Household linens. Underappreciated crafts of the past, these are a treasure trove of folk embroidery, tatting, cutwork, edgings, etc. for instant embellishmends. Also, quality fabrics.

- Contact your local clothing collector, keeper of the bins. Cook up collaborations.

- FABSCRAP. These adored visionaries collect fashion industry rejects. Buy it cheap or, if you're near, volunteer some time in exchange for free fabric. Amazing quality pieces.

---

* *Stuff* = fabric.

Vintage Haberdashery

I'm far from the only one with this fetish and many delights of past eras are now fetching a premium as more and more menders are minted. This can go only one way—the same way as garments, with increasing numbers of us chasing dwindling numbers of them. If you crave an original Speedweve or a copy of Maureen Goldsworthy's *Mend It!* (yes, her title inspired mine), you're in for a fat three figures. A late nineteenth-, early twentieth-century store display case of cottons or even silks (I got my pride and joy, below, many years ago for small money) will set you back closer to four. But, as with vintage clothes, if you're good at hunting—dogged, intrepid, resourceful, diligent—you will be rewarded, because these things are often hiding in plain sight.

If you like a bit of graphic design, there's another reason to love this stuff. Needle books are the most fun in this department. I prize my Virginia Slims "You've come a long way, baby" cigarette ad needles (page 99), which have confusingly printed "It used to be that men had the problem of women's rights all sewed up" right on top of a fine set of agents of domestic drudgery. And I don't know what message my Witch and Hexe needle threaders think they're sending. Are they related to each other?

We're at the tail end now of a few decades of moms' and grans' sewing supplies bequeathed to

thrift or eBay when they were no longer understood. Intact kits break my heart, in a good way: they're portraits in notions. And while I never knew your late great-aunt, there's something so intimate about sewing by hand that I feel great empathy with her, this anonymous dead person connected to me by a thread. To imagine a weary workingwoman painstakingly repairing the latest ladder in her worn-out lisle stockings with this very Belding Heminway Corticelli Handy Midget or Brettle's Silkestia and Lustrina I am using is charming and poignant. I realize I'm now ruining my supply forever, but these precious pieces deserve to be loved and used, and, though I'm giving it my best shot, I can't collect them all.

Remember

- As for the "Where," search the same places for vintage fabrics, as above.

- Vintage spool cotton is often degraded beyond use. Inquire before bidding if you can. Test any new-to-you batch by simply pulling a strand. If it snaps easily, toss it. There is no remedy.

- Beware cards of mending wool; they're susceptible to moth attack. Again, no saving them.

- We reached peak knitting years ago. Knitters often purge their stashes, and this is good news for us darners. I'm tempting fate, but I've never yet bought moth-eaten stash ends.

- I have quite the collection of half-done rug-making and cross-stitch kits: great for darning yarns.

- If bidding on needle books, check the state of the actual needles: intact, missing, or rusted?

Someone else's kit, abandoned mid-mend

Treasure Goals

- The whole kit. Study the contents on max magnification: reject infestation, dust, any signs of unscrupulous upkeep. Even random or new collections are good if you're just starting out.

- Used mending kits. Not to everyone's taste, but I find it satisfying to stitch a new mend story using supplies that themselves embody a mending narrative.

- Related: thread collections. My best was a stranger's great-grandmother's; it'll last forever.

- And floss. Whether deadstock in shop cartons, an embroiderer's orderly tray of cards, or just an assorted lot, I like this better than new—at least when it consists of premium brands.

- Trimmings. The best tend to go for real money, but add such élan you may wish to invest. There are some great dealers of passementerie and French mercerie on the interwebs.

- Lace, ditto, and look at pre-1950 underclothes for dismembering. Nylon lace is a mixed blessing.

- Soutache, piping, etc., that is, everyday trim, can be really useful for VM and goes cheap.

- Ribbon. Grosgrain or petersham, the ribbed sort in hatbands, is strong, versatile, and ubiquitous. Even fancy gift ribbon is worth keeping on hand for edging, hemming, and lining jobs.

- Bias tape, rickrack. Home dressmakers bought it by the mile. Boring, but has its uses.

- Needle books. Adorable! Sewing Susan ones made in occupied Japan are common. Promotional giveaways can be low quality. Victorian/Edwardian English or German packets are gold standard but can feature very mini needles.

- Forgotten notions—bachelor's buttons, Dorset buttons, hook-and-eye strips—snap 'em up.

- I dislike inserting them, but when needs must, metal zippers are superior. Also, decorative.

- Sewing birds, ebony and silver darning eggs, needle cases, beaded lace bobbins—it all comes back around. If you can't afford one, try the next auction. Putting in the time pays off.

Where to Keep Clothes

Now for the targets and results of all this renovation, rejuvenation, and reevaluation: your clothes. No normal person is satisfied with the size and state of their closet, and by "normal" I don't mean Mia of *The Princess Diaries* or Cher of *Clueless* but someone with less than a spare room. (And Sara Berman's closet of perfection here is not realistic—it was literally an *art installation*.) If you purged during the decluttering trend of five minutes ago, you will have recluttered by now, because of the law of physics called the set point of stuff,[4] and keeping an orderly wardrobe will have become the same old battle.

I have two words for you. Give in.

Not give *up*, but surrender.

Embrace a limited amount of controlled chaos. The trick is to tame the chaos gradually and regularly, a bit every day or week, rotating within your own shelves and racks, according to a system you yourself devise. There are multiple experts forming a line into your closet these days, claiming they know better than you how to organize you. It's a shame. Wardrobe consultants have professionalized something we can all do quite naturally, and, I'd venture to say, we should do ourselves. I know so many people who felt steamrollered by their consultant or went into mourning for the half of their dear old clothes they rashly Kondoed.[5] As they discovered the hard way, there's nothing virtuous about throwing stuff out. Clothes wrangling should be a pleasure, not a chore, and definitely not a service rendered.

Sara Berman's Closet, art installation by Alex and Maira Kalman at the Mmuseumm NYC, 2015

The Ten-Step Closet Mend

If your wardrobe has really been getting on top of you, perhaps literally, then start with a reboot, perhaps literally. This ten-step, reality-based plan will get you organized. Also, it will help you rediscover delights you already own, find new combos with old friends, refile according to current wear patterns, and concentrate and refresh your own unique style.

1. Decide on a category: pants, dresses, sweaters. Or pick one shelf, or a single drawer, or the clothes-that-hang.[6] You can even tackle the whole lot at once. This will take as long or as short a time as you care to give it. Do it alone or with a friend.

2. Throw it all on the floor, then pick things up one by one. Try some on and prance about. Do whatever it takes to divide them into three categories: *Tops* (most loved), *Middles* (occasionally worn), and *Bottoms* (underworn/meh).

3. Fold all shelf and drawer items nicely. Pile them up on the bed in the above groups. Pile the hanging garments alongside. Anything stretched, torn, or stained goes in the mend pile.

4. Now for the assessment. Start with the Bottoms. If it's old, and you liked it before, you will like it again. *For God's sake, keep it.*

This is the number one idiot advice from the experts, who invariably say if you haven't worn it for a year, it must go. Nonsense. Something five years unworn often turns into my favorite. Half my clothes have gone vintage in my closet.

5. Find a space to house these.[7] This is your reserve collection, because your wardrobe is not inert, but organic and responsive. It works with you.

6. Still in the Bottoms, weed out only those pieces you really hate, complete mistakes (though you *did* love them enough to buy them). Put them aside. Sort and rehouse them in step 10.

7. Now for the Middles—I bet the biggest pile. These are the hardest.

   a) If it's new(ish) and under- or unworn, it goes in the rehousing pile. Last in is first out. Learn from this next time you shop.

   b) Rediscover gems to put with your favorites. This is the famous shopping your closet. Move these to the Tops pile.

   c) The rest: you'll still wear them sporadically. Start restocking your closet, with these as the first layer, under your best things, along with any Bottoms you've promoted.

Before you start restocking, create your system, really thinking it through first. The prime directive, naturally, is like with like. The general rule is to put your most worn garment types (Tees? Jeans?) in the most accessible places—the shelf just below eye level; the middle drawer. File the rest according to usage. Out-of-season piles go in back, down low, or up high. You'll rotate out according to season. See "How to Make Space and Time," page 156, for more on this.

8. Now place the Tops piles on (duh) the tops of the piles in drawer and on shelf.

9. Replace all hanging garments. File these purely by color. Or, if you have space, by type (jackets, long dresses, short dresses, etc.: like with like), then by color within each section.

10. Rehousing. It's complicated, so make it a fun project. Here's how.

The entrance and inside of my magic basement clothes library. Decades in the making, this is the accidental result of all that collecting and adoption. It is the opposite of a commercial operation.

Where to Lose Clothes

New Wave Redistribution

- Yes, resale is an industry. Rookies should research online before attempting to monetize rejects. You really need to shop with an eye to flipping if you're to make a go of it.

- Or hold your own sale: stoop, garage, rummage, stall at local flea. If there isn't one . . .

- Start a local flea! Or community consignment store. Or hold an at-home pop-up with friends.

- Your best rejects can enter one of the proliferating personal garment rental markets.

- If you must donate, write a note with the garment's story to insert in pocket or tuck into hem.

- The future lies in a whole raft of creative, cashless redistribution methods. Try these . . .

  - ○ Organize a swap. Swapping is *everything*. Write labels with the clothes' stories.

  - ○ Create a generosity project. Be a clothing yenta. Curate pieces for individual friends, a tote bag each of things they'll love.

Stoop sale, July 2019

  - ○ If you have space, start a clothes library. Among friends, or for profit.

  - ○ Make mending materials, as above. Cut them up; unravel or boil the sweaters.

  - ○ Alter, dye, or remake. Experiment! Find a fashion upcycling class. Or start one.

- Be a craftivist: Make patchwork, pompoms, cushion covers (and stuffing), etc.

- If nothing else works: use as rags instead of kitchen paper. Save a tree or two.

Mend, Tend, Lend, Spend

My mantra. The last one is what we need to add to keep the flow going, investing in quality new gear so as to insert good pieces back into the puzzle. The dream and the aim is a more communal attitude to wardrobe—and it's happening! When I launched Refashioner, reselling or swapping to keep the life force in the garment was a downright peculiar idea. In the ten years since then incredible changes have occurred. Resale has scaled; rental and subscription are normal; takeback schemes and in-brand mending services are spreading. Most of this is great, but not necessarily when the main goal is an IPO. Our personal wardrobes shouldn't be cash machines for money-men who care nothing for clothes. That said, the profit motive is what will spread the solutions far enough to avoid a *Wall-E* future. The missing concept here is iteration. Instead of one or two megalithic category killers crushing every startup in their path, let's multiply the many small-scale, fashion-forward models that are for us by us. Tons of local consignment stores; buy-sell-swap stores; farmers' markets of used and upcycled clothes; a fashion library on every Main Street—all with a modest website and app. Designers should sell their own vintage pieces, their back catalog (Marimekko's self-sold old pieces cost more than the new ones). It all works together to the benefit of all, especially us clothes hounds and fashion addicts, who get our hands on the great pieces, enjoying higher turnover for way less outlay.

Above all, remember the first law of wardrobe metaphysics: it's not cluttering, it's keeping.

Remember

- Rehousing does not equal donating. Donating is a last resort, barely better than trashing.

- Of thrift store donations, just 10 to 15 percent are resold. Some African countries have banned imports of our reject clothes because it's killing their indigenous textile industries.[8]

- Though many are trying to update the technology, currently anything polyester or Lycra blend can't be recycled—and this is nearly everything we wear.

- Before feeding clothes collections bins, research the company. Not all are legit.

- But the good ones are excellent. Don't dump dirty, sweaty, disgusting clothes. Consider the humans sorting this stuff by hand. The for-profit companies depend on higher quality mixed in.

- Charitable collections like Dress for Success are now highly specialized, so don't be surprised when your discards don't make the grade. New with tags is often the rule.

- You don't need me to tell you, resale is an art and a science. Too much to go into here. But eternal turnover is an illusion, and a dangerous one.

Look after your clothes pets. You are a saver of stuff. You are the solution.

Peace of mend for all.

how

How do you visibly mend? You just start.
That was a really short chapter.

But honestly, there's only one thought that stops anyone from doing anything, ever, and that is, "I can't." But you *can* mend, even if you've never held a needle. Ever since sewing skills melted away, a perception has taken hold that clothes are as impenetrable as a car or an iThing, fixable only by experts—it's a big reason for our disposable culture. Or do you think sewing isn't for you anyway? That it belongs to an alien aesthetic and personality: someone who has time and likes tapestry. Maybe you tried, and it was like threading a wet noodle into a keyhole, then the fabric got puckered and the thread knotted, and there's no YouTube tutorial about *that*. So this how-to chapter is more real-world strategies and hand-holding than normal stitch guide—though there's also a mending-specific one of those. The stitches are mostly basic, taking some cues from dressmaking and other bits from embroidery. Some instructions are slightly unorthodox, because regular rules can be found in one second online if you want them. I find those can make sewing sound impossible, as if to guard the oldest, simplest skill from beginners, with confusing instructions ("bring needle up at A, down at C, back up at B, double back to A . . .") that omit the peculiar things that actually happen and that tell you which stitch to use where, as if there were laws. There were indeed many rules in sewing once upon a time, but we can discount them now. If you like, you can easily stop at the first stitch, running stitch, and still mend for life. Don't be perfect. Seriously, this is the freest kind of sewing in the world—no wrong way, no pressure, unique fashion item made every time.

How to VM: The Six Rules

1. **Any mend is better than no mend.**

2. You've **nothing to lose.** It's broken; you'd probably toss it.

3. **Fortune favors the bold.** If it sucks, unpick your hot mess and start over.

4. Better still, if you don't like your mend, **double down.** More is more.

5. You're welcome to mend by sewing machine, just **not in this book.**

6. Actually, I lied. **There are no rules.**

There's very little to learn: you practice visible mending by doing it, and in my experience, everyone is always delighted with their very first mend, no exceptions. After how to make mends, we'll cover how to make other things, for example, space, time, and your clothes safe from moths.

How to Start

This first part is for the complete novice. To rehearse, use a piece of scrap fabric, or, better, for verisimilitude, one of those garments you plan to cut up for parts. Since it's VM, start with three strands of embroidery floss, any color, and let's say, a Crewel (Embroidery) needle, size 3. Or whatever needle you have. (Ordinary thread will do, too.)

Needle and Thread 101

1. Cut the thread

There's a reason the traditional length is 18", about the length of your forearm: shorter than that and you're rethreading too often. Much longer and you get tangly. *Langes Fädchen, faules Mädchen*, as my mother used to, nonseriously, say: "Long thread, lazy girl." I am very often a lazy girl, but only with thread that I know is not too prone to knots. Make the cut clean and sharp, with all ends even. Embroidery floss normally comes in skeins of about eight yards, secured by two bands. Of its two ends, one—usually the one near the longer band—pulls out smoothly, leaving the rest neatly bound; the other will stick and snarl the whole thing into a clump of misery. So pull gently till you know you're on the right path.

2. Split the floss

Floss is formed of six individual threads plied or twisted together. We'll work with three, so start the separation, half-and-halfing the threads to an inch or two down. Now hold each three-thread strand up on each side of your chin, and slooooowly pull them up past your ears and over your head, letting your chin do the splitting. Do not rush it. You can do the same thing without your chin, but this almost infallible comedy method was taught to me by a sixth grader, and I like it. For a single strand, it's easier to pick one thread and pull it, holding the rest back and letting them bunch up, then smoothing them back.[1]

3. Thread the needle

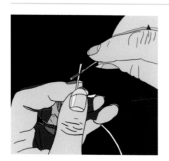

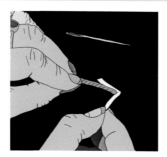

Lick the end and pinch it with finger and thumb so it's flat and rigid. Hold it upright and position the needle above it, its eye parallel to the floor. Carefully lower the eye over the thread. This beats stabbing the thread sideways at the needle by a thousand percent. You almost never need to use a needle threader, except for this scrappy magical fat-yarn threader. Simply cut a strip of paper a little thinner than the eye, fold it, sandwiching the thread inside, and push.

how

To knot or not to knot? The debate rages on, though strict knot-lessness is for embroiderers and needlepointers and perfection-ists, not really for VM. See the box opposite for methods.

6. Finish

Same as beginning: knot or not? You could knot as you sew, inserting the needle through the loop of the final stitch and tightening it. Or make the final few stitches backstitches.

Positioning

- Sit in a chair, or cross-legged on the floor, and hold the work in your lap, resting on a board, a big book, or a cutting mat if you like. Or sit at a table. Whatever's comfortable.

- Hold the fabric by gripping it loosely between the first two fingers and thumb of your nondominant hand, thumb on top. The other fingers provide support beneath. (Lefties, please forgive me if I call the nondominant hand *left* from here on.)

- Hold the needle between thumb and first two fingers of your right hand, palm down, pointing to the left.

- If you're working a garment, hold it by inserting the left hand inside it, to separate the layers. Stitching a thing's front to its back is a popular mistake that we all like to make.

- Stitch right to left. When reversing the direction of stitching, turn the whole thing around so you're still stitching right to left. When you get to darning, darn away from the body. Some stitches are done in different directions, which will be noted in the stitch guides.

Knot or Not

1. The tailor's (or quilter's) knot

  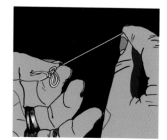

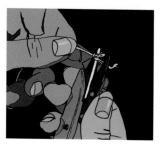 

Wind the thread three times around your forefinger, then roll those loops off the finger, which twists them together. Run your fingers down the thread end behind the loops, pulling them to the end, and tug to form the knot. Snip off the ends to form a little tuft.

2. Ordinary knot

You know how. Make it a double if you like. Trim the end.

3. Knot as you sew

Working from the back, take a tiny backstitch and stop before the thread's all the way through, leaving a loop. Insert the thread in that loop and pull it through to tighten. Repeat, if you like, for extra security.

4. Waste knot

A needlepoint technique. Start with an ordinary knot on the front (face) an inch away from your starting place. Once you've sewn your first few stitches, snip off the knot and pull the thread through to the back.

5. Away knot

Again, start with an ordinary knot, this time on the back about three inches away from your starting place. After sewing, cut the knot, thread a needle with that tail, and run it through the original first stitches to secure.

6. Not a knot

My preferred method. It's exactly like the waste or away knot, but without the initial knot. A few backstitches secure the thread at beginning or end; split stitch is even securer.

Running Stitch

Welcome to your first stitch. It's the most basic, and the only one you really need to know. It joins layers, whether that's a patch on a holey place, or an entire seam. Varying the direction or size of the stitch, the shape of the line, or repeating rows makes it decorative. Because you're just starting, try the alternate styles here if they appeal. When I learned sashiko, I realized I'd always sewn that way (not the hand position, just the part about moving the fabric instead of the needle). The point is, whatever works for you is correct. If you want to sew backward or hold the needle with your teeth, go for it.

Regular

Pass the thread in and out at regular intervals, moving the needle along the fabric to the left. Down and up is another way to put it. You should not turn the fabric around to the back: keep your needle on the surface (technical name: the face) and dip the needle in and out from there. You only turn the piece over to secure the thread at the beginning and end (whether or not by knot).

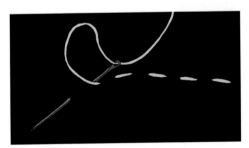

Sashiko

The exact same stitch, but here you move fabric rather than needle, loading several stitches at once onto a long needle, gathering as you go, then pushing the needle through.[2] At the end of every pass, stop, pull the thread through, and smooth the fabric so the stitches lie flat.

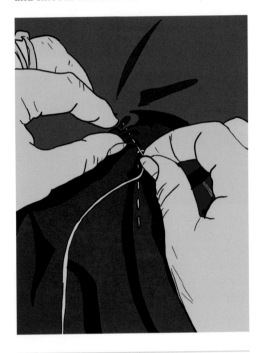

Kantha

Same again, but kantha uses a kind of rocking motion. Hold the needle with second finger and thumb, and place the index finger ahead of the stitch to pull and advance the cloth.

Running Stitch Relations

Got the hang of that? Good. Now you've got five more sewn up—all variations of the exact same thing. Written descriptions of stitches are incomprehensible, so do study the illustrations.

Basting or Tacking

A big, long, sloppy running stitch in contrasting thread. It keeps things in place, then is removed.

Seed Stitch

Tiny, sloppy running stitch, randomly scattered, using thin or thicker thread, is both decorative and functional.

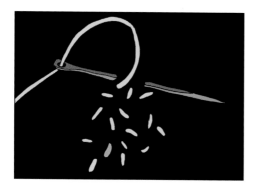

Backstitch

Running stitch that's two steps forward, one step back is a mighty strong stitch.

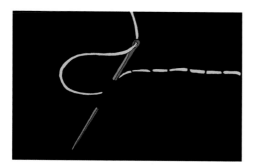

Split Stitch

Backstitch, but with the next stitch going back through the previous. Nice strong, solid lines.[3]

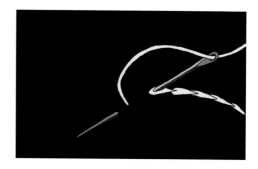

Stem Stitch

Same, with the next stitch laid just to the right or left halfway back alongside the previous. Good for curved lines. Stick to the same side every stitch or it gets ugly.

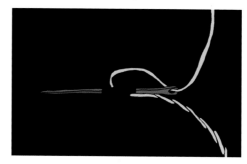

How to Continue

Come back, expert sewers. You know the stitches, which come from both dressmaking and embroidery directions; now meet them afresh dressed up in their mending clothes. Also see the box on the next page for tips and tricks and reassurance: that weird thing that happens to you actually happens to everyone.

Secret Sewing Truths

- Thread often has a nap. Run fingers down it to check, and thread the needle to pull the thread in the smooth direction.

- Thread will always twist. It's like when you wind up a swing till it goes into a crazy whizzing spin. Slightly rotate the needle counterclockwise every pass to avoid the crazy whizzing knots.

- If it's getting worse, just reverse. Sometimes clockwise is the way to counter the spin.

- If you reversed too late: use the detangle dangle. Drop thread, let it untwist or run fingers down. Resume. With some kinds of thread you will do dangles *all the time*. This is normal.

- Alternatively, slide the needle's eye all the way to the fabric, then run your fingers down the length of the thread to untwist it before bringing the needle back to sewing position.

- Slow is better than knots. When a knot threatens, *do not proceed*. Stop, detangle.

- Start in a hidden place. Your first stitches are like the first pancake: misshapen.

- The iron is your friend. Press everything before, during, and after. It saves time in the end.

- Nobody said an ironing board has to be set up every time. A towel or heat-proof blanket on floor works.

- Tension is everything. You cannot check it too often. Too loose is better than too tight.

- Insert a cutting mat, piece of cardboard, or magazine inside the garment you're working so you don't sew the front to the back. Put same on lap: don't sew garment onto your jeans.

- Wax the thread to sew through tough things: Velcro, trim, fat seams. Soap works at a pinch.

- Unthread the needle and unpick a mistake immediately. It will bug you when it's too late.

- Use a loom knot (page 130) to attach new thread to old for continuity or to change colors.

- Seams are boring. Use the machine. No need for a serger: use zigzag to secure edges.

Edging and Joining Stitches

These next four are all you need to attach thing to thing, also for edges and stretchy bits.

Whipping

This over-and-over stitch done with a circular hand motion is the simplest way to join two bits together, do a hem, or attach a patch. Can and should be executed with contrast and élan. Neatness is overrated.

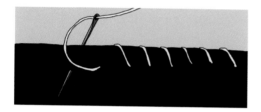

Overcasting

The same round-and-round stitch when used on a single edge to limit fraying. Worked gapless around a hole, it makes a porthole mend (page 188).

Felling

A.k.a. appliqué stitch: it's similar to the whipstitch, but with tiny perpendicular stitches spaced with diagonals. The Proper Patch (see page 166) is known as a felled patch for its use of this stitch. It's generally very useful in VM.[4]

Herringbone

Attachment with stretch, this is super useful, needless to say. Work it along two parallel lines (drawn or imagined), taking a small stitch in the normal direction (<<<) alternately on the bottom line, then the top, and moving from left to right, to form a connected row of long-legged crosses. See third picture on page 202 to see how this looks on the reverse side.

Feather Stitch

Another stretchy one, good for decoration as well as joinery. Sew vertically, top to bottom, and imagine (or draw) a center line. Your needle dips in from either side of this line, slanting toward it, downward at forty-five degrees, and coming out alternately to its right and left, over the top of the working thread. This forms a chain of crooked double vees (as I said, easier to copy the diagram).

A Joining Knot

The loom knot is used in hand weaving where a thread must be continuous, and, aptly, I use it continually. The great thing about this is its security: the more you pull on the new thread, the tighter the knot gets. It can be done with a very short end, but I leave more than I need, just in case. It might take a few tries, but do persist, it's worth it. Sometimes it's fun to knot on the surface, leaving a tiny tuft.

- Point the fresh thread (the pink) to the northwest (top left) and make a loop with the tail in front.

- Hold the loop at the crossed threads and insert the ending thread from front to back (left to right, heading northeast). Now bring the ending thread's tail around the whole thing and insert it through the loop, front to back (right to left, heading northwest).

- Grasp both tails in your left and the fresh thread in your right hand, and pull gently to tighten the knot. Tug the new leading thread to test and secure it, and snip the tails.

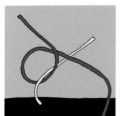 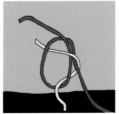

Framing Stitches

A group of standard stitches thoroughly repurposed to become the MVPs of your repertoire. See them applied as mends in Chapter Seven, "Which."

Eyelet

The love child of overcasting and satin stitch, eyelet excellently edges holes.

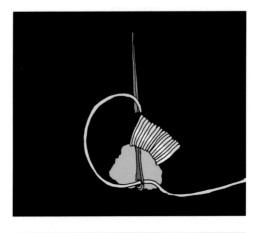

Buttonhole Stitch

Another hole outliner, with extra structure. This is the exact same stitch as the blanket stitch that follows, only with the stitches laid snugly next to each other, without a gap. Who says a buttonhole needs a button?

Blanket Stitch

Its traditional job is to edge things and stop them fraying, though it's equally happy in the middle of something, or as a cheeky novelty hole-framing device (see page 188). Work vertical stitches, left to right, dipping the needle in from the face, downward, out and over the working thread, before looping around for the next stitch. Alternatively, for a firmer edge, pull the needle most of the way through, then pass it back through the loop you made, essentially knotting it every pass.* In fact you can mess with blanket stitch any way you want, going right to left, upside down—just be sure to use the same variation every stitch. Though it is officially for edging, this is a versatile decorative stitch. You can work successive, slightly overlapping rows to make battlement stitch. Working successive interlocking rows is an alternate darning technique.

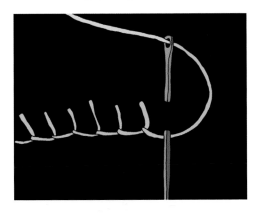

Drawing and Decorating Stitches

For all the stains and splatters, for tiny-hole networks, for boring patches and adorning a mend, or just because you're feeling it, I give you pure embroidery. Or impure embroidery.

Chain Stitch

The classic of classics, this has endless uses and is especially good for outlining boldly, and also for word mends. Working right to left, bring the needle out from the back, back down *in the same spot*, and out again over the working thread, pulling it through to form a loop. Next stitch, place the needle inside the previous loop and repeat, forming a chain.

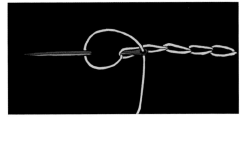

---

* When this is worked with stitches close together, it's the nice secure and professional tailor's buttonhole stitch.

Satin Stitch

The ultimate filler, with tons of variants, this is essential for fatter word mends (see statemend, page 179) and for all sorts of decorative stitching (embellishmend, page 180; paintypant, page 191). Simply bring the needle round and round, placing each stitch precisely adjacent to the previous. Since the effect—of glossy, smooth satin fabric—depends on accuracy, it's best not to slant the needle, but to place it vertically into the fabric; exactly the opposite of the illustration, oops. Missing a spot is not a disaster; it's fairly easy to go back around next pass to fill it in. You will almost certainly want to mark out your design before stitching, maybe even sewing the outline, then working the satin stitch just outside this running stitch guide.

Laid Stitch

False satin, or laid stitch, is similar but uses a fraction of the thread, so it's useful for similar effects on thinner fabrics. It's also economical with thread. For this, definitely sew a running stitch outline, and also place the needle vertically, not slantwise. Place each stitch on the face, across the design, taking a tiny, tiny perpendicular stitch in back before the return journey horizontally in front. The second illustration shows this, but you should sew the whole thing from the front, not turning the work over. In order not to get gappy, you may be catching only a single thread in back, so the fabric should have enough integrity to support this. PS: I worked all the words on this book's cover in laid stitch.

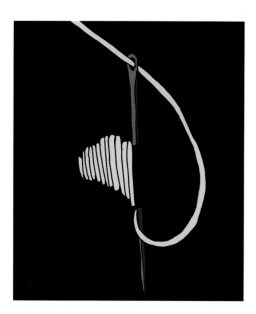

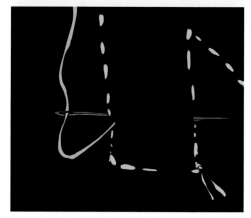

Cross Stitch

Detach it from its tapestry roots and this is just the handiest of shapes. Also see variations with additional arms, making stars and foundations for web stitches. It is also a fundamental component of sashiko stitching, placed this way, or, more often, as little plus signs. If accuracy and evenness matter to you, mark out guide lines, as in the illustration.

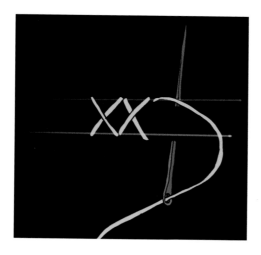

French Knot

This stitch has a reputation for difficulty. Au contraire, it's really satisfying, though it might take a few tries to perfect. Grip the thread with left thumb and forefinger two inches above the surface, and, holding the needle flat, wrap this lower thread three times around it. Now place the needle back in the same spot it exited and gently push with your left hand to slide the loops down onto the fabric—a smoother operation than it sounds. When you push the needle vertically down through the loops and pull it out the back, a roselike knot tightens on the surface. Use a needle with a slim eye, or it might get stuck. This is the stitch that makes sprinkles (see page 194), and all sorts of dimensional effects for embellishmends.

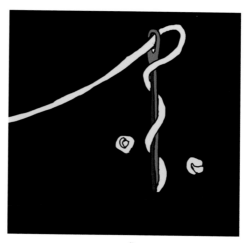

how

Couching

When Opus Anglicanum goes slumming . . . The way to use all those impossible fancy threads. You need two threads, a thicker one (the laid thread) to make the shape, and a thin one (the couching thread) to secure it—contrasting or matching, depending on the effect you want. All you do is lay the fat thread where you want it and sew catch stitches across it at short intervals to fasten. Pull the laid thread tight periodically. You can make any shape this way: writing, outlines, or even solids, by laying the thread in adjacent lines—when deliberate placing of catch stitches can make fancy effects with fancy embroidery names. In Opus Anglicanum–style underside couching, the thin thread pulls the laid thread through to the back, disappearing into the fabric to make near-unbroken lines. This is more useful for solid gold wire than our old yarn stashes.

Little Ding Stitches

Embroiderers call them detached stitches. I call them the most fun ways to close a small hole. Since these double as the mends themselves, instructions are in Chapter Seven.

Web Stitch

Renamed carbuncle by my husband, when applied to his cardigan that is now my cardigan. (See page 195)

Ribbed Web Stitch

A.k.a. whipped wheel, this is more spidery than the web stitch, hence its new specifically mending name of spider. (See page 196)

God's Eye

It's a whipped cross, with great color opportunities, even nicer in Spanish as *ojo de Dios*, and nicer still when you call it a goddess's eye. (See page 197)

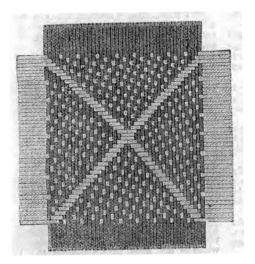

Darning

And now, my favorite thing. You may think of it as needle weaving, because that's exactly what it is: you're creating a plain weave fabric directly over a hole on (mostly) knitted garments, laying the warp then alternating the weft threads over, under, over, under, but doing it in miniature, and with needle instead of shuttle. The plain weave is as far as you may ever go, since you can produce so many effects just with color and shape, but there's a world of complexity, of forgotten diaper[5] and damask darns, available for the needle nerd. Here's a bit of an 1885 child's instruction for "one of the simplest examples of damask darning" (see left):

> 1st Row.—Under 3; over 4 and under 1, 7 times; over 4, under 3. 2nd Row and every alternate one are returning rows, and start, of course, from the left hand side.—Over 1, under 3, over 1, under 1; over 4 and under 1, 6 times; over 5, under 3, over 1. 3rd Row.— Over 2, under 3, over 1; under 1 and over 4, 6 times; under 1, over 3, under 3, over 2 . . .

And so on, for forty-five rows, all different. This isn't darning as we know it; it's a form of embroidery. Nobody used pattern darning to mend, because even the ablest could manage only about half an inch per hour, and it's generally executed on fine linen or cotton cloth. It was reserved for showing off, passing the time, and torturing schoolgirls. So here we'll concentrate on the simple, functional darn, with a word about . . .

Swiss Darning

Or mimicking the knit structure with a duplicate stitch (an alternate name) to reinforce worn areas— hence its mendy name, stitch on stitch. All darning instructions are in "Which."

How to Not Sew

Extra mending ruses to add to your repertoire.

Crochet

Look, I can't knit, okay? I did learn, but it didn't stick. I knit not. I suspect it's a whole other mindset, not to mention skill set, but crochet is different. Hooking the thread through itself is a bit like sewing, or like the knotting at the end done over, and over, and over. Clever crocheters do wonderful patterny things, but I am a dumb hooker and only do this one. Details are in the next chapter.

Knitting

Though I can't suddenly knit since the last paragraph, I do know Amy Twigger Holroyd, and she has kindly agreed to share the knowledge. Her Reknit Revolution, on page 136, breaks down the steps of extreme repair in a yarnspirational infographic a dozen years in the making. Of course, I can't help you with methods, but just pop over to reknitrevolution .org for info and knit tricks, including the essential cardiganizing that is sure to change the world. (Or try my sewing version on page 201.)

REKNIT REVOLUTION

reknitrevolution.org
#reknitrevolution

Use your knitting skills to rework the knitwear in your wardrobe

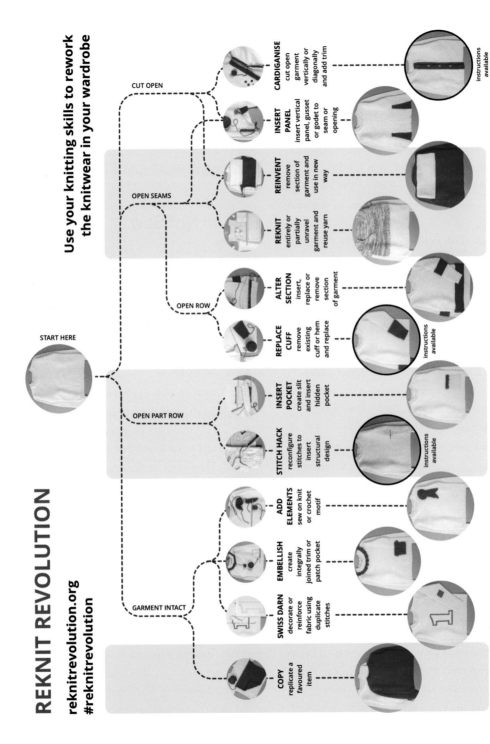

START HERE

CUT OPEN

CARDIGANISE
cut open garment vertically or diagonally and add trim

instructions available

INSERT PANEL
insert vertical panel, gusset or godet to seam or opening

OPEN SEAMS

REINVENT
remove section of garment and use in new way

REKNIT
entirely or partially unravel garment and reuse yarn

OPEN ROW

ALTER SECTION
insert, replace or remove section of garment

REPLACE CUFF
remove existing cuff or hem and replace

instructions available

OPEN PART ROW

INSERT POCKET
create slit and insert hidden pocket

STITCH HACK
reconfigure stitches to insert structural design

instructions available

GARMENT INTACT

ADD ELEMENTS
sew on knit or crochet motif

EMBELLISH
create integrally joined trim or patch pocket

SWISS DARN
decorate or reinforce fabric using duplicate stitches

COPY
replicate a favoured item

Version 2.3 April 2019

Needle Felting

Felting is a whole subculture revolving around baby animals, but felt needn't lead to cute. Instead, you can mend every hole in most every wool sweater by prodding it with a sharp stick. It is magic. Full instructions are on page 206, but you just get some roving (pre-yarn wool), a mat, and a felting needle and stab away. There is nothing to learn—oh, except the fact that only pure animal fibers will felt, so your acrylic sweaters are out of luck. I didn't mean to diss cute: felted kitten mends are totally fine.

Iron-Ons

Since ironing is my least favorite aspect of mending, I confess I find these charmless and baffling. Anyway, they exist, and they come with instructions, so no need to go into it.

Readymade patches: age-old low-sew mend

How to Wrangle Fabric

Behold, this huge subject squashed down on a need-to-know basis. The things to know are how to tell what you're mending *on*, what you're mending *with*, and how to match them up.

How to ID Fabric

Fabric, to risk being obvious, is made of fiber. Fiber is its fundamental component part, the stuff from which thread is made; then that thread is woven or knitted into countless thousands of variations. But, because we're not constructing garments, we can ignore most of the weave and knit structure business, and get straight into what you're actually wearing and how *it* wears, that is, the wear patterns of you and your clothes relating to mending. First off, you can divide all material into natural and synthetic fibers, though lots of your closet (if not all of it) will be blends of both—a great and horrible issue in the recycling world, if easier to care for.

Natural Fibers

Derived from organic, living sources, they're completely biodegradable, which is excellent, until they biodegrade in your closet. Natural was all that existed until midcentury (twentieth), which makes pre-1950s vintage all the more vulnerable and precious. Here's a natural fabrics breakdown.

Fiber to Fabric: The Naturals

TYPE	FABRIC	SOURCE	USES AND FABRICS
Cellulose	Cotton	Seed boll of cotton plant	USES: shirts, blouses, tees, spring/summer/fall dresses, skirts, jeans, pants, chinos, dungarees, overalls, shorts, light jackets, suits, sweats, socks, underwear, leggings, towels
			FABRICS: jersey, denim, corduroy, calico, canvas, duck, chintz, chambray, lawn, muslin, voile, cheesecloth, gabardine, twill, gingham, flannel, flanelette, fleece, terry, sateen, seersucker, poplin, damask, organdy, velour, velvet, velveteen
Bast	Linen Jute Hemp	Stem of flax, jute hemp, ramie, etc.	USES: shirts, blouses, summer dresses, skirts, T-shirts, pants, shorts, light jackets, coats, suits
			FABRICS: linen, flax, jute, hemp, ramie, kenaf, jersey, hessian, burlap, damask
Protein	Wool Hair Silk	Sheep fleece Animal hair *Bombyx mori* moth cocoons	WOOL USES: sweaters, cardigans, coats, winter dresses, skirts, pants, suits, socks, stockings
			WOOL FABRICS: jersey, tweed, gabardine, twill, tartan, melton, merino, crepe, challis, suiting, serge, worsted, jacquard, felt
			HAIR USES: knitwear, coats, jackets, dresses, skirts, pants
			HAIR FABRICS: cashmere, mohair, angora, alpaca, camel
			SILK USES: blouses, dresses, gowns, suits, pants, stockings, lingerie
			SILK FABRICS: silk, jersey, faille, tulle, voile, georgette, satin, peau de soie, taffeta, jacquard, velvet, organza, shantung, moiré

The Skin Thing

Missing from the chart, because not fibers, is the oldest natural fabric of all: animal skins. Needless to say, fur and leather are controversial, never mind how they present conservation issues all their own. Here's my pitch. I feel we should love and use the vintage kind. We couldn't have saved those animals, so let's keep them in circulation so that they didn't die in vain. And no, PETA, vintage fur is not a gateway drug to evil fashion animal slaughter. Also see silk. Sericulture boils the cocoon, killing the caterpillar (silkworm) midmetamorphosis, so . . .[6]

Cellulosics

Between natural and artificial lies this huge and growing category of natural fibers formed into fabric by industrial processes: cellulose, often wood pulp, is dissolved, extruded in filaments, then chemically solidified and woven into fabric. Rayon is the generic name for this first ever man-made fabric, known as artificial silk, or art silk, when it went into production in the late nineteenth century—so it is *all* over the vintage market. Other names and types: viscose, cupro (a Comme des Garçons fave), acetate (in heavy use for linings from the 1920s onward), modal, and lyocell (Tencel). Research continues, with new rayon being made from orange peels, soy husks, coconut shells, you name it, at least partly in the commendable quest for circularity.

Synthetics

Nylon, said *Fortune* magazine in 1940, "flouts Solomon. It is an entirely new arrangement of matter under the sun."[7] Three years later came Terylene, the first commercially marketed polyester, and Orlon, the first commercial acrylic. Then, just in time for the 1960s, spandex, and, millennially, microfiber. The first year polyester outsold cotton was 2002; now it's about four to one and rising, and a brief glance in your closet will tell you where Lycra's at. Microfiber fabrics are choking entire oceans as they leach, well, their microfibers.

As the Marvel documentaries show, arranging matter in entirely new ways while not being God is dangerous. But here we are, buried in performance fabric athleisure and stretchy jeans. What would Solomon do? Mend it.

How to Discern Mendability

Mendability is a function of cleanability and integrity, and is decided on a case-by-case basis. Nevertheless, each fabric has its tendencies, summarized in the following chart.

Shattered silk: unmendable

Can You Mend It?

NATURAL FIBERS	NOTES: CARE AND MENDABILITY	EASY	HARD
Cotton			
Broadcloth, poplin, percale, etc.	The quality of your plain weave cotton matters very much. Better lasts longer, duh.	✓	
Jersey, 100% cotton	Splendidly mendy but good luck finding it! Jersey curls if unhemmed; tricot doesn't.	✓	
Fleece, 100% cotton	If made now, its purity is a feature. Vintage sweats tend to holeyness, but are prized.	✓	
Denim (plus canvas, calico, duck)	95% of mends are denims; 5% lack Lycra.[8] More stretch, less strength is the rule.	✓	
Gabardine, twill, chino	Workhorse cottons of pant and jacket; nearly always worth mending and fun to do.	✓	
Flannel, brushed cotton*	Think plaid shirts, PJs, camp sheets. Colorful, supersoft, but can run to holes fast.	✓	
Lawn, batiste, voile, organdy*	The filmiest of cottons are also the weakest. Layering patches is a nice work-around.		✓
Corduroy, velveteen, velour*	Pile weaves/knits aren't always hard to mend but need special care: watch the nap.		✓
Velvet*	The luxury nonstretch pile weave is more unforgiving: hard to press, easy to ruin.		✓
Gingham, madras, chambray	Lightweight, yarn-dyed check fabrics, or white + color make great mendees or patches.	✓	
Chintz, sateen, damask	Glossy finish or woven-in pattern make these potentially awkward, though hardy.		✓
Seersucker, plissé*	Texture built into the weave adds a level of difficulty for achieving patch flatness.		✓

* These fabrics are also made in synthetic versions but can generally be treated similarly regardless of fiber content.

NATURAL FIBERS	NOTES: CARE AND MENDABILITY	EASY	HARD
Linen			
Linen, flax, hemp, ramie	Smooth, durable, lovely to mend, creases like crazy. Good linens improve with age.	✓	
Jersey, 100% linen	It's fairly easy to find these days, cool and uncrushable, but very, very weak.	✓	
Hessian, burlap	Unlikely to be in your closet, unless vintage, but fun to mend with its open weave.	✓	
Wool			
Knitwear, 100% wool, chunky	Watch for unraveling/moth attack; darn with big yarn. A felting patch candidate.	✓	
Knitwear, 100% wool, fine	Moth food. But the funnest to mend. Darning is usual, but also consider felting or even patching.	✓	
Wool jersey	Moths' very favorite candy. Accepts all mend types though: embellishmend to felting.	✓	
Tweed, tartan, herringbone*	Hardy, yarn-dyed patterned cloth for jackets, coats, kilts, etc. Needs durable patching.	✓	
Twill, gabardine, worsted, serge	Long fibers, tight weaves, think fine suiting: you need precision to mend it well.		✓
Crepe,* challis	Can be challenging because textured/superfine; just take care going in.		✓
Melton, felt, boiled wool	Rarely comprises the whole garment but good surfaces for many applications.	✓	

* These fabrics are also made in synthetic versions but
  can generally be treated similarly regardless of fiber content.   *(Continued)*

NATURAL FIBERS	NOTES: CARE AND MENDABILITY	EASY	HARD
Hair / Down			
Cashmere, alpaca + blends	Cashmere is notorious for pilling, blends less so. Alpaca, usually blended, resists this.	✓	
Mohair + blends	In knits its signature loose hairiness makes it a bitch to mend. Can be done though.		✓
Angora + blends	Ditto. Don't even try to replicate the kitten-belly soft fuzziness in your darn.		✓
Camel hair, vicuña	Hardly seen now, this beautiful, smooth, expensive cloth is worth some extra effort.	✓	
Silk			
Habotai, China silk, broadcloth	Modern silk is easy care but can be thin/weak; vintage tends to have more substance.	✓	
Shantung, doupioni, Thai*	Slubs and uneven yarns make unmendably weak places, less so in synthetic versions.		✓
Satin, duchesse, charmeuse*	The signature smooth luster shows every pull and fault; difficult to VM successfully.		✓
Taffeta,† moiré, faille*	Fine-ribbed, textured, stiff gown fabrics are challenging to VM in suitable style.		✓
Silk noil, tussah, brushed silk	Noil, or raw silk, frays. Tussah is wild: tough and valuable. Brushing adds substance.	✓	
Crepe, crepe de chine*	The granular face provides a forgiving canvas for mends. Synthetic versions, ditto.	✓	
Georgette, organza, voile, chiffon*	The floatiest, thinnest fabrics represent obvious mend hazards. Finest needles needed.		✓
Brocade, jacquard*	Woven-in pattern and tight weave might be no trouble at all, but finer ones need care.		✓

* These fabrics are also made in synthetic versions but can generally be treated similarly regardless of fiber content.

† Recognize taffeta by its *scroop*, the term for the sound made by a fingernail running down its fine horizontal ribs. Moiré, a.k.a watered silk, is calendered taffeta, given a wood grain pattern via heating and rollers: think 1950s prom dresses and evening gowns. Faille is a far finer, more flowy version of taffeta. Unless you're in the couture end of the market, or get lucky (or spendy) with vintage, you're far more likely to find acetate versions of these.

MAN-MADE FIBERS	NOTES: CARE AND MENDABILITY	EASY	HARD
Cellulosics			
Rayon, viscose	So many variations it's hard to generalize, but easily handled fabrics on the whole.	✓	
Cuprammonium (cupro)	From a tough, drapey jersey to a hard, shiny woven cloth: just watch the washability.	✓	
Acetate	You know how old linings go all brittle and splitty? It's acetate's fault. Best replaced.		✓
Lyocell (Tencel®)	It's so soft, smooth, and pliable it'll need support: mend it on table not lap.	✓	
Modal®, micromodal®	Made from beech, usually a jersey; it's even slipperier, so can be hard to manipulate.	✓	
Bamboo	Also soft, but, like all rayons, it varies a lot, so do select a patch fabric that matches.	✓	
Synthetics			
Nylon	Shiny stretchiness, random discoloration, pulls, smells: vintage nylon can be awful.		✓
Polyester	So many types but can't think of one that's especially pesky. Polyester thread is best, obviously.	✓	
Acrylic, modacrylic	Sweaters and 1970s sportswear are frequently found; there are no special mend issues. Can't be felted.	✓	
Microfiber fabrics	If you can stand it catching on your skin it mends like butter. Not that butter mends.	✓	
BLENDS	NOTES: CARE AND MENDABILITY	EASY	HARD
Cotton + polyester	Probably your entire wardrobe, so it's just as well it's easy to handle, and wash.	✓	
Cotton/silk + rayon	Rayon adds strength and luster, but can be less easy care in the laundry department.	✓	

(Continued)

how

BLENDS	NOTES: CARE AND MENDABILITY	EASY	HARD
Linen + cotton	Such a good compromise: that linen look with less ironing/cost. Mends like cotton.	✓	
Natural fibers + elastane/ spandex	Keeps its shape, loses its integrity. Built-in weakness means mending earlier and often. Use a stretchy stitch.	✓	
Synthetics + elastane/ spandex	Athleisure. Period. Tricky to mend if too stretchy/ sweaty. Patch with similar fabrics and stretchy stitch.		✓
Acetate, etc. + elastane/ spandex	A common rib knit called "slinky" in the trade is hard to mend: *waaaaay* too stretchy.		✓
Acrylic + wool	Less breathable and stain resistant than wool, but more mothproof. Cannot be felted.	✓	

SPECIAL CONCERNS	NOTES: CARE AND MENDABILITY	EASY	HARD
Historic	Do not visibly mend museum-quality historic pieces. Did I really say that? I did. They need conservation: more science than art. Scrappy pieces are fine to mend.		✓
Weighted silk	Adding metallic salts to counteract sericin loss in silk processing was common ca. 1870–1918, resulting in *shattering*—complete loss of integrity. Can't be repaired.*		✓
Embellished	Sequined, embroidered, beaded, rhinestoned— visibility of mend is hard to pull off.		✓
Lace	Real lace is precious and deserves specialist restoration. Yours is probably machine made and fine to mess with; can also be removed and used to mend other pieces.		✓
Metallics	Generally tricky kinds of fabrics, with special sewing needs; also, hard to clean.		✓
Dimensional	3D effects—matelassé, embossed, waffle, plissé— add surmountable difficulty.		✓
Multifabric	Patchwork, illusion, quilted: treat according to the most delicate of included fabrics.	✓	

* Weighted silk inevitably, eventually shatters—it looks like broken glass, shredding, or honeycomb made by insane bees. The process was used to give the illusion of more expensive material. Museums often deaccession these silks, because conservation (usually holding the shards in place with a net overlay) is so expensive.

SPECIAL CONCERNS	NOTES: CARE AND MENDABILITY	EASY	HARD
Textured	Pointelle, Swiss dot, dobby, eyelet, etc.: let the decoration dictate the mend.	✓	
Intarsia, patterned knits	The issue is merely aesthetic: making the mend visible with the right kind of clash.	✓	
High pile	Faux fur is likely to be the hardest mendee in your closet. Evade/avoid.		✓
Swimwear, lingerie	Fit in swimwear is obviously an issue; lingerie may be too worn out. Use for parts.		✓
Net/mesh	Athletic mesh, power mesh, tulle, fishnet . . . Too much airspace in it to mend it well!		✓
Technical fabric	If it's weatherproof or sweatproof it might also be needleproof. Get the machine out.		✓
Bonded (Neoprene, GORE-TEX)	Any mend will compromise the integrity of functional garments. Forget pleather, too.		✓
Pleated	Perma press pleats will keep their shape, but it's a hard shape to mend around.		✓
Hand finished	Don't fear painted or embroidered surfaces, as long as you're careful. No washing!	✓	
Special finish	Calendering, ciré, glazed, flocked, moiré, etc.: match the patch and you'll be fine.	✓	
PVC	The technical term is inherent vice: the plastic fabric breaks down all by itself, cracking and going sticky and icky. It also off-gasses to spoil its neighbors. Avoid.		✓
Leather	As long as it's been well kept, it's mendable, though you will need specialist needles and extrastrong thread. Cracking may be alleviated with leather food if you're lucky. If it's dried out/brittle, forget it.		✓
Suede	Stains and shiny patches are probably permanent and soft suede tears easily. Difficult.		✓
Fur	Furs need cool, dark, dry storage. Badly kept they dry out; the damage is permanent.		✓

how

How to Match Your Patch

Having given a big buildup, this is actually very easy indeed, and you already know the main thing: like with like. To break it down, these are the qualities by which you'll assess your prospective patch, in order of importance:

1. Weight (thickness)

2. Hand (feel)

3. Fiber

4. Color

How to Keep Clothes

As stated, no one is satisfied with their storage. This is because (nature abhorring a vacuum), possessions will always expand to the limits of the space allotted, and clothes are particularly rampant breeders. All we can do is manage the situation. This is about space (see 156), but also care. Our tending habits are really old-fashioned. They are hangovers from the post-war boom, the nuclear family plastics era of your first washer-dryer and hygiene paranoia. The plan outlined here is a combo of museum conservation practices, old-school washing day fun, and efficiency ruses. It is very mendy.

Wash Less

Washing is killing your clothes. Every laundering shortens a garment's life by, oh, a month (see endnote 8). I bet the source of the one-wear wash idea was Procter & Gamble's *Mad*

Patch Selecting Tips

- Like with like. But deliberately mismatched can work: a lace fragment on a sweater, etc.

- Use common sense. Don't patch your jeans with silk or your silk blouse with denim.

- Jersey fabric is best for T-shirts. Poly-cotton on rayon is fine as long as the feel is similar.

- If you can, mend vintage with vintage fabric. Brand-new modern weaves don't match.

- Watch washability. Sweats patched with velvet can no longer be thrown in the machine.

- Watch stretchability. Patch stretchy with stretchy and—important!—use stretchy stitch, e.g., herringbone.

- A patch of easily fraying fabric should be hemmed, or overstitched patchiko-style.

- The integrity of the patch fabric itself is important; fragile vintage cotton will not last.

- The no-patch solution: chain or split stitch an outline on a stain or eyelet around a hole (see Frames, page 188).

- There is no patch for shattered silk, PVC, dried out fur or leather, or shredded gauze/chiffon.

- Do not resuscitate: swimwear, worn lingerie, torn suede, holey net/mesh, split shantung.

- Very vintage cotton or silk that tears easily is also probably too far gone to be patched.

Men—era marketing team: overwashing sells more Tide (it can also redeposit soil on clothes and set stains permanently). Not washing is getting awfully trendy now, for green reasons, but the main mend-related reasons are that less washing—and definitely less tumble drying—paradoxically saves your favorite clothes, and probably time, too. There are three reasons to wash a clothe: removal of stain, or of germ, or of smell. I daresay smell (or fear of) is what propels us fastest to the washing machine. But listen up.

Less Laundering ≠ More Stinking

To overgeneralize, but not really, because athleisure, clothes get stinky when they're made of synthetic fiber. Ridiculously, the clothes manufactured expressly for sweating into are the most petrochemical of the lot. Yes your performance fiber top wicks your sweat, but then it hugs it to its bosom, maybe refusing to let it go, *ever*, in a phenomenon scientifically named *perma-stink*.[9] Synthetics are hydrophobic but oleophilic—they hate water, but love oil—so they cling jealously to body odor compounds, but refuse the advances of your washing machine. The more you fight your running tights, the more they resist—dryer sheets and extra detergent and heat drive the smell-causing bacteria deeper into the fibers, where they take up residence. Antimicrobial finishes such as silver chloride don't deter them at all. It is gross.

I'm not here to lecture on eco-water-saving detergent-minimizing, though this is a happy side effect of many old-new methods.[10] I'm here to keep good clothes alive and mendable.

I confess I'm a bit conflicted about stains. Set-in stains invite mending, and mends invite conversation, and then you can tell everyone about the bacteria partying in their pants. So I'll ignore stains, aside from the kind that attack and degrade fabric or can't be mended or spoil the overall beauty of a thing. Speaking of ignoring, follow only the bits that sound appealing: the last thing we want is the return of washday labor and guilt. I've been around the laundry block—never owned a washer-dryer till I was a mom; been a student, a traveler, dirt poor, addicted to wash-dry-fold service—and after all this, I've discovered that tending clothes is actually fun. Anyway, decide for yourself. Here are assorted old-school and costume specialist hacks to mend your cleaning routine and keep your favorite garments alive.

- **Gym stink.** Sweat is odorless. The smell is bacteria breaking down proteins into acids. Left in a swampy pile, these reproduce like a horror film. Arrest the breeding! Rinse gym things out in plain water and hang to dry right after committing the sweat.

- Or switch to **all-cotton** workout wear. It's hydrophilic and oleophobic, the opposite of synthetics, so absorbs and holds or wicks sweat, but resists oils and smells.[11]

- **Aromatic pits and the crotchal region.** Sorry to be graphic, but you know what I'm talking about. Try these professional theater costume department and vintage dealer no-wash fixes.

  o Give it a drink. Spritz generously with pure (cheap) **vodka**; let dry. No alcohol smell!

  o Connect to earth. Sprinkle **fuller's earth** on the bits overnight. Vacuum up, with stink.

  o Acidulate. For allover smell, steam garment over a hot bath of **white** vinegar solution.

  o A paste of **baking soda** and water is much cheaper than Febreze and often works better.

- **SOS: Save Our Sweaters.** Handwashing in cool water is the only way. You don't need to do it often.

Invest in perfume-priced cleansers or use **baby shampoo.**[12] Rinse thoroughly, squeeze gently, then . . .

- Reshape (it's called blocking) the wet sweater on a fluffy towel, **Swiss roll** it, and kneel on the roll to squish out water. Never wring knitwear. Dry on a fresh towel, turning it periodically.[13]

- **Air dry** whatever you can, especially vintage, most of which should never go in the dryer. Your hand mends last longer when air dried, too. Use ordinary hangers if you lack line or frame.

- Add a few drops of lavender essential oil to water in a spray bottle to **spritz on while ironing.**

- **Yellowed cotton** might have gotten that way from dry-cleaning. Add **borax** to the wash. And hang out in the **sun**—which is mostly terrible and verboten for fabrics, because of this bleaching effect.

- **Care labels** are often as generic as the website cookie disclaimer that you never read and fulfill a similar legal function. Nearly everything can be **gently handwashed.**

- **Exceptions are:** velvet, satin, taffeta, brocade, some silks, anything tailored or structured, and everything under Special Concerns in the chart on pages 144–45. **Beware rayon:** very tricky and variable.

- **Spot clean and steam**[14] fancy clothes—or, in fact, most clothes. Vintage dealers do.

- For embellished items, borrow the **museum conservator** method: vacuum on low with open vent and flat nozzle through a gauze screen edged with tape.

- Forget wasteful sticky-sausage lint cleaners. Use an old-school **clothes brush** or the kind that picks up lint one direction and deposits it on the reverse journey.

- **Mildew.** Omnipresent fungal spores that feast on your damp natural fibers. It's serious and contagious. Dry, vacuum, dry-clean, revacuum. It may be too late for this poor garment.

- A final little trick. Scribble all over metal **zippers** with graphite pencil: nonstick magic.

How to Keep Clothes . . . Safe from Moths

Tineola bisselliella evasion is the number one thing I'm asked about. But, without the multitudes of ravenous moth children, where would darning be? After mending awhile, you may find you are confusingly unsad when you discover a herd of *lepidoptera* have had a private picnic on your cardis. Because there is no official collective noun, I propose we call them an opportunity of clothes moths.

And yet.

It is vexing and and even heartbreaking to find your favorite woolens all beholed and spattered with frass (moth poo), and, because they are stealthy little buggers and apparently invisible, often perplexing. You can be sure there is a source somewhere though, in the nethers of a cupboard or a rug in the garage or that muffler you never wore. It will be the only place you didn't look, for example, beneath your husband's closet where a wool baseball cap he claims not to recognize caused a mothpocalypse I am still tackling to this day. For example.

Sweater enemy #1: *Tineola bisselliella*

How They Work

The webbing clothes moth (and the less common casemaking *Tineola pellionella*, which behaves a bit differently) hates light.[15] They're small and golden and if you do see one she'll sit with wings folded or flitter aimlessly but not hungrily (she lacks mouth parts), having already laid her fifty miniature eggs in an unknown wool baseball cap. Hatching into tiny larvae, these spin webbing cocoons using partly your clothes, and devour your stuff, defecating with abandon. They prefer keratin but they'll eat everything. Bad tenants that they are, they may stay a month, or it may be two years, they're not sure, it depends. Eventually they pupate and by then it's too late for your cashmere crewneck. Then they have about a month to locate your most secret, perhaps soiled, sweater stash upon which to attach more babies.

How to Beat Them

Prevention is ideal, but if you're reading this it may be too late. So move on to elimination, monitoring, and further prevention.

Moths Like . . .

Dark, undisturbed places—in closet (backs and bottoms), on garment (under collar, in folds, in pockets), and in basement. The larvae feed on wool, hair, fur, down, feathers, lint, and felt. Dust, dirt, and stains attract adult females. If other fibers, especially those mixed with wool or spattered with delicious dirt and stains, are nearby, they may be endangered, too. Also inspect toys, piano felt, upholstery, rugs, blankets, down comforters and pillows, taxidermy mounts, and wool baseball caps.

Prevention

Inspect, move, rotate, and wear garments of the above composition regularly. Take everything out to brush, air, or shake periodically, and clean it all thoroughly before putting it away for the season. Food spills, even if antique, make attractive nurseries for moth moms. Vacuum everywhere, including shelves and crevices.

- Inspect closely *every single* new-old acquisition of a wooly nature. If you suspect your vintage find of the slightest infestation, quarantine it, as described opposite.

- Cedar blocks, lavender bags, spice sachets—sadly, none of these work to repel moths.

- A cedar chest works, but only if it's of fresh heartwood and is completely airtight.

- Old-fashioned mothballs of naphthalene and paradichlorobenzene do work, but again, only if in high concentration at the top of a tightly sealed case, where the heavy vapors descend over the garments. Unfortunately, mothballs are toxic and carcinogenic. Cruella de Vil was probably killed slowly by her coats.

Monitoring

- In addition to those steps, and especially if you've had past infestation, install pheromone traps—glue boards baited with female sex hormone—to catch adult males. It's an early warning system not a solution, because the men aren't the problem. Repeat: traps do not end infestations.

- The pheromone lure is species specific so if you suspect *T. pellionella*, get some of that type, too. Webbing moth larvae stay attached to your woolens (right), whereas these casemaking caterpillars make separate tubes they drag around, then attach to nearby shelf or ceiling to pupate.

- Quarantine. Seal any suspicious garment in a clear baggie to inspect for signs of incubation. Or skip this step and move straight to just-in-case mothicide. Remember eggs are invisible to the naked eye.

- Take any infested item(s) outside, pick off cocoons with disposable gloves, brush, and vacuum. Tired toothbrushes are great for this, then discard them, along with the vacuum bag.

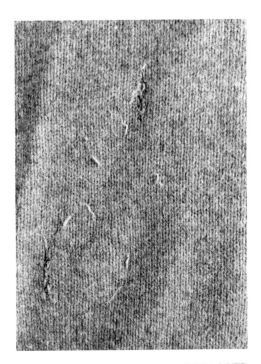

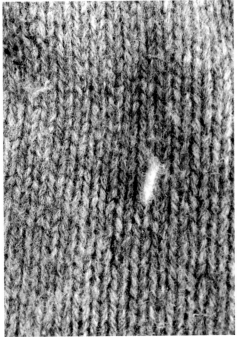

Mothicide

When infested, any of these three methods work. They must be carried out meticulously.

Freezing

Seal each moth-eaten item completely in its own airless zipped bag, the flatter the better (i.e., fewer folds) to increase rapidity of cooling. Place in freezer. How long you leave them depends on whether you have a deer-sized chest in the barn or a leaky snowed-up icebox atop the fridge—that is, temperature. Conservators say certain death occurs after one week at -4°F (-20°C), but I leave mine for a month, at which even a balmy 5°F (-15°C) will do the job.[16] I don't trust my freezer. After taking them out, leave the things in their bags for twenty-four hours to return to room temperature. Follow the postmortem procedure.

Heating

Moths of all stages are killed by surprisingly low heat, and all you need is an oven. In fact, the problem is keeping the temperature low enough: 130°–140°F (55°–60°C) is the sweet spot, so your oven needs a "warm" setting, or a warming or proving drawer. Mine starts at 170°F so I leave the door slightly ajar and keep a close eye on the thermometer. All you do is place a pan of water on the lowest rack to keep up the humidity, then place your garment(s) on the middle shelf, refolding halfway through. Alternatively, prevent desiccation by roasting your sweaters in oven bags, or even regular zippy bags.[17] Heat for three hours (one will do, but let's be thorough), switch off the oven, and leave the clothes to cool

inside with the door shut (or shut the door if it was open). Bingo, moths murdered. Go to post-mortem. PS: *Do not microwave.* Too many risks, too uneven temperature, too much likelihood of metal bits.

Sunbathing

Solar bagging was developed for rural and lower-tech areas, and uses the same baking principle, but with the sun as the heat source.[18] You have to like a project, to be sure, but it's good for bulk disinfestation and anyone nostalgic for a science fair. You parcel up your garments in light cotton as a buffer, seal them in black plastic (which shields them from damaging UV rays), then leave them in the sun. It's best to raise the packets off the ground, enclose the whole thing in clear plastic sheeting, and monitor the interior temperature by thermometer with a probe: 130°F kills the beasts; above 140°F is bad for clothes (vent the bags). It's like wearing black nylon in summer and will easily kill all insects in one sunny day. Allow twenty-four hours before unbagging the clothes and moving on to the postmortem.

Postmortem

This is simply a question of inspecting and cleaning all remaining debris from the formerly moth-infested garments. Nervous persons may opt to place the still-sealed packets in quarantine for a week to be sure of death. But before putting them away, you must remove all clothes from areas near which the moth has veered, and vigorously inspect, shake, and brush them all. Then vacuum the areas incredibly thoroughly down to the tiniest of crevices.

How to Do Vintage

I'm sure you're already doing vintage, but what is it though? Officially, any garment made twenty or more years ago (twenty-five say some) is vintage; age ninety or older and it's designated antique. However, thanks to Big Fashion, the manufacture of the good clothes we talk about when we talk about vintage started to slow around 1990, with the output of not-worth-keeping accelerating insanely with the new century. Since 2005 we have made very little future vintage. This is why people tag the real thing #truevintage to distinguish it from vaguely retro-style dresses, or indeed the copious crap copies of actual twentieth-century pieces. The sad truth is the clothes of the past are going extinct and it's our job to look after what's left. So, to spot it in the wild, knowing what you've got, understanding its needs, its mending, and how it looks best with combat boots is data of value. And these are garments of value: rare or even unique living history, and high-ticket items, if they're lucky. Historians call ordinary clothes from real wardrobes, as opposed to designer pieces, *vernacular clothing*, and these are almost more exciting. Then, as now, early-career name designers and talented unknowns worked for mass-produced brands. So just because the label is modest doesn't mean the garment isn't splendid. Vintage has special mending needs. Know its age and fabric before stitching anything permanent: first, do no harm. But then again, it's yours now. Have fun with it.

How to Shop, Style, Know, Own It

- Vintage that got away is tragic. If it's an "on" shopping day *buy it*. Or mourn it forever.

- Fashion frowns on costumey— single-era top-to-toe, overdone, embellished. Fashion exists to be disobeyed. I like like with like. Be lady, mod, hippie, punk . . . Dress the hell up.

- Playing the opposites is classic: floral + stripe, tulle + leather, gown + boots, couture + cutoffs.

- If it doesn't fit right, wear it back to front, belt it, hem it. Reversed cardis were a 1940s fad!

- Collect punctuating pieces in clashing colors for unzipped glimpses of tank, bra, bandeau.

- Wear short sleeve over long, tightness over volume, T-shirt under strapless, pant under dress.

- Bunch brooches and pins, switch out buttons, bring back the scarf, the kipper tie, the bolo.

- Matchy is marvelous. Do suits, shades of a single color, toning tights. All black is back.

- Develop a signature look. Which era liked your body type? Ignore current trends. Do you.

Instant Expert Vintage Cheat Sheet

SILHOUETTE	DECADE	STYLE SIGNATURES	DATING HINTS	DESIGNERS
	1920s	Flapper, Jazz Age Drop waist Flat bust Silk, chiffon, lace, beading Linens, striped blazer Cloche hat	Easily recognizable, but hard to source the real thing. More likely to be 1980s-does-1920s (also 1930s). Hems rose higher later; only button flies till 1928.	Vionnet, Patou, Molyneux, Erté, Sonia Delaunay, Jeanne Lanvin, Callot Soeurs
	1930s	Bias-cut gowns Lean, long, midcalf Waisted, boxier later Small shoulder pads Snood, platform shoes Hollywood, Art Deco	Can be hard to tell 1930s from 1940s; zippers on dresses only started in late '30s. Lots of slinky rayon. ILGWU-CIO Union label dates it from 1936 to 1940.	Madame Grès, Schiaparelli, Mainbocher, Adrian, Valentina, Norman Hartnell
	1940s	Tailoring, trench coat Utility, siren suit Plaid, gingham, crepe dress Zoot suit, aloha shirt Wedge heel, beret Film noir	1940s suits (they said "costume") can still be found. Hems longer late in the decade. ILGWU-AFL label dates it from 1940 to 1955. Metal side-seam zippers in dresses.	Claire McCardell, Charles James, Norman Norell, Dior (New Look, 1947), Balmain
	1950s	Hourglass, peplum Full, pencil, circle skirt Bullet bra, sweater girl Beaded cardigan Clamdigger, side-zip pant Stiletto heel	Look for high, fitted armhole and three-quarter sleeve. From late 1950s: center-back zipper, sack-back gown, and trapeze dress. ILGWU AFL-CIO label from 1955.	Balenciaga, Jacques Fath, Griffe, Ann Lowe, Hubert Givenchy, Scaasi, Hardy Amies, Pauline Trigère

SILHOUETTE	DECADE	STYLE SIGNATURES	DATING HINTS	DESIGNERS
	1960s	*Mad Men*, Jackie O, Twiggy Mini, baby doll, sleeveless shift Space age, op art Sergeant Pepper, military Hippie, cheesecloth, beads Hendrix, Joplin, Bardot	Nylon gets going now, including zippers. Hippie styles start at end of the '60s. Sleeveless cocktail shifts in synthetics are common. "Made in Hong Kong."	Mary Quant, Rudi Gernreich, Paco Rabanne, Yves Saint Laurent, Oleg Cassini, Thea Porter
	1970s	Flares, bell-bottoms, hot pants Midi, maxi skirt Spread collar, fitted knits Granny dresses, patchwork Studio 54 to punk Perfecto jacket *Annie Hall*, *Shaft*	Garment care labels in the US start in 1972; ILGWU label is red, white, and blue from 1974. Novelty print polyester jersey shirts are easily found.	Biba, Halston, Stephen Burrows, Bill Gibb, Willi Smith, Fiorucci, Ossie Clark, Jean Muir, Vivienne Westwood
	1980s	*Dallas*, *Dynasty*, *Miami Vice* Madonna, MC Hammer pant Shoulder pads, power suit, mini Leotard, *Flashdance* sweatshirt New Romantic, pirate shirt Neon, LBD, gold lamè	Shoulder pads in *everything* (but removed by reseller?). Lycra begins. Deep armholes. Last decade of "Lot" numbers. Care label updated in '83.	Versace, Chanel (Lagerfeld), Gigli, Patrick Kelly, Armani, Dapper Dan, Lacroix, Moschino, Kenzo, Gaultier, Alaïa, Mugler, Ferré
	1990s	Grunge, goth, heroin chic Rap, hip-hop Slip, prairie dress, flannel shirt Minimalism Crop top, camisole, fanny pack *Fresh Prince*, *Clueless*, *Buffy*	End of ILGWU labels: 1995. Start of "Made in China." Last decade of Woolmark label. If the RN# is listed on ftc.gov database, it's post-1998. Lycra in everything.	Donna Karan, Cross Colours, Calvin Klein, Rei Kawakubo, Issey Miyake, Helmut Lang, Margiela, Marc Jacobs, Dries van Noten

How to Make
Space and Time

So, having refreshed your relationship with your clothes in the Ten-Step Closet Mend and taken care of your mending kit needs, here you still are, somehow cursed with insufficient space and always short of time. Here we all are. But after many, many years of defiant and relentless too-much-stuff-having, I've discovered some things that help keep order, which in turn makes space and saves time. But first a word about the kind of space a textile prefers. Clothes have needs, too.

Saving Space

Such a funny phrase, as if you could put some space in the bank and cash it later, or maybe you're rescuing it? Anyway, my space-saving thesis is based on the truth that what you see is what you wear.[19] To make use of all your lovely clothes, you need to rotate the seasons—not just the four seasons, but *your* seasons. Whatever your intentions, you will grab the thing that's right in front of you, so switch out that thing (on middle shelf, in top drawer, etc.) for the ones you're feeling right now. If you repile, refile, and rehang on a regular basis, you'll keep refinding dormant treasures and dress more interestingly. Also, you'll continuously weed out the fails, and get some space in the bank. You can find store-under-the-bed tips online. These are more personal.

Remove one-third to half of your clothes to a reserve collection, completely separate, even off-site (Closet Mend, Step 5). Changing out your hangers for the slimline velvet kind doubles your space and stops slippage. Use padded ones for delicate fabrics, and watch the shoulder stress: hanger ends can pierce holes. Hang nothing stretchy or very heavy. Double-decker your closet rails. Bottoms on the bottom, tops up top, obviously, and utilize inside-door and back-of-closet space. Hang belts by their buckles on door-mounted mug hooks. Hooks on the wall behind the clothes are good for your rarely worn best pieces (on hangers, in covers). Install shelves all the way up; use the top level for boxed out-of-circulation shoes or sweaters. I Space Bag sweaters all summer. This is naughty, because it's bad to squash fibers, but it mothproofs them, too. Drawers are simple: fold everything, then instead of the final, vertical fold, roll it up and store it visibly, sideways, like colorful monkey bread.[20]

Consider doubling down on your space savings by joining the nonownership movement. With rental services of all kinds proliferating it's getting easier to source for your taste and borrow your occasion wear, or work wear, or all wear. Better still, start your own in-friend network, then you can all mend it together.

Mending supplies are not such real estate hogs as clothes, but don't let floss take over. Whenever you bust out a new skein, simply take a strip of any old cardboard, snip notches up the sides and slits to secure thread ends. I make thread palettes all the time, it's quite satisfying. Also, pre-thread every color you have and store these needles on fridge magnets. I stick mine on the actual fridge. See picture on page 212.

What Clothes Like

- Darkness. Light damage is cumulative and irreversible—look at your faded curtains. Don't keep your clothes on an open rack. Coat hooks should be out of direct sunlight.

- Cool. Organisms, moldy and mothy, like it warm.* Store away from heat sources.

- Dryness. Damp is an obvious no-no, but too dry and fibers are desiccated. Relative humidity around 50 percent is ideal, but if you can't be perfect, then just avoid constant fluctuations or sudden spikes in humidity, which can encourage mildew, a virulent pest.

- To breathe. Squishing together leads to wrinkles and hiding places for moths.

- Lying flat. When out of use for long periods, for example, in storage, padded hangers are fine, but a boxed bed of acid-free tissue paper is nicest: protects from dust, buffers any folds.†

- Dust protection. Cover if not in use, an old cotton sheet will do; calico garment bags are gold standard. Dust contains mold spores, proteins that moths like, and abrasive particles.

- Steaming. Gentler, safer, and more effective than pressing—just ask vintage dealers and museum conservators. A steamer is a compact little guy that can fit into any closet.‡

---

*   But mildew likes it cold and damp. Ever left damp washing sitting awhile by mistake? It's one reason why everything textile is shipped with those little packs of desiccating beads.

---

†   Acid-free tissue paper is a museum mainstay that really does help preserve even modest clothes of natural fibers. Buffered tissue has a slightly alkaline pH, which is good for cotton, but bad for silk and wool, so get the unbuffered. Archival materials tend to cost a lot and come in bulk: the best prices for top quality and reasonable quantity I've found are at gaylord.com, which caters to the home archivist and collector as well as the professional.

---

‡   You'll still want an iron for your mending projects, but I've been less wrinkly (in wardrobe if not face) since discovering the joy of the Jiffy—the industry-standard manufacturer—about twenty years ago.

How to Find Time

- What can you *not* do? Start with the obvious: social media. It'll still be there after you've mended your thing. Then you can post it and join in the #visiblemending family. We are friendly.

- Turn off notifications. Do a mend, then switch on and enjoy a bunch of activity all at once.

- Aimless surfing. Need I even mention? Clickbait is designed to eat your time, and it will.

- That game. It is designed to eat your time, and it will. Also, it wants to eat your money.

- Shopping. Until Big Fashion dies, it's boring and demoralizing. Shop and mend your closet.

- It is the era of peak TV. But who says you can't stream and sew simultaneously? Try it.

- Millennial or younger, you've already dumped email. If not, then limit it to one hour twice a day.

- Bring back the phone call. It's oddly efficient. Salvage hours from email and text chains.

- Lunch hour, sandwich at desk. Add a mend. If you're in an office, you might even attract a crowd, start a trend.

- Don't drive during rush hour. Commute early or late. Use quiet saved time to mend.

- Carpool and use your passenger seat time to mend. Any car service or taxi use is also good mend time.

- Virtual meetings can be used for simultaneous, surreptitious mending.

- I love a party, but sometimes suddenly bail. That's four free hours for mending.

- Airports are made for mending, flights, too. A train seat is the perfect mendvironment.

- Irony alert! Planners and spreadsheets and calendars can waste time. Limit or ditch productivity tools.

- Save hours by not mislaying stuff. You're organized in closet, be organized everywhere.

- Put. Down. The. Phone. Selfies, TikTok, cat videos, whatever it is, it adds up to one big time suck.

Making Time

Where on earth are you going to find the time to mend, when you can't even [fill in this space]? Refer to the first line of this chapter: Just start. Time will appear. (Unless you're a new parent, in which case you have absolutely no time whatsoever. I'm sorry. It passes.) I know you're busy and this sounds ridiculous, but we've been sold a bill of goods about time—and I do mean sold. Time, they say, is money. You save time and buy time and sell it to the highest bidder. If nobody wants to buy yours, you're a failure. If you don't spend it wisely, you're wasting time or squandering it; don't work fast enough and you're losing it. If you live too long, you've borrowed it. But from whom? Nobody owns time.

Then again, we all *have* it. And our time isn't the same shape as money at all, that is, linear and directional (well, money is conceptual, too, but that's another story). Consider friend time, for instance—when you haven't seen so-and-so for months or years, but then you drop right back in where you left off, as if no time had passed. As shopping for vintage taught me, putting the time into something pays off, but often in a distant, apparently unrelated, place. Everyone knows how elastic time is, how it drags when you're bored and how summer lasts five minutes. But everyone has forgotten how new and artificial is time-as-we-know-it. It's not even a century old. So-called civil time was finally, globally adopted in 1925 (except in India) after fifty years of bickering among railway engineers, astronomers, and naval authorities.[21] No, nobody owns time, but it has worked for the Western white man ever since, trapped in timetables and clocks, all efficiency, uniformity, and "progress." I always thought Greenwich *mean* time was well named, in both the British sense of stingy or cheap, and the American sense of deliberately cruel.

With the spread of the movement erroneously called mindfulness (because the point is to be free of mind stuff, or thinking, should it not be mind-*less*-ness?), tagged #liveyourbestlife, #selfcare, and so on, it is widely understood that the only time that exists is now. This seems faddish, yet is absolutely, self-evidently true. If the concept has eluded you, or you can't stomach the Goop of it all, then mend. Mending is pure menditation. I can't prove it, but it somehow seriously, mysteriously mints time. Stitches represent time itself, captured in visible increments. On the left are some things from which you might steal time and pick up the needle to prove for yourself that mending is ordinary magic.

Making Mending Money

If you get good, offer your services via the Menders Directory on visiblemending.com.

which

As Emma Lazarus said: give me your tired, your torn, your huddled garments yearning to breathe free, the wretched refuse of your teeming drawer. Get your kit out, it's mending time. "Which" refers to the choice of mend. I'm not going to issue orders, but rather provide nudges and suggestions: it's half lookbook, half cookbook. Not that there aren't instructions. There are instructions, for thirty individual techniques I've affectionately titled over the years (some names have caught on by now—I'm the proud mother of some hashtags), but mostly it's for you to jump off from as you evolve your own mending style. This is an inevitable and natural process. Me, I'm a happy, messy mender. I like to see the hand. I'm congenitally un-crafty, enjoy an edge of comedy, and find perfection almost repellent: perfection comes from factories. Or is it that I just *can't* sew neatly? You be the judge. Which sort of mender are you? Only one way to find out. Here's a rundown of the process that precedes a mend. You can plan more formally of course, but that seems way too serious.

Which Mend?

- Pick your patient. The one that's speaking to you right now.

- Lay it out. Just sit with it and gaze. What does it need?

- Let the garment and its damage suggest ideas and solutions.

- Pick some supplies, a range of possibilities for what you have in mind.

- Whether contrasting, clashing, or toning, it's color that makes the effect.

- Place fabrics and yarns on the garment, one by one. Picture the finished look.

- When you've selected your supplies, decide your plan of action.

- If you're a sketcher, draw your idea, try it out on paper.

- Visualize the stages, lay out the tools. Practice any new stitches.

- Prepare: press the mend region and any patches. Pin, then baste in place.

- Or mark out stitch patterns, attach stabilizer, fit the embroidery hoop, etc.

- Or transfer your design to the garment with fabric marker or chalk.

- If it's a darn, outline the area in running stitch if you like (I don't).

- Start stitching. Relax, breathe, smile, laugh. You can't go wrong.

- By all means, alter course midstream if you're feeling it.

In all the mendstructions that follow, I will assume you've done the prep work from Chapter Six, "How," and therefore will only mention pressing if it's an unexpected extra. Always read through the whole recipe before starting. Later mends build on foundational ones, and if you're just starting out, it's a good plan to try those first. Refer to the Periodic Table of Mend Elements and the Pick-a-Mend Chart at the end of the chapter for guidance in selecting which mend goes where.

Patches

Patches and darns had a fight over which should lead, and patches won because jeans. The reason there aren't any here is that I once decided blue jeans hate me, and never grew out of it, but I *do* do jeans of another color, so you can imagine the pants in blue if you like. I feel there've been enough faux-boro denimends already anyway. Poor darns are way down on page 182.

Underpatch

Nothing says visible mending like a good underpatch. (Well, aside from a good darn.) Essentially this is an inset patch or set-in patch, depending on whom and when you ask; or, in normal sewing, it's reverse appliqué: two layers of fabric with a figure cut out of the top one, its edges stitched to the now revealed foundation. But your convenient hole means you don't need to cut out anything! Nor stitch its edges down. Unless you want to. I enjoy leaving

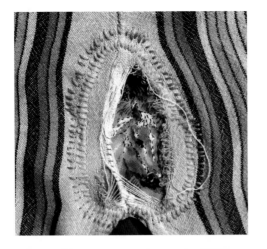

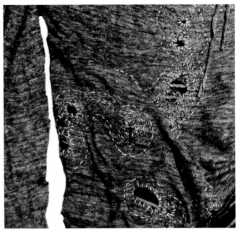

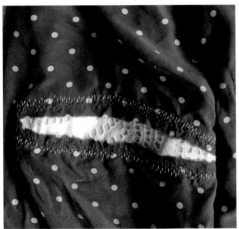

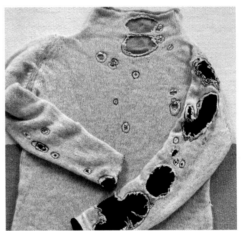

frayed edges, and exaggerating the gap to show more patch. An underpatch can also be added for reinforcement, in the absence of a hole, as seen in the target-shaped Flag mend on page 177. For my most extreme underpatchings, I insert an endoskeleton out of a waste garment, as in this linen top with stripey ex-dress inside, or this cashmere sweater, shredded by a mouse for nest building, which was saved by a holey but equally wispy-soft cashmere scarf.

1. Cut out your patch, ensuring it covers the entire hole plus any weak fabric. Make it even larger than needed if you like. Consider the final shape of stitching you're after.

2. Turn garment to wrong side and line up the patch beneath the ragged-edged hole, right side of patch to wrong side of

which

fabric. Turn right side out and inspect. Like the look? You may, of course, neaten up the hole, trimming loose threads and so on.

3. Then pin the patch in place and check it's smooth. Baste it and remove pins. If you've done an oversized patch, baste close to the hole edges and also at the patch edges.

4. Garment turned right side out, start attaching the patch, working a line of running stitch near to the hole, following its contours perpendicular, as here, or straight, as in the linen sweater. Check for smoothness all the while.

5. Keep stitching consecutive rows until you've reached the patch edge. You could alternate the stitches so they align with the gaps of the previous row, line them up exactly, increase or decrease the stitch size, alter the shape gradually, stitch a spiral instead of consecutive rows, use a different color for each row: go wild.

EYE EYELET

You might not have any eye fabric, nor wish to embroider an eye, but you may still use the pun.

1. Cut a round patch not too much bigger than the hole, ideally, from fabric depicting an eye.

2. Pin and baste as described opposite, then sew on the patch with ordinary thread, matching or not.

3. Now go around the hole in eyelet or buttonhole stitch: a porthole (see page 188). There's no need to sew through the patch.

4. You can of course use a bigger patch and add running stitch in contrasting floss, as here, but this tends to look best when the eyelet thread is the only pop of color.

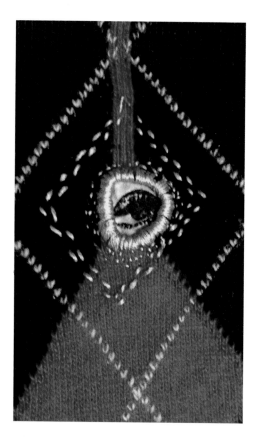

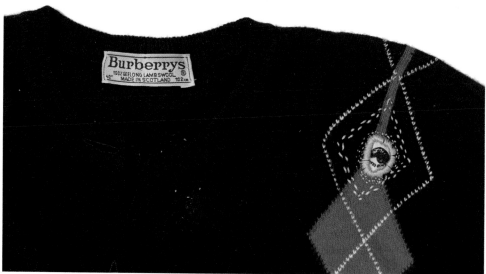

PROPER PATCH

For the neater person, this is a felled patch done correctly, where the patch itself supplies the visual interest and the stitching is not featured.

1. First, cut a square patch to cover the hole and then some. Fold its edges ¼" to its *front* (face), and press. You can miter the corners by opening out the folds and cutting across (see Pocket Patch, page 172, picture 2) so the edges lie flat at the corners with a forty-five-degree angle, or leave it with layered corners as here.* This patch is square, but other shapes work. For curves or circles, snip triangles into the edges before folding and pressing.

2. On the wrong side of the garment, baste the patch in place (you'll see its back; edges turned inward to its front, tucked underneath), check it, then fell it, or sew it on with whipstitch.

3. Turn right side out and trim the hole, snipping it into a square smaller than the patch.

4. Clip diagonally ¼" into each corner and turn the four edges in to the back, creasing them with a fingernail to lie flat (some fabrics you'll need to press instead).

5. Still on the right side, whipstitch/ fell the hemmed hole edges onto the patch.

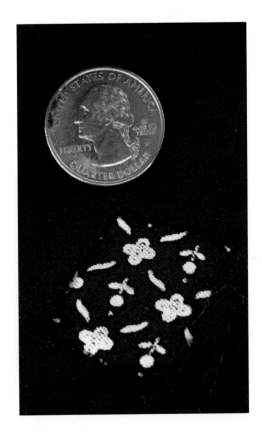

---

* This is a cut-rate version of the real way to miter a corner, which involves turning the hem allowance twice. I believe for VM, the fast way is the best way. Not mitering at all, as here, gives quadruple-fold corners, so if your fabric is on the heavy side, it's better to miter.

mend!

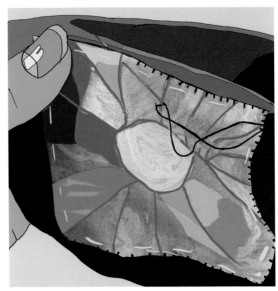

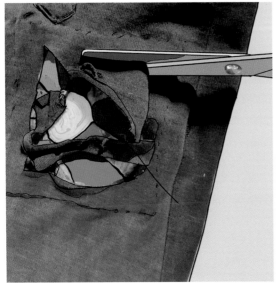

FAUX MOLA

Mola, rare and extraordinary multilayered textiles made only by the Kuna people in the San Blas Islands of Panama, are the mendspiration for this super underpatch.

1. Sew two or three layers of patch fabric beneath the hole—or as many as you dare.

2. Trim the hole in a pleasant shape close to the patch edge and whipstitch/fell around it, turning the edges under ¼" as you go. Snip into dramatic curves or corners as needed.

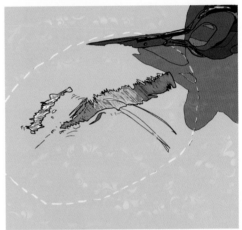

3. Pinch up the next patch layer, pierce it, then snip it into a smaller shape. Hem that the same way.

4. If you have further layers, repeat step 3. You might wish to mark out all the shapes first with fabric marker, or sketch the whole thing out before you start.

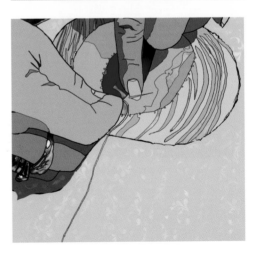

A real mola

Patchiko

I apologize, Japanese people, for taking sashiko in vain. This easiest of all mends, a patch-sashiko hybrid, just riffs on a repeated running stitch, but I named it years ago and now can't get the toothpaste back in the tube. This is easy, fast, and durable—good for your first ever mend and works exceptionally well on denims.

1. Cut a patch, big enough to easily cover the hole, with some to spare. Place it on the front, over the hole, right side (face) up. Pin and baste.

2. Stitch it on with multiple lines of running stitch, going way over the edges. Remove basting. Done. You could use little crosses, or seed stitch, make the lines wavy or circular or random, your call.

which

Band-Aid

What appliqué is called when it's rescuing clothes. This is a classic technique for attaching letters (see my "The Opposite of Hate Is Mending" sweater, on page 178), and yes, you can use woven fabric to repair knits—like the glazed chintz applied to this merino wool cardi. The green felt "Dovima" was my first ever visible appliqué, while the elbow patches are a classic of the genre.

1. Cut your patch in any fancy shape you wish. It shouldn't be a fraying material.

2. Pin, baste, then attach it with contrasting blanket stitch, using yarn, floss, or regular thread. Herringbone, whipstitch, or felling also work well, or you can make the stitching less visible to feature the patch itself. Add interior stitches to a large patch for extra security, and an extra design element.

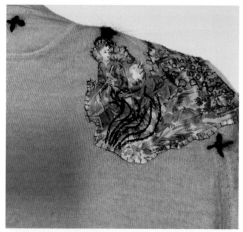

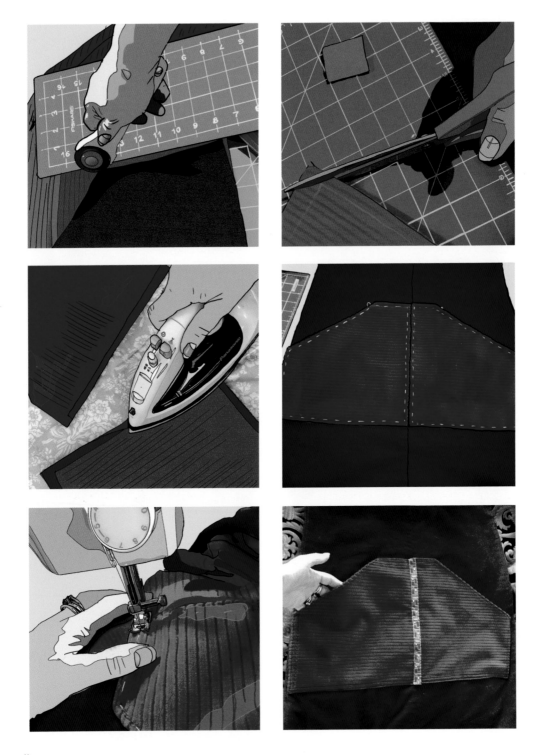

Pocket Patch

If your stain or hole is kind enough to appear where you'd like a pocket, congratulations: you get a twofer. Though you can hand sew your patch pockets, this one is better done on the machine.

1. Decide your pocket shape and make a pattern from an old T-shirt or paper. Don't forget to add ¼" to ½" for turnings. (Since it's VM we are turning the edges only once, unlike real dressmakers.) Use the pattern to cut your pocket fabric, which should be of a similar weight to the garment. You could also use your smocking practice piece as a pocket. (See Elasticize, page 198.)

2. On the reverse side, mark a quarter to half an inch line all around, and snip the corners as shown to make a nice neat forty-five-degree miter when you fold. Turn the edges in to the reverse side and press.

3. Baste all around the pocket(s) to secure the hem, then machine sew it. You can get away with skipping that step if the fabric isn't too flimsy. Apart from the top, do machine that edge.

4. Pin, then baste the pocket(s) carefully in place (adding trim or decoration as you like) before attaching by machine and removing basting. Obviously, don't sew up the top where your hand goes in. Work a few extra stitches over the top corners to reinforce the stress points. In case you hadn't noticed, this is the only machined mend in the book.

which

Selfiepatch

Do you have a printer? And a photo of yourself? You're all set. Well, one more thing. Though I first did this by glueing an old sheet to paper, it's *way* better to invest in printable fabric sheets.[1] This mend is funny, obviously, but also a mom's-face patch is good for young kids' clothes if they're experiencing separation anxiety. And kids' clothes always need mending.

1. Select your shot or shots, and size them to fit the patch you want.

2. Print according to printable-fabric instructions.

3. Attach patch as for underpatch, eye eyelet (as here), or proper patch, previous page.

Mendstruation

This Band-Aid variation is for awkwardly sited gusset mends and increasing the mend pun count. People love it, but mostly women for some reason. It's pretty obvious how to do it but do be sure to use something fray-proof, such as red felt.

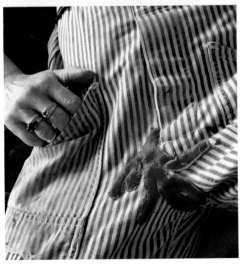

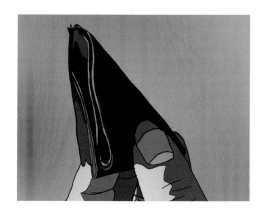

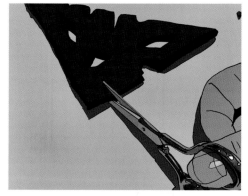

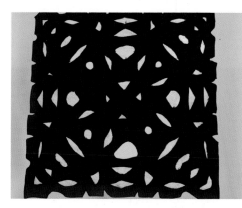

Kindergarten Lace

As a child, did you ever make paper snowflakes? Now relive preschool and do it with an old T-shirt. Covers stains or a network of small holes. Use a good sturdy cotton jersey, or felt, or something else nonfraying,

1. Cut your chosen fabric into a square, and fold it diagonally in half, then again in quarters. You can stop there, or, for a better snowflake, fold in half diagonally one more time. A circle also works, and is more snowflakey.

2. Using sharp embroidery scissors, snip into the wad of fabric, cutting a variety of small shapes into the sides, and through the middle, all the layers at once.

3. Open out it out, et voilà! Attach it as you would any patch, by felling or whipping in contrasting thread, or matching thread if you want to emphasize the lacey shape itself. You'll want to secure at least some of the internal holes, not just the perimeter.

Cheatos

As you know, there's no such thing as cheating, but I apply this term when I've made instant patch prettiness by cutting out someone else's embroidery from a stained old tablecloth, dismembering old lingerie, or using lovely ribbon. My best cheat was some incredible battlement couching made by Jen Rose @fiberenabler for the #mendandmakefriends patch swap created by Erin Hogue @gatherwhatspills (a little insight into instagram-mending: you must join in). Anything iron-on also goes in this category, as does any use of fabric glue.

Unpatches

It's very visible mending to not actually mend the damage (also see Frames, page 188). May not be for you, but it's a fun way to look at a hole and widens your repertoire considerably.

The Flag

This is anything that points to the wrecked state of your garment. Almost any method can be utilized to achieve this, so there are no specific instructions. Some examples: I did a sun around the damage in a black stripey cardi the day I managed to miss the total eclipse; outlined paint blobs alongside a statemend put hearts on a sleeve and a target on a butt; inserted giant curly brackets around a bleach stain.

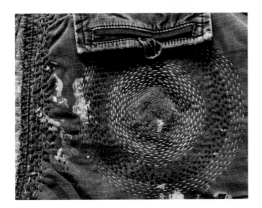

Statemend*

Wordiness can be achieved in several ways. I do quick word mends in running, chain, or split stitch (stem stitch or backstitch also work), which I improvise: I outlined the word *hole* in pretentious font surrounding a hole, and mended the "Underarm" hole in my London Underground T-shirt. Appliqué works, as you know, but the most classic of word mends are achieved with satin stitch—some lines from "View of the Menders" (see page 213) along the hem of this hand sewn apron; a November 2016 "ooops America" pit mend—or laid stitch: that Bowie quote; all the words on this book's cover!

1. Select your font, or use your own handwriting. The font is the entire effect.

2. This is definitely one to mark out. You might end up coloring outside the lines, but you'll still need an initial guide. Except for appliqué, an embroidery hoop is essential.

3. If the lettering is very large or complex you might outline it in running stitch before filling in. If the fabric is fine, use laid stitch for the lettering.

4. If you like a raised, dimensional effect, outline the letters in split stitch, then fill with seed stitch lengthwise before satin stitching horizonally over the top, in the most basic version of stumpwork, popular in Elizabethan England and American Etsy.

* Thank you, brilliant Elsa Buijs @Fie_derelsa, who coined this term, and Embellishmend, too.

Embellishmend

This covers anything decorative, as well as functional. It might involve beading or passementerie or fancy stitches. Some examples of mine: a Vivienne Westwood dress with suitably punky safety pins couched in silver and gold thread; a favorite T-shirt with its mushroom print echoed in mushrooms; a rose on a stained 1990s Comme des Garçons frock, and lavender on a 1970s Leonard; a satin-stitched shredded black shantung jacket; a running stitch on a stained collar.*

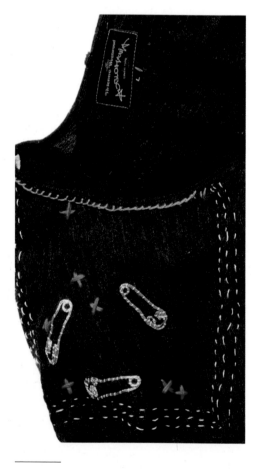

---

* Note how the Leonard and Anglomania dresses and the T-shirt have underpatch reinforcement.

Darns

The heroes of VM, whatever the patches say. They only ended up this far down owing to thematic progression, but they're not insecure so they don't mind being dozenth in the list.

Needle Weaving

I have stolen this term from a drawn thread technique (also called Swedish stitch) because nobody does that, and everybody does darn. Also it describes exactly what darning is. At least, everybody did used to darn, and for centuries (see Chapter Three), and it is my dream that everyone will darn again. This is not as moonstruck as it sounds, because weaving with a needle makes you happy.

1. **Prepare.** After any necessary mothicide, and handwashing of garment, examine the hole. Neaten it up if you wish, trimming dangles, or leave all the mess to incorporate into the darn.

2. **Design.** Select your yarns, according to weight (like with like) and choose your colors (unlike with unlike). You can change them out later as you go, but it's good to have an idea of the look you're after. Hold the work as shown on page 184.

3. **Lay the foundation.** Starting at least an inch below and to the right of the hole, secure the yarn and, working away from the body, weave in and out vertically, using a running stitch. At the end of the line, turn the work around so you're still working away from you, and sew the opposite way, placing each stitch opposite the first, like a checkerboard. Keep turning and stitching; three or four lines will do it. Watch the tension on the turn stitch: not too tight.

4. **Warp it.** When you reach the hole take the yarn across, laying each strand beside the previous one, catching it on the opposite side and continuing an inch beyond it with running stitch before turning, like before. Keep laying down the warp threads this way till you've covered the hole. Keep the same tension on each strand and leave leeway at the turns. The hole should be undistorted, the warp a little loose. Execute three or four lines of running stitch after the hole, as before.

5. **The weft.** If you're using a contrasting color, switch now, perhaps attaching new yarn to old with a loom knot. Turn the work ninety degrees and work lines of running stitch as before, horizontally across the area outside the hole, placing the stitches approximately between the vertical ones, or in whatever arrangement looks attractive to you.

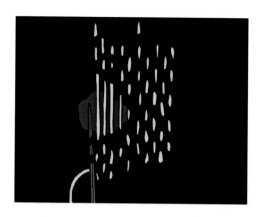

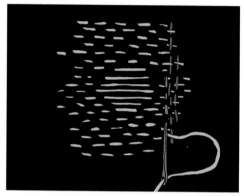

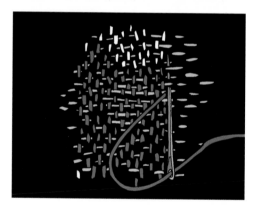

6. Weave. Now you've reached the hole, and the best bit. Take the yarn over, under, over, under, over the warp threads one by one, then continue beyond with running stitch as far as your vertical stitches go. At the end of each row take a small perpendicular stitch on the back, or simply reverse the direction and, being careful not to pull too tight, turn the work to go back the other way. At each pass alternate the stitches, under, over, under, over, weaving the yarn opposite the previous row. Tamp down each row you finish with the needle to keep the rows close and tight.

7. Finish. When you've filled the hole, continue for a row or two, as in Step 3. Secure the yarn. Done.

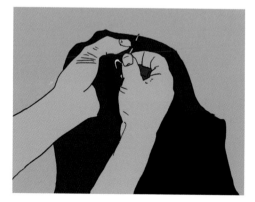

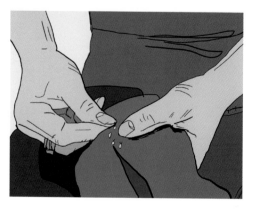

Darning Tips and Hacks

- Above all, don't stress and go slow. Adjust each row as you go. You'll improve fast.

- Threading needles with fat yarn is easy with the paper-helper method. See illustration, page 123.

- Tension, even more than with sewing, is everything. Stay focused, check it continuously.

- Do leave an allowance at the turns; don't pull the thread tight when reversing direction.

- The traditional advice is to darn on the wrong side. Pretty sure this is to make it less noticeable, so, obviously, I prefer the right side. Then you can see what you're producing.

- Traditional advice is to outline and stabilize the area with running stitch. It's optional.

- The problem with darning mushrooms: stretching the hole over it can make a lumpy darn.

- The problem with eggs: nipple darn. If you're not mending toes, don't use the egg.

- The problem with hoops (on thin knits): stretching too tight, therefore wavy darns.

- Alternative stabilizers: people use rubber balls, oranges, even light bulbs.

- You will miss stitches and go over two. It doesn't matter. It won't show much in the end.

- You will mess up in all sorts of ways. It doesn't matter. It'll still work and look good.

- A blunt tapestry needle is best but not necessary. If you split the yarn, doesn't really matter.

- Or feel free to reverse the needle and lead with the eye when working the weft.

- Variegated yarn makes a fancy darn with zero effort. People will think you're really good.

- Huge holes on thin knits: tack net fabric behind for support and darn through it.

- Huge holes on thick knits: use a cutout piece from a waste sweater or perhaps a lace doily, as on the left cuff on page 186.

- A scattering of little catch stitches far outside the hole area can be a nice effect.

- Think about the shape when laying down the warp so you don't do relentless oblongs.

which

Stitch-on-Stitch

This is officially called Swiss darning for un-known reasons, or duplicate stitch for known reasons, i.e., that's what it is. It reinforces thin-ness of knit. I've read countless instructions—mostly in nineteenth-century schoolbooks to be fair—and every single one makes this sound completely impossible. But it's simple, especially for knitters—not necessarily easy peasy, but simple. You just copy exactly what you see. It is ten times harder to draw it than it is to stitch it. Only attempt this where you can see the stitch; fuzzy knits are hard; warp or raschel knits are impossible. You can use this technique to fill a hole if you first lay a founda-tion of warp threads to support the duplicate stitches. That's called a stocking web darn, and it's one for the sequel; we are ignoring it.

1. Embrace the knot, it's not going to be invisible. Secure the yarn an inch past the bottom right corner of the area.

2. Follow the existing stitch. It's that simple and that tricky. Concentrate. Don't worry though, you can reverse any mistake and redo, or just accept it. Lead with the eye of the needle, even if you're using a blunt or ball tip one. Extra-chunky knits can even be Swiss darned with a bodkin.

3. At the end of the row, loop around and come up over two stitches, as shown below. Now turn the whole thing around so you're still working right to left. End with a knot.

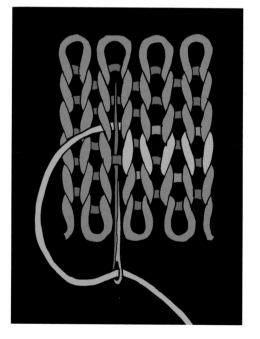

Frames

If an unpatch flags the damage, a frame features it as the star of the movie. These are the boldest of VMs for the fully committed, which also makes them in many ways the best.

Porthole

This is very easy, pretty fast, and really funny. You saw it in the eye eyelet, but here there is nothing but hole beneath. Success depends on color. Spend extra time selecting hues. Remember that outlining in eyelet stitch—or buttonhole—on a knit will about double the diameter of any hole, so work that into your plan. It's not only for knits, though, as you see here on the stripey dress.

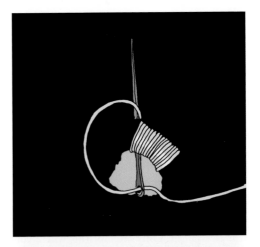

1. Secure the thread ½" outside and behind the hole, then turn and work from the front.

2. Go carefully round the hole in eyelet or buttonhole stitch. Insert the needle vertically as close as possible to the previous stitch, keeping the same distance from the hole.

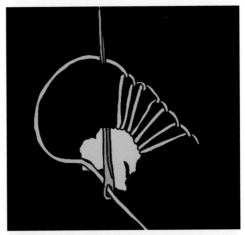

3. Keep the tension steady and push the stitches into place as you go to make them even and adjacent. A porthole looks nicest when it's smooth and gapless.

A porthole can also be worked in blanket stitch to make, uh, a blanket wheel.

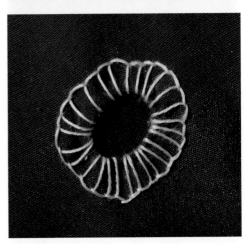

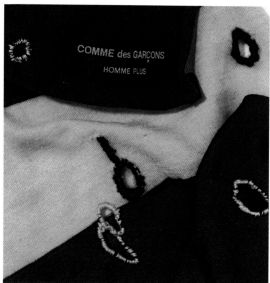

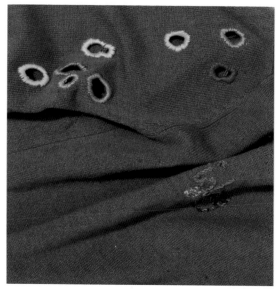

Greasytee

As a fake grown-up I find my fronts are usually spattered with dinner. The more I like a top the more likely it is to be embellished with embarrassingly noticeable grease spots. So rather than relegate to the only-indoors pile, I came up with this simple fix. The collared shirt was my first greasytee; I believe the first anywhere. Remember my favorite Loomstate T-shirt in Chapter Two? The one whose double I never wear? Here they both are, the fave spattered and mended, then later extremely respattered and remended. I still don't wear the other one.

1. Draw around the stains or spots in erasable fabric marker.

2. Follow those lines in your favorite straight stitch. You could couch it, too, that would be fun. I must try it.

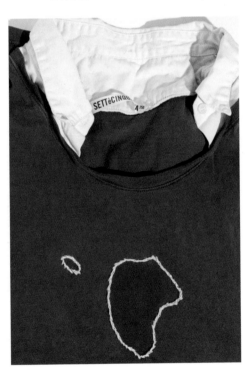

Paintypant

This sibling of the greasytee was born when I'm just touching up this wall; I'm sure I don't need to change first. I should change first. Obviously works on not-pants, too. And not-paint.

1. Do satin stitch to precisely cover every tiny splotch of paint. Or other splotch.

2. That's the only step, but it's very repetitive. I like a rainbow effect, which is why I pre-thread every single color in the house and stick the needles on a fridge magnet.

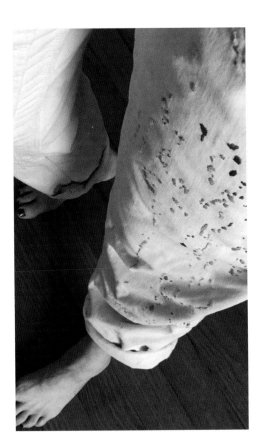

Attachment Issues

When parts get separated, or splits happen, or things fall off, these are your fixes.

Frankenstein

Named, wrongly, after the mad scientist, maker of the monster, but you know what I mean: it's the zipper effect of sutured flesh rendered in embroidery floss.

1. Ensure there's enough integrity at the edges to be joined; you may need to hem or overcast first.

2. Use a whipstitch to reattach your parts. Use thick enough thread to make it visible. Or fell the join for a neater look.

Featherweight

This is a fancier version of the Frankenstein and a different sort of misnomer—you're more likely to use a herringbone than feather stitch, frankly, but *herringweight* doesn't work at all. Anyway, this repurposes a couple of embroidery stitches for joinery. They have the great advantage of being stretchy, so this is your go-to for joining and patching all that Lycra, the old T-shirt collection, and, if you're me, the stretched-out knees of your cotton sweatpants. I can't lay claim to the beautiful blanket here: Amish did it.

1. Again, check the integrity of your edges. It's advisable to sew up the seam or tear for extra security, being mindful of stretch—you don't want to negate the flexibility of the stitches. If the seam is very weak, machine it with zigzag. If a patch is likely to fray, hem its edges.

2. Work a herringbone or feather stitch along the join. If you didn't reinforce the seam, check every stitch as you go to ensure you've attached it securely.

Baubles, Dangles, and Beads. And Buttons

When your sequins are snowing, your beading is bailing, or your paillettes are popping, don't try to replicate; replace with something else entirely. As with the related embellishmend, there are too many variants to supply instruction, but here are a few ideas. Also, as attachment issues go, nothing needs mending more often than a button. Obviously, you should pick a contrasting one.

- Substitute lines of running or chain stitch for missing sequins.

- Keep a collection of drops, beads, pendants, etc. to exchange for missing dangles.

- Repair balding sequined items with patches of wrong-colored assorted sequins and paillettes.

- Replace zipper pulls with jewelry parts, chandelier crystals, etc.

- Get a beading needle: they have extratiny eyes. Invisible nylon thread is permissible here.

- Couch strands of fake pearls, thin gold chain, anything.

- Buttons. Reinforce behind with square of cloth or small back button.

- Space the shank by inserting a matchstick, toothpick, or pin behind the button while you sew.

- Replace all the buttons with a nonmatching assortment.

- Fix a gaping neckline with a fancy button and loop—buttonhole stitches on a loop of thread.

- Use buttons as design elements, or replace sequins with them.

Spots

Single dings, as well as scatterings of little, probably moth-related holes, or smatterings of dirt, grease, paint, rust, what have you, are such common damage, especially when dealing with vintage, that this kind of mend comes in very useful. I sometimes wonder if *Bombyx mori* moths—silkworms—work so hard because, in a sort of moth math, they're trying to pay the karmic debt of their sister clothes moths.

Sprinkles

This is merely a whole host of French knots, but it makes a lovely effect: the more knots the lovelier. Great on stains, but I've also done it on tiny holes. Avoid placing any knot right on top of a hole. I like to use variegated thread, so the sprinkles are effortlessly multicolored. You can also use bullion knots to mimic classic ice cream sprinkles, or the moth cocoons you just removed.

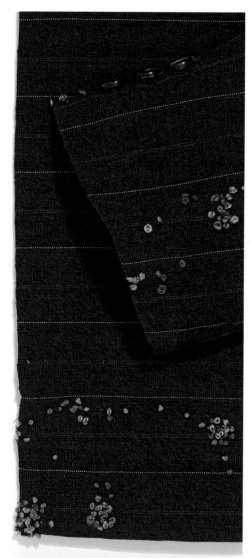

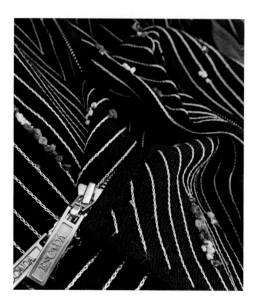

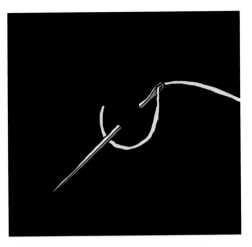

Carbuncle

The isolated embroidery stitch called a spider's or woven web does look more like this kind of blobby protuberance. It covers a sizeable hole in double-quick time and makes a good 3D polka-dot effect in groups. Below is the original carbuncle, as named and rejected by my husband.

1. Work a five-spoke star, of your carbuncle diameter. Technically this is a fly stitch with two extra straight stitches. End in the center, taking the needle down and to the back.

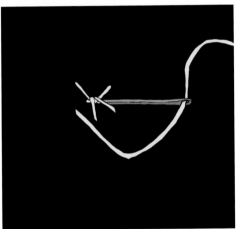

2. Coming back up the center, weave under and over the spokes till you reach the edge. Use a blunt needle, or, better (and unlike the illustration), turn the needle and lead with its eye because splitting the foundation thread or picking up the ground fabric spoils the thing.

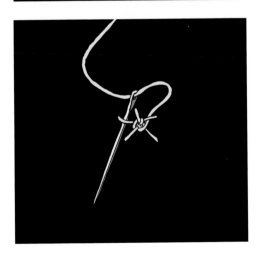

Spider

This is a ribbed web and looks more spidery than the preceding stitch, hence its mendy name.

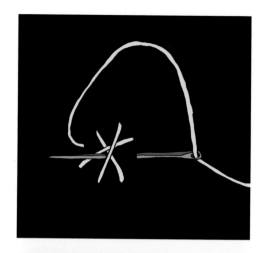

1. Work a cross, then another, for an eight-spoke star, securing the center, downward.

2. Come back up through the center, and pass the needle under two spokes, to the left, remembering to go eye-first.

3. Whip around that spoke, then under the next. Repeat to the edge, adjusting the thread manually as you go.

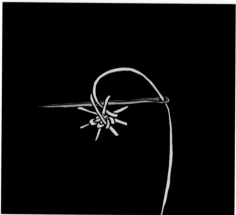

Goddess's Eye

The third in this group is the best, I think, with its bicolor effect. I've heard that summer camp consists entirely of making giant versions of god's eyes in craft workshops.

1. Work a single cross, with a long foot in the desired direction, probably downward.

2. Using a new thread color, come up at center and, leading with the eye of the needle, whip counterclockwise around the cross to the ends of the arms.

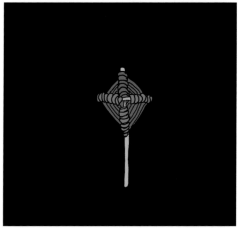

Loafer

This is shisha work by another name, specifically the shoe called penny loafer, traditionally adorned by a penny in its leather pocket above the tongue. Shisha is named after the Persian *shisheh*—"glass"—on account of the little mirrors it uses, but the visible mending version prefers to insert shiny pennies, foreign coins, paillettes, pins, medals, circular souvenirs—anything thin, small, and durable—inside the stitched frame.

1. Place your penny, or flat roundish thing, and hold it to the fabric while you secure.

2. Stitch across at the bottom, then the top, bringing the needle up vertically as close to the penny thing as possible, and still holding it in place. Check you're not puckering.

3. Stitch vertically on one side, then the other, threading under and over the horizontals (whipping).

4. Adjust the frame before finishing and knotting, ensuring the penny is firmly held, but not pulling.

5. Work buttonhole stitch around the frame, checking for puckers all the while.

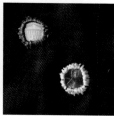

Rebirth

When the garment is past mending, or is completely ill fitting, or only partially pleasant, you have to go large and interbreed your visible mending with upcycling or refashioning.

Elasticize

If your newfound thing is oversized, your old thing is overstretched, or any thing is just too boring, smock it. Normally associated with little girls' party frocks or national costumes for tourist shows, I have reassigned smocking to Fashion. This is a basic honeycomb version, for practice, making a foot-wide piece out of a yard. If you like it, apply as you wish, or take it further into decorative madness. Another approach is to extemporize with rows, columns, whorls, and random curves of running stitch, which you pucker and gather as you go, in an exercise of controlled chaos. My free-form elasticizing takes inspiration from the marvelous shirt works of Nui Project makers (see pages 88–89). There is no instruction for this: you have to be willing to stitch freely, make it up as you go. It is pure menditation.

1. Mark out your fabric with dots spaced evenly, in straight lines.

2. Take one yard-long piece of thick thread per row of dots, knot securely, and weave in and out of the dots along each row, completing all of the rows. The illustration is truncated: your yard of fabric will yield many more columns.

3. Gather the fabric evenly, pleating up toward the knots. When done, knot the far ends.

4. Carefully even out the gathers. Then, starting at one corner, sew two pleat peaks together with parallel stitches. Repeat all along the row.

5. On the second row, skip the first pleat and do the same, but contrapuntally, sewing the second and third pleat together, and then every pair to the end.

6. The third row, sew together pleats one and two and repeat as in the first row. Continue alternating pleat pairs until all rows are done. Remove the gathering thread.

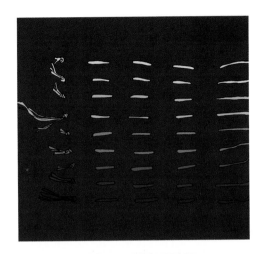

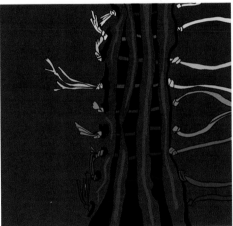

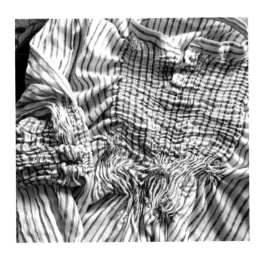

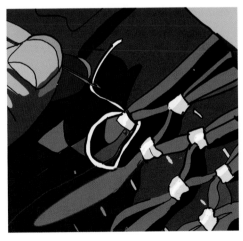

which

Longerize

An obvious fix for too-shortness or embellishing a trouser cuff. Just sew on a supplemental strip of fabric, and hem it, or use wide ribbon. It's a bit boring, so do machine it if you like.

Pocketize

This is the only invisible mend in the book, and it's not even a mend. But I have no use for pocketless things, especially dresses, so am doomed to pocketize everything that's inadequately finished by inserting on-seam pockets. I'm very bad at it, so often end up adding a VM. In fact, I'm so bad at it, I recommend you use someone else's instructions, easily found. If it turns out you're also crap at pocketization, work in a Band-Aid or an eye eyelet at the top seam, as done here. This has the additional virtue of adding strength at the stress point.

Monsterize

When T-shirts don't fit right or have bad logos, or to use up leftovers after mining for patch material, combine them into a Frankenstein's monster of a top. There's no one way to do this because it entirely depends on your parts, but in general, success lies in the planning. Select the bits you like—this one's sleeve, that half of printed front, this neckline—and lay them out together until you have a whole shirt's worth. You have to be willing to wing it. When sewing together (machine is best TBH), go piece by piece and keep checking your work. Strange shapes are more than fine; they are the point. This is all very Comme des Garçons. In fact, the bottom left in the group is actual CDG. Bottom right is another professionally

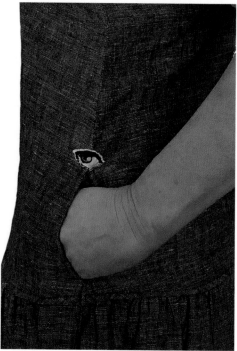

monsterized top, by Patagonia. The others are mine. And why stop at tees? This cardigan used to be two dull sweaters.

Monsterizing Variation

CARDIGANIZE

An Americanized spelling of Amy Twigger Holroyd's best reknit but, in case you are as yarn-compromised as I, without knitting. It has the great merit of being the only known use for those miles of bias tape that are otherwise pointless.[2] Also the merit of making cardigans from every boring sweater—and cardigans are life. Well, I say *every* but it doesn't work so well on chunky knits, owing to the slimline nature of the tape. You could make your own bias tape, but that would defeat the object of being a shortcut.

1. Cut carefully down the center front of a boring sweater. Blanket stitch along the edges like mad.

2. Open out your widest double fold bias tape and pin, then baste, accurately along each edge, sandwiching the sweater inside. Be precise here, tucking every millimeter of blanket-stitched edge all the way into the crease of the tape.

3. Using regular thread, attach the tape with backstitch, ensuring you're always picking up both of its edges through the sweater. This stitching shouldn't be visible. Remove the basting.

4. Work buttonhole stitch to close and neaten the top and bottom of the tape, at neck and hem.

5. Sew lines of a decorative stitch evenly down the bias tape in contrasting thread. Herringbone, as here, is good both for its security and appearance. (Here you can see how the reverse side of herringbone comes out.)

6. Add fasteners, such as oversized snaps attached with contrasting thread. Large hooks and eyes also work well, including the decorative frogging kind. Buttons mean buttonholes, which take a lot of work, but then you get to have an extra design element.

If you're doing buttons, you might replace the contrasting decorative stitch with more invisible backstitch.

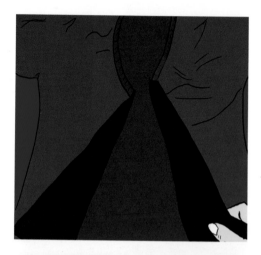

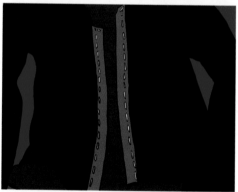

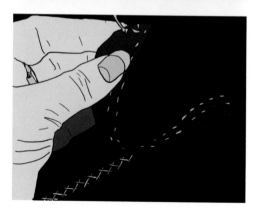

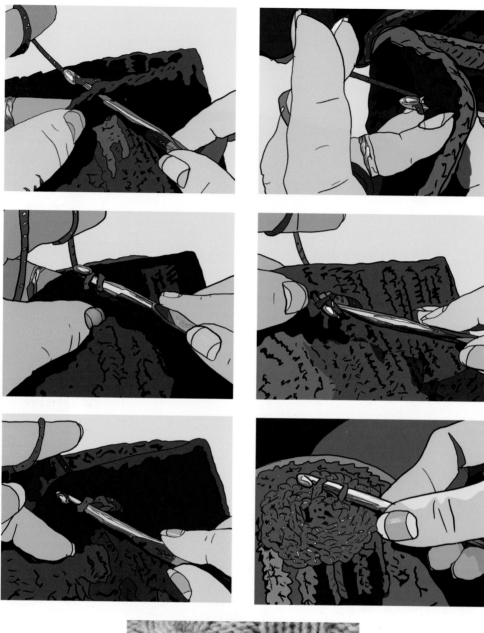

No Sew

And finally, no needles. Or not that kind.

Knit Not

Crochet is a world unto itself from which I've borrowed the most basic of stitches for the most basic of knitwear holes. Don't sue me; these are not the official crochet instructions. Real crocheters should now step away from the book.

1. Secure the yarn in back outside the hole edge; work from the front. Hold the hook with thumb and first two fingers of your right hand.* With your left hand, hold the work between your thumb and your ring and little finger, picking up the yarn from the ball and winding it one and a half times onto your extended middle finger.† It will feel super awkward at first. You'll be incessantly readjusting the tension of this yarn feed—steady tension is key throughout.

2. Poke the hook through from front to back and pick up the yarn with it, twisting the hook as you draw the yarn to the front through the sweater hole you entered.

3. Keeping this loop of yarn (that you just pulled through) on the hook, poke an adjacent hole in the sweater, locate the yarn in back, and hook it back through to the front in the same way as step 2. Now you have two loops on the hook.

4. Staying in the front, twist the hook to pick up the new loop and reverse twist to pull it back and through the earlier loop. You're left with one loop on the hook. Poke the hook into an adjacent spot and continue, repeating steps 2 to 4, all around the perimeter, to form the foundation row.

5. Now just keep going round and round, poking the hook through the stitches of the foundation row for the next row, and then the next, continuing to spiral inward. The only difference is that you skip a stitch or two as you move inward, to reduce the diameter.

6. When you reach the middle, knot the yarn inside. It might end up a bit nippley, but you'll still be proud as punch.

---

* Again, excuse me for assuming right-handedness. In this case I confess I am not at all sure whether left-handed crochet works differently, so I suggest you southpaws consult the experts—as you're no doubt used to doing. Sorry.

---

† Some prefer using the index finger as yarn holder and tension regulator.

Punchdrunk

Because you'll be drunk on the power of the punch. Needle felting is completely idiotproof (as long as you realize only pure wool works) and so gratifying, in a Victorian asylum way, it being all about stabbing. You do need some supplies: roving, felting needle, and mat. The barbed needle frays and recombines the fibers in the unspun cloud of wool and the hole edge, fusing them together, as you punch it through into a protective mat. You can use a rolled up towel, but I recommend investing in a small purpose-made pad (under ten dollars) and the kind of felting tool that has several needles in a handle—no use to pros who need accuracy, but fine and faster for sweater felters. Introductory packs of many colors of roving are easily found. You can get ambitious with shapes, use stencils, make pictures, or just stab-stab-stab in pretty colors and fix your hole. Bonus. Got cat? Brush her and felt with her spare fur. Double bonus: fewer hair balls.

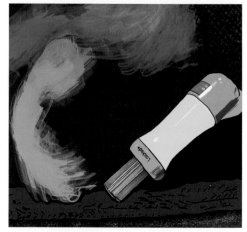

1. Select your roving color(s), position the hole on the mat center, with a small piece of roving on top.

2. Stab. Stab. Stab. Stab. Stab. Stab. Stab. Stab. Stab. Stab. Stab. Stab. Stab. Stab. Stab.

3. In between stabs, gently peel the felt you're forming off the mat, or it'll stick.

4. More roving. Repeat.

5. Done.

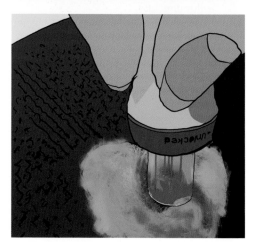

Which Mend Where?

You'll soon get a feel for mend selection, but here's an overall guide, starting with the scientific classification of mends.

Periodic Table of Mend Elements

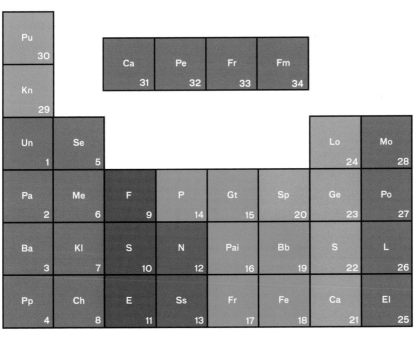

| Patch | Unpatch | Darn | Frame | Spot | Rebirth | No Sew |

PATCHES

1. Un — Underpatch
2. Pa — Patchiko
3. Ba — Band Aid
4. Po — Pocket Patch
5. Se — Selfiepatch
6. Me — Mendstruation
7. Ki — Kindergarten lace
8. Ch — Cheatos
32. Ee — Eye Eyelet
33. Pr — Proper Patch
34. Fm — Faux Mola

UNPATCHES

9. F — The Flag
10. S — Statemend
11. E — Embellishmend

DARNS

12. N — Needleweaving
13. Ss — Stitch-on-Stitch

FRAMES

14. P — Porthole
15. Gt — Greasytee
16. Pai — Paintypant
17. Fr — Frankenstein
18. Fe — Featherweight
19. Bb — Baubles, Dangles, and Beads. And Buttons

SPOTS

20. S — Sprinkles
21. Ca — Carbuncle
22. Sp — Spider
23. Ge — Goddess's Eye
24. Lo — Loafer

REBIRTHS

25. El — Elasticize
26. L — Longerize
27. Po — Pocketize
28. Mo — Monsterize*
31. Car — Cardiganize

*includes use for parts

NO SEWS

29. Kn — Knit Not
30. Pu — Punchdrunk

Pick-a-Mend Chart: Which Goes Where

GARMENT	DAMAGE	TYPE	LOCATION	MENDS
Accessory				
Scarf, knitted	Hole	Any	Any	12 N
Scarf, silky	Hole, rip	Torn	Any	3 Ba; 8 Ch; 9 F; 28 Mo
Gloves, knitted	Hole	Any	Any	12 N
Gloves, leather	Split	Unraveled	Seam	17 Fr
Athletic Wear				
Top, tank, performance fiber	Hole, rip	Any	Any	1 Un; 2 Pa; 3 Ba; 9 F; 15 Gt
Tights, yoga pant, stretch	Hole, rip	Any	Any	1 Un; 3 Ba; 9 F; 15 Gt
Tights, yoga pant, stretch	Hole, rip	Single	Gusset	1 Un; 3 Ba; 6 Me
Fleece, sweatshirt, coverup	Hole, rip	Any	Any	1 Un; 2 Pa; 3 Ba; 9 F; 15 Gt
Blouse, Shirt				
Cotton, linen, blend	Hole, stain	Single	Front, back, hem, cuff	1–5; 7–8; 33 Pr; 9–11; 22–24
Cotton, linen, blend	Hole, stain	Multiple	Any	9 F; 15 Gt; 16 Pai; 20–23
Silk, rayon, blend	Hole, stain	Single	Front, back, hem, cuff	1–5; 7–8; 9 F; 10 S; 11 E; 22–24
Silk, rayon, blend	Hole, stain	Multiple	Any	9 F; 15 Gt; 16 Pai; 20–23
Silk, rayon, blend	Stain	Double	Underarm	1 Un; 2 Pa; 3 Ba; 15 Gt
Synthetics, jersey	Hole, stain	Single	Front, back, hem, cuff	1–5; 9–11; 22–24
Synthetics, jersey	Hole, stain	Multiple	Any	9 F; 15 Gt; 16 Pai; 20–23
Synthetics, jersey	Stain	Double	Underarm	1 Un; 2 Pa; 3 Ba; 15 Gt
Any	Loss	Buttons	Placket, cuff	19 Bb

GARMENT	DAMAGE	TYPE	LOCATION	MENDS
Coat/Jacket				
Cloth, wool or blend	Hole, stain	Single	Front, back, hem, cuff	1–5; 33 Pr; **9–11**; **12 N**; **14 P**; 21–24
Cloth, wool or blend	Hole, stain	Multiple	Any	**9–11**; **12 N**; 20–24
Cloth, wool or blend	Thin places	Pre-hole	Elbow	1 Un; 2 Pa; 7 Ki; 8 Ch; 33 Pr; **12 N**
Cloth, cotton, linen, blend	Rip, tear	Single	Front, back, hem, cuff	1–5; 33 Pr; 34 Fm; **9–11**; **14 P**; 21–24
Acetate or similar	Rip, tear	Not hem	Lining	1 Un; 2 Pa
Any	Loss	Buttons	Placket	19 Bb
Dress				
S/S cotton, linen, silk, blend*	Hole, stain	Single	Any	1–5; 7 Ki; 8 Ch; 33 Pr; **9–11**; 22–24
S/S cotton, linen, silk, blend	Hole, stain	Multiple	Any	**9 F**; **11 E**; 15 Gt; 16 Pai; 20–24
S/S cotton, linen, silk, blend	Rip, tear	Any	Any	1–5; 7 Ki; 8 Ch; 33 Pr; 17 Fr; 18 Fe
S/S cotton, linen, silk, blend	Stain	Double	Underarm	1 Un; 2 Pa; 3 Ba; 15 Gt
S/S cotton, linen, silk, blend	Ill fitting	Stretched	Bust, waist	25 El; 28 Mo
F/W wool, jersey, blend†	Hole, stain	Any		1–5; 7 Ki; 8 Ch; 33 Pr; **9–11**; **12 N**; 21–24
F/W wool, jersey, blend	Rip, tear	Any		1 Un; 2 Pa; 33 Pr; 17 Fr; 18 Fe
Special fabric: velvet, lace, etc.	Rip, stain	Any		3 Ba; 8 Ch; 33 Pr; **11 E**
Formal, structured	Rip, stain	Any		1 Un; 3 Ba; 8 Ch; 33 Pr; **11 E**
Embellished, sequined, etc.	Loss	Pieces	Any	**11 E**; 19 Bb
Any	Split	Unraveled	Seam, hem	17 Fr; 18 Fe
Any	Pocketless	Sadness	Side seams, front	4 Pp; 27 Po

(Continued)

* S/S = Spring/Summer   † F/W = Fall/Winter

GARMENT	DAMAGE	TYPE	LOCATION	MENDS
Jeans				
Denims, dungarees	Hole, rip	Single	Knee	1 Un; 2 Pa; 3 Ba; 5 Se; 32 Ee; 17 Fr
Denims, dungarees, cutoffs	Hole, rip	Single	Gusset	1 Un; 2 Pa; 3 Ba; 6 Me
Denims, dungarees, cutoffs	Hole, rip	Multiple	Any	1 Un; 2 Pa; 3 Ba; **10 S**; **11 E**; 17 Fr
Denims, dungarees, cutoffs	Detached	Pocket	Rear	4 Po
Denims, dungarees, cutoffs	Stain	Any	Any	**9 F**; **11 E**; 16 Pai; 20 S; 21 Ca
Denims, dungarees	Thin places	Pre-hole	Knee, butt, thigh	1 Un; 2 Pa; 33 Pr
Denims, dungarees	Length	Too short	Cuff/hem	26 L
Knitwear				
Sweater, wool, blend, synthetic	Hole	Single	Front, back, hem, cuff	**9 F**; **12 N**; 14 P; 29 Kn
Sweater, wool, blend, synthetic	Hole	Multiple	Any	**10 S**; **12 N**; 14 P; 21–23; 29 Kn
Sweater, wool, blend, synthetic	Thin places	Pre-hole	Elbow	**13 Ss**
Sweater, wool, blend, synthetic	Boring	Boring	General	31 Ca
Sweater, wool, cashmere	Hole	Any	Any	**10 S**; **12 N**; 14 P; 21–23; 29 Kn; 30 Pu
Sweater, wool, cashmere	Pilling	Pile	All over	19 Bb; 20 S
Cardigan, wool, blends	Loss	Buttons	Placket	I9 Bb
Pant, Shorts				
Casual, cotton, canvas, blends	Hole, rip	Single	Knee	1 Un; 2 Pa; 3 Ba; 5 Se; 32 Ee; 17 Fr
Casual, cotton, canvas, blends	Hole, rip	Single	Gusset	1 Un; 2 Pa; 3 Ba; 6 Me
Casual, cotton, canvas, blends	Hole, rip	Any	Any	1–5; 7–8; 32 Ee; 33 Pr
Casual, cotton, canvas, blends	Stain	Any	Any	**9 F**; **11 E**; 16 Pai; 20 S; 23 Ca

GARMENT	DAMAGE	TYPE	LOCATION	MENDS
Cotton, canvas, linen, blend	Length	Too short	Cuff/hem	26 L
Linen, blend	Hole, rip	Any	Any	1–5; 7–8; 32 Ee; 32–34; 17 Fr; **11 E**
Linen, blend	Stain	Any	Any	**9 F; 11 E;** 16 Pai; 22 Sp; 23 Ge; 24 L
Dress, wool, suiting, blend	Hole, stain	Single	Front, back, hem, cuff	1–3; 33 Pr; **12 N;** 21–24
Dress, wool, suiting, blend	Rip, tear	Single	Front, back, hem, cuff	1 Un; 2 Pa; 3 Ba; 33 Pr; **12 N;** 17 Fr

Skirt

GARMENT	DAMAGE	TYPE	LOCATION	MENDS
S/S cotton, linen, silk, blend	Hole, stain	Any	Any	2–5; **9 F; 11 E;** 15 Gt; 16 Pai; 21–23
S/S cotton, linen, silk, blend	Rip, tear	Any	Any	1–5; 7 Ki; 8 Ch; 33–34; 17 Fr
S/S cotton, linen, silk, blend	Length	Too short	Hem	26 L
Dress, wool, suiting, blend	Rip, tear	Any	Any	1–5; 33 Pr; 34 Fm; **12 N;** 17 Fr
Formal, structured	Rip, tear	Any	Front, back, hem	1 Un; 3 Ba; 8 Ch; 33 Pr; **11 E;** 17 Fr

T-shirt, Top, Tank

GARMENT	DAMAGE	TYPE	LOCATION	MENDS
All: cotton, rayon, linen, blends	Hole, rip	Single	Any	1–5; 32 Ee; **9–11;** 14 P; 22–24
All: cotton, rayon, linen, blends	Hole	Multiple	Any	**9–11;** 14 P; 20–23
All: cotton, rayon, linen, blends	Stain	Any	Any	**9–11;** 15 Gt; 22 Sp; 23 Ge
All: cotton, rayon, linen, blends	Ill fitting	Any	General	26 L; 28 Mo
All: cotton, rayon, linen, blends	Ugly	Boring	General	**11 E;** 28 Mo

Undergarment

GARMENT	DAMAGE	TYPE	LOCATION	MENDS
Sock	Hole	Any	Toe, heel	12 N
Tights, stockings	Ladder	Any	Leg	13 Ss
Tights, stockings	Hole	Any	Toe, heel	12 N

which

whether

There are the movers and shakers of the world,

and then there are the menders.

The menders are the innocent and wise.

They are innocent of cynicism and despair,

and they are wise in not waiting for
the world to be otherwise than it is.

They patch up the wounds the world
inflicts on itself

without question and without grimace.

The greater half of the world, when something
is broken,

has the instinct to throw it away and
get a new one,

but that lesser better half has the instinct to
mend it, to make it well.

You'll never guess where that poem is from. *Vogue*! It's the first half of *"Vogue's* Eye View of the Menders," from March 1953, when the magazine was the absolute fashion bible. Can you imagine it being published in today's mag? And yet, it resonates. Today the movers and shakers still seem to run the world, but secretly, underneath, the innocent and wise are gathering strength. Now that "the wounds the world inflicts on itself" are graver than ever, the most crucial interrogative word might be *whether.* Whether the menders can indeed make the world well. Whether the current interest in slowing down production cycles, consuming less and better, and fixing things that already exist grows into the dominant mindset or fizzles out is one great and urgent question of the day.*

We can't mend the world by fixing clothes, but it's a fine place to start. Sewing up old stuff infects you and those around you with— what's the opposite of cynicism and despair?— optimism and glee. Just try to mend spitefully: you can't. Mending can't help being sweet.

So, before we part, I'd like to introduce another ten menders of fabric, who are also (though too modest to admit it) mending the very fabric of society. Why these particular ten? It's simple: I know them; I'm their fan. Some I met once, some are my sister, but it's all grossly subjective. Still, it works as a compact cross section of a growing movement, and I hope it helps galvanize you into joining in. Because whether this all continues to accelerate is up to you. We really do need *you.*

---

* And, as I revise this in the early pandemic, whether fashion even still exists in a form that needs the same resetting as before.

Ten More Menders

Elizabeth Cline. In 2013, Elizabeth published *Overdressed: The Shockingly High Cost of Cheap Fashion*, and, six years later, ***The Conscious Closet***, an indispensible guide to the care and keeping of clothes.[1] *Overdressed* has had an immeasurable impact: to read it is to immediately renovate your wardrobe thoughts, and for years it was just about the only readable book with reliable, independent data on the economics of clothes. There've been a few books on Big Fashion published in the UK, but transatlantic cross-pollination of ideas, not to mention actual collaborations, has been curiously elusive. Anyway, please get those books.

Tamsin Lejeune. Speaking of the UK, Tamsin founded the nonprofit **Ethical Fashion Forum** (EFF) in London in 2006, relaunching it ten years later as **CO** (Common Objective), a global *for*-profit database matching fashion brands and buyers with sustainable suppliers. Tamsin cut EFF and CO from whole cloth, with no training (she was an architect), slogging doggedly through many difficult patches to create a platform that's a visionary multibenefit business for the future. Do go take a look.

Orsola de Castro. When she cofounded **Fashion Revolution** in 2013 (see page 7), Orsola was already a force of nature—and fashion—having started the green arm of London Fashion Week in 2006 and her label, **From Somewhere,** whose collections were cut from other companies' overstock, way back in

1997. Pioneering circularity before most people had even heard the term, Orsola has been the very embodiment of better ways in fashion for over two decades, a beacon for us all.

Sam Robinson. In 1996, Sam opened **The Cross** and slightly changed London. Why did this exquisite, compact local store wield such influence? In a word: taste. Crammed with fluid displays of fresh designers, heritage labels, and adorable home stuff, The Cross is a tiny world, casting a spell against mass-ness. The formula caught on, yet not far enough—if every shop were such an experience, retail would be thriving.

Brandon Giordano. And if only every vintage emporium operated like Brandon's, vintage would be saved. With husband Collin Weber, Brandon runs **James Veloria** like a sexy club, a delightful cornucopian party in a closet, to which all are welcome. The secret is not just precise selection and profound knowledge, but generosity: pieces are priced to move, so the frock can find the right home. Way more fun than profit.

Liisa Jokinen. Similarly, Liisa's **Gem** is a specialist search engine that does right by vintage. Created with her tech whizz husband, Sampo Karjalainen, Gem is a deceptively simple cross-platform app that works so well because this street-style blogger (check out Hel, SF, and NYC Looks) deeply knows her stuff. And because she respects the clothes and their spirits, it is done for love not money. Silicon Valley should learn from this.

Ngozi Okaro. And fashion, all of it, should learn from Ngozi, whose NYC-based **Custom Collaborative** models a scenario that is just about ideal. The nonprofit trains low-income and immigrant women in business, design, and production, but more than that, it teaches them equitable and sustainable practices for people and planet—and, hallelujah, pattern cutting to suit all the planet's bodies. As I write, the eighth CC cohort just graduated, mid-lockdown, but Zoom couldn't dilute the spirit of Ngozi's powerful vision. A taste of fashion's future. Let's hope.

Jessica Schreiber. Jessica was (deep breath) senior manager in the Bureau of Recycling and Sustainability at New York City's Department of Sanitation, but left that noble-sounding job, disillusioned. After witnessing the tragic lost opportunity to repurpose the local fashion industry's discarded textile, Jessica founded **FABSCRAP** to work directly with companies to recycle their textile waste. FABSCRAP is mendy heaven. Volunteer to sort at the warehouse and you earn five pounds of free fabric. There's a wonderful retail store, too. Jessica gives me further hope for the future.

Adam Baruchowitz. Wearable Collections, cofounded by Adam in 2004, is—and this is a crucial factor for supporting sustainable business—a *for*-profit waste management company that prioritizes environmental sustainability. Adam models and invents new solutions alongside the traditional recycling bins, shredding, and such, most recently partnering with scientists to manufacture textile made from reclaimed mixed fibers. This is the absolute recycling grail, a game-changing world saver. We wish Adam all the luck.

Veronica Sekules. After we left my sister in Chapter Four, Dr. Sekules the medieval art historian spent three decades on the art coalface, curating and running education at a major university art museum. Then, in 2016, she renovated an abandoned Modernist building in King's Lynn and opened **GroundWork,** a gallery showing "art which responds to our changing environment." Now she's taking a lead role in the resurgence of a moribund city, while punching way above her weight in mounting stellar exhibitions of ecologically aware artists—many big names—plus related events and seminars. Also there's **GroundJewels,** her collection of contemporary recycled jewelry makers. Yes, I am shameless in my admiration, but also, it's a personal joy to find we've come full circle and joined up on the other side. Now that Veronica is all entrepreneurial, I am studying to be Dr. Sekules II (Doctor of Mending), and both of us are full-time committed to environmental world healing.

Obviously, full circle is the overall theme here. Circularity will save fashion. It is the only viable economic future. In economist Kate Raworth's splendid model, the circle is a doughnut shape—the Doughnut of social and planetary boundaries that replaces the grievously out-of-date linear GDP growth charts that got us into this mess.[2] The default mental image at the word *economics* is a graph with a jagged red line going diagonally up or down. That represents the make-take-use-lose trajectory of the industrial era, in which a garment was manufactured, we bought it, we wore it, we tossed it. Sadly, many wardrobes are still living out this olden days scenario instead of the circular mend-tend-lend-spend of the Doughnut, where social and environmental benefits are built in. In the Doughnut economy, a company is heavily taxed for using virgin materials, and given tax breaks for employing more workers. You could say it's a win-win, except that it's no longer a competition at all. It's about whether the whole planet can work together.

It's important, says Raworth, to literally redraw our economic future so we can picture change and work toward it. So, in that spirit, here's the refashioning manifesto painted as a scenario of how clothes could be done. This all depends on whether we can replace scale with iteration and insert a million small righteous independent enterprises where the monolithic monopolies now lurk.

On my magic Main Street is a thriving row of indie stores: The Cross, a James Veloria, and dozens more, digitized supportively by CO. There's a Custom Collaborative Training Institute with its own shop, a community-run rental place, a clothes library, or several libraries, each catering to different demographics—for men, kids, queen-size designer lovers. Local entrepreneurs run similarly stratified consignment stores, clothes swaps, and exchanges—like Beacon's Closet in New York or Wasteland on the West Coast. Empty storefronts are temporarily filled by versions of England's charity shops, where nominal rent is charged for thrift stores that are run by, and that fund, individual nonprofits—only these are more selective, like the retail guru Mary Portas's Living and Giving stores and the Fara shops in London. The donation leftovers (the quantity has been dropping sharply from the current 85 percent) are processed by thousands of disparate versions of FABSCRAP and Wearable Collections—that is, if they're not snapped up by the new breed of remaker-designers, who monsterize reject clothes into fabulous hybrid outfits. There is at least one mending storefront on every street.

On the grander avenues, designers have broken free from Bernard Arnault (currently the richest man in the world, having overtaken Bill Gates, because Gates spends billions philanthropically), and now stand or fall on their talent and sales. Normal people shop their creations because they save up to afford one special piece instead of squandering their paychecks piecemeal at H&M. Well, they can't shop at H&M because it's now a foundation researching circular solutions in textile, the Persson family having finally admitted their lofty CSR goals are incompatible with their profiteering. In fact, all the Big Fashion companies have gone the way of Forever 21: they died of starvation when young consumers boycotted the lot of them. The former factory workers benefited from Third World debt cancellation, their life transitions now supported by various NGOs as they establish microfinanced sewing collectives connected to the vast number of thriving indie designers worldwide. Those who still can't afford new designer pieces shop the own-vintage racks every label now carries, or search Gem for their vintage fix.

New department stores are blossoming on the boulevards. They resemble bazaars more than sad old Saks; you never know what you'll find. You've still got your cosmetics and accessories and designer concessions, but most floors are mazes of pop-up boutiques of every style, new and old clothes, interspersed with cafés and wine bars, music booths, makeries and classes, and little GroundWorks–style galleries showing affordable art. You can do customized store tours, evening champagne shopping, attend the cabaret, drop off garments for restyling, reserve the immersive fitting room suite: it's experience shopping.

Okay, my fashion fantasy may not match yours, but it's surely better than today's actual Main Streets of vacant storefronts turning slowly derelict, or replaced by banks, real estate agents, and drop-in medical facilities, deserted because nobody wants them—and don't even start on the chains. I like how the "View of the Menders" says we are "not waiting for the world to be otherwise than it is." This is important. The future may depend on whether we're willing to upend everything, but for now it's whether we can ditch the convenience of Walmart, the instant fix from Uniqlo, the free next-day delivery (it's not free, it costs the earth). It's whether we invest in a single object of desire instead of multiple impulse-click buys, keep a few pairs of socks darned instead of running through ten-packs from Target. It's whether we can mend our ways along with our clothes. Let's start right here.

acknowledgments

Penguin, I am proud as punch to be shelved with your iconic orange spines. Thank you, Shannon Kelly, who understood this book so completely and saw it seamlessly through to launch, then "orphaned" me—but in the nicest way. I was so lucky to be adopted by the amazing Victoria Savanh: thank you for shepherding the book elegantly and drama-free, even as the pandemic hit. Thank you, Patrick Nolan, for believing—I hope we've had the mending sessions by now. I bow to you, Roseanne Serra, for your genius cover idea, and my hair twin, Claire Vaccaro, for your vision and for giving me the exceptional designer Shubhani Sarkar. Shubhani, it was a spooky mind meld and an utter joy, and you made the book sing and dance; you are so darn talented. Thank you, Erika Storella at the Gernert Company—dream agent, you just made it happen, no fuss. I am so impressed, and eternally grateful. This book has been gestating for years. Thank you/sorry, Markus and Natasha, for taking on previous versions, and Caroline Wood, for your faith. Zoe Pagnamenta, you were so generous with advice and introductions, and, Leigh Newman, you held my hand and steered me right. Thank you.

My friends, I love you. Thank you for being especially adorable during lows in this saga (lucky you) Nora Meyer, Annabel Jankel, Gaby Darbyshire, Susan Pottinger, Craig Seligman and Silvana Nova, Anya von Bremzen and Barry Yourgrau, Peri Lyons, Adam Cjivanovic, Liz Adams, Jan Woroniecki and Sam Robinson, Jenny Raymond, Catie Lazarus and Lily Malcom, Ulli Barta and Robert Arbor for the party, and, of course, my kin Ambrosia Parsley and the core mend club: Holly Miranda and Brian Ogle. Big thanks to Cathy Crawford—such photo fun! Thank you, Marysia Woroniecka (fashion sage), Angela Tribelli and Andrew Cohen, Danielle McConnell, Jamie Pallot, and Pavia Rosati, for kindness during Refashioner; thank you, Cyrena Lee, I couldn't have done it without you. Thanks, John Kalinowski, wise transition enabler; Sass Brown, great bringer-together; badass compadre Dr. Jen Ayers; and supreme truth speaker Elizabeth Cline, I'm so glad we're friends.

Thanks for helping me pupate into a very happy scholar, Pegi Vail, Tamsin Lejeune, and Janet Mayo—and Janet also for inspiring this whole dress-academic thing. From NYU, thank you immensely, Nancy Deihl, Elizabeth Morano, Elizabeth Marcus, Sarah Byrd, Daniel Cole, and, for curation inspiration, Mellissa Huber. Thank you, my conservation and collections gurus from Museum at FIT, Anne Coppinger and Michelle McVicker. And my beloved cohort, Aanchal Bakshi, Madeleine Luckel, Kerstin Heitzke, and Nandini Gopalarathinam: in this together. Also thank you, Michele Majer and all at BGC: I can't wait.

In mending world, thank you immeasurably to all those in the book; may you continue to inspire. I wanted to include my mendfriends from Instagram, but space didn't allow. Special thanks, then, to the original Mendmarch crew: @Fie_derelsa, mendpun queen (and for the lambs); sweet, funny @Trollkjerringa1 and @Tails andtextiles, for all the mendingmayhem; patch matchmaker @gatherwhatspills; @mending.my.life and sidekick Lego Emei; the Speedweve ninja @Roberta.cummings; @heartfulstitches, @Jessiejessyg, @morrissews, @raheliharper, @squaremerry, @lindzeanne, @milli_and_the_bee, fellow mendauthor @Erinlewisfitzgerald—and so many, many more. We are a surprisingly genuine, unruly community. I guess it can't last.

Finally, my family. Veronica, you're in the book, but I send extra enormous love and thanks—you've been my inspiration, best friend, and wise counsel all my life, and I'm beside myself with admiration. Sandy Heslop, you probably don't know how huge an inspiration you've always been, too (also in the bread department)! Clio and Jack Heslop, you are both so extraordinary, and I hope you know how much I adore you. Ma, the original mendspiration, thank you for everything. Scott and Bea, it's simple: you are the lights of my life and you mean the world to me. *Thank you* doesn't begin to cover it.

notes

Chapter Two: **why**

1. This is not counting the June 8, 1938, *New York Times* headline "Shoes Are Bought in 'Fast Fashions,'" a story about industrial shoe production speeding up to meet sudden fashion demands. There are other early uses, but the popularization of the term is fairly recent.

2. Compare and contrast "Big Pharma" for the pharmaceutical industry.

3. This one's old, but we tend to only focus vaguely on a headline, then remember it for years.

4. McKinsey & Company and the Business of Fashion, *The State of Fashion 2020*, November 2019, 7–10.

5. This situation is unfolding as I write. It's impossible to know what will happen in overseas factories, unsafe, insecure environments even before the pandemic. How many Western brands paid for their millions of canceled orders? How many factories had to close, or reopened too soon, with fatal consequences? What happened to the millions of unemployed workers? Domestically, in late March, the activist organization the Garment Worker Center (https://garmentworkercenter.org) launched an emergency COVID-19 relief fund for the tens of thousands earning an average $6/hour in LA garment factories who were either laid off or obliged to continue working in lethal sweatshops. It won't have been enough. Fashion month will not have taken place. There's a lot more to say, but it's old news by now, so I'll desist.

6. It is sometimes still said that fashion is the second most polluting industry on earth. Though this may well be true, there is no research basis for the claim and nobody can trace it to its origin. And yet it is frequently repeated by reputable news outlets, including *Forbes*, *Washington Post*, *Guardian*, and, uh, Wikipedia. The aggregate of the most recent and verifiable research puts fashion definitely in the top five, but because apparel production has hard-to-measure crossover with other industries— agriculture, power, transportation—it could actually end up being the single most polluting industry of all.

7. Sources in this section include: Environmental Protection Agency, Shippers of Recycled Textiles Association, Association of Wiping Materials, Used Clothing and Fiber Industries, Institute of Scrap Recycling Industries, Council for Textile Recycling, US Bureau of Labor, Goodwill Industries, *Grist*, Friends of the Earth, Greenpeace, International Labour Organization, Congressional Research Service, Labour Behind the Label, Clean Clothes Campaign, Fashion Revolution, Sustainable Apparel Coalition, Common Objective, Ethical Fashion Forum, Environmental Justice Foundation, Centre for Sustainable Fashion, the Clean Clothes Campaign, Global Labor Justice. Demographic and income data are from World Bank, United Nations Population Division, and US Census Bureau.

8. Figures in this section are based on Common Objective's, whose research group aggregates multiple independent reports and continuously updates its data (full disclosure: I am on the advisory panel); I did further research on top of these.

9. The bulk of US-China trade quotas expired in 2005. Currently, of course, this is controversially being reversed, but we won't go there.

10. Two measures were brought in after Rana Plaza: the Bangladesh Accord on Fire and Building Safety, signed by 150-plus mostly European corporations, and the Alliance for Bangladesh Worker Safety, with around twenty-six North American signatories. Both enforced, slowly, the most basic safety measures that should always have been standard practice. Walmart refused to sign.

11. The Garment Worker Diaries, a project led by Fashion Revolution in partnership with Microfinance Opportunities, has data collected and collated from yearlong field research including weekly interviews with an average of 182 Bangladeshi clothing factory workers. It found hardly any improvements in conditions, safety, or wages; https://workerdiaries.org.

12. "To know and not to know, to be conscious of complete truthfulness while telling carefully constructed lies, to hold simultaneously two opinions which cancelled out, knowing them to be contradictory and believing in both of them, to use logic against logic, to repudiate morality while laying claim to it . . . Even to understand the word 'doublethink' involved the use of doublethink." George Orwell, *1984* (Houghton Mifflin Harcourt, 2003), 120.

13. This was LVMH at a conference they'd called to explain their environmental agenda in September 2019—while dissing archrival Kering's dueling environmental agenda. Of course, if any of them meant to really change anything, they'd be working together, not fighting for market share based on stories they

tell the concerned consumer. The opinion is my own; the conference was reported here: Sarah Kent and Laure Guilbault, "LVMH Gets Competitive About Sustainability," *Business of Fashion*, September 26, 2019, https://www.businessoffashion.com/articles /professional/lvmh-gets-competitive-about-sustain ability.

14. "'It is important to note that offsetting isn't actually tackling the reduction of a company's footprint,' says Ilishio Lovejoy, project manager for policy and research at Fashion Revolution. 'It is making the overall global situation 'less bad' by 'doing good' somewhere else.'" Ellie Violet Bramley, "Is Carbon Neutrality the Silver Bullet Fashion Has Been Hoping For?," *Guardian*, November 12, 2019, https://www .theguardian.com/fashion/2019/nov/12/is-carbon -neutrality-the-silver-bullet-fashion-has-been-hoping -for.

15. Recycling 19,500 tons at 1,000 per twelve years; producing 500 tons per day. Based on numbers from the H&M take-back scheme, from the H&M Annual Report 2017 and reported by Lucy Siegle, "Am I a Fool to Expect More Than Corporate Green-washing?," *Guardian*, April 2, 2016, https://www .theguardian.com/commentisfree/2016/apr/03/ rana-plaza-campaign-handm-recycling.

16. "Garment Workers Are Waiting for an Answer—Will H&M Deliver on Its Promise to Pay a Living Wage in 2018?," *Clean Clothes Campaign*, November 25, 2017, https://cleanclothes.org/news//25/garment -workers-are-waiting-for-an-answer-2013-will-h-m -deliver-on-its-promise-to-pay-a-living-wage-in-2018.

17. "Kering Commits to Full Carbon Neutrality Across the Group," Kering, September 24, 2019, https:// www.kering.com/en/news/kering-commits-to-full- carbon-neutrality-across-the-group.

18. The environmental profit and loss report—EP&L—is a self-explanatory metric, and a great one, if a com-pany's growth is included in the calculations, which it isn't. Gucci's EP&L value was €289 million in 2018, up 80 percent from 2015, but these being the barnstorming Alessandro Michele growth years, that figure actually reflected an 8 percent year-on-year *decline* in environmental impact. This also goes for its parent company, Kering, which invented the EP&L. Sarah Kent, "Can Kering Grow and Be Sus-tainable at the Same Time?," *Business of Fashion*, June 6, 2019, https://www.businessoffashion.com/ articles/news-analysis/can-kering-grow-and-be- sustainable-at-the-same-time.

19. Hannah Moore, "Vivienne Westwood Gives Her Ad-vice on New Designers and Fashion Waste," *BBC Newsbeat*, June 13, 2017, http://www.bbc.co.uk/ newsbeat/article/40260489/vivienne-westwood -gives-her-advice-on-new-designers-and-fashion -waste.

20. Jeff Beer, "How Patagonia Grows Every Time It Amplifies Its Social Mission," *Fast Company*, February 21, 2018, https://www.fastcompany .com/40525452/how-patagonia-grows-every- time-it-amplifies-its-social-mission.

21. The other ten richest men in fashion, listed with their 2019 company revenues and personal net worth (in billions): Hermès, $7 (Nicolas Puech, $4.3); Nordstrom, $19.9 (Bruce Nordstrom, $1.2); Ar-mani, $2.3 (2018) (Giorgio Armani, $11.5); Dolce & Gabbana, $1.54 (Domenico Dolce, $1.7, Stefano Gabbana, $1.7); Prada, $3.1 (2018) (Prada family: Miuccia Prada and Patrizio, Alberto, and Marina Bertelli, $9.4); L Brands (Victoria's Secret, etc.), $13.2 (Leslie Wexner, $4.5); Under Armour, $5.2 (Kevin Plank, $1.8); Levi's, $5.7 (Mimi Haas, $1.2); Arcadia Group (TopShop, etc.), $2.3 (2018) (Philip Green, $2.6); Lululemon, $3.3 (Chip Wilson, $4.7). You will notice that three of these "men," Miuccia Prada, Marina Bertelli, and Mimi Haas, are in fact women. Data sources: GDP, International Monetary Fund, World Bank: Forbes Real-time Billionaires Rankings, Bloomberg Billionaires Index; individual companies' annual reports.

22. Jason Burke, "Muhammad Yunus Appeals to West to Help Bangladesh's Garment Industry," *Guardian*, May 12, 2013, https://www.theguardian.com/world/2013 /may/12/muhammad-yunus-bangladesh-appeal.

23. This is a lie. In spring 2017 I was verifiably (https:// www.instagram.com/p/BTJyIAxFHcr/) seduced by a dress in H&M. Hypocritical, much? I am no angel. Nobody can resist always and completely, and if they can, they might not be telling the whole truth. I have worn this dress twice. I apologize.

24. Luxury conglomerates LVMH (Vuitton, Marc Ja-cobs, Fendi, Dior) and Kering (Gucci, Saint Laurent, Balenciaga, McQueen) had record revenues of $55 billion combined in 2017, and LVMH topped those record earnings for the following two years, Source: company annual reports.

25. With due reverence to Michael Pollan, who did so much to popularize the good use of food with his 2009 book *Food Rules: An Eater's Manual* (Pen-guin), and the seven-word distillation of the sixty-four rules in that book: "Eat food. Not too much. Mostly plants." The parallels between food and clothing consumption have been pointed out before.

26. Allyson Payer, "The #1 Fabric to Avoid, According to Science," *Who What Wear*, October 10, 2019, https://www.whowhatwear.com/worst-fabrics-for -skin.

27. Compare Pollan, *Food Rules*, rule #37: "The whiter the bread, the sooner you'll be dead."

28. Pollan, *Food Rules*, rule #41: "Eat more like the French. Or the Japanese. Or the Italians. Or the Greeks."

29. Pollan, *Food Rules*, rule #44: "Pay more, eat less"; rule #45: ". . . Eat less." Vivienne Westwood: "Buy less, choose well, make it last."

30. *Parks and Recreation*, season 4, episode 4, "Pawnee Rangers," directed by Charles MacDougall, written by Alan Yang, aired October 13, 2011, on NBC; see https://www.youtube.com/watch?v=AUOh7TlZGO4.

31. Pollan, *Food Rules*, rule #49: "Eat slowly"; and rule #48: "Consult your gut."

Chapter Three: **when**

1. The research of Ralf Kittler, Manfred Kayser, and Mark Stoneking, "Molecular Evolution of *Pediculus humanus* and the Origin of Clothing," *Current Biology* 13, no. 16 (August 19, 2003): 1414–17, was superceded by that of Melissa A. Toups, Andrew Kitchen, Jessica E. Light, and David L. Reed, "Origin of Clothing Lice Indicates Early Clothing Use by Anatomically Modern Humans in Africa," *Molecular Biology and Evolution* 28, no. 1 (January 2011): 29–32, https://doi.org/10.1093/molbev/msq234. The "new" dates from Toups's research put the emergence of clothing lice between 83,000 and 170,000 years ago, so clothes might in fact be nearer to two hundred millennia old.

2. Same with its raw material, as archaeologist and linguist Elizabeth Wayland Barber points out in her magnificent 1994 book, *Women's Work: The First 20,000 Years* (Norton, 1994), nobody ever recorded the history of textile, it being vanishingly perishable and done by women.

3. Jinyu Liu, *Collegia Centonariorum: The Guilds of Textile Dealers in the Roman West* (Brill, 2009), 72.

4. John G. Gager, ed., *Curse Tablets and Binding Spells from the Ancient World* (Oxford University Press, 1999).

5. Jinyu Liu is the primary historian of these *centonarii*; these facts are from her book cited above, *Collegia Centonariorum*, 72–73, 90. She credits Dr. O. M. van Nijf with having corrected the mistranslation in 1997.

6. "World's Oldest Needle," *Siberian Times*, August 23, 2016, https://siberiantimes.com/science/casestudy/news/n0711-worlds-oldest-needle-found-in-siberian-cave-that-stitches-together-human-history. How recently

it was discovered! Denisovans are an extinct subspecies of us that coexisted with Neanderthals. For an excellent sewing needle history see Mary C. Beaudry, *Findings: The Material Culture of Needlework and Sewing* (Yale University Press, 2007), 44–85.

7. Eliso Kvavadze et al., "30,000-Year-Old Wild Flax Fibers," *Science* 325, no. 5946 (September 11, 2009): 1359.

8. Sheila Landi and Rosalind M. Hall, "The Discovery and Conservation of an Ancient Egyptian Linen Tunic," *Studies in Conservation* 24, no. 4 (November 1979): 141–52. Date reviewed in Alice Stevenson and Michael W. Dee, "Confirmation of the World's Oldest Woven Garment: The Tarkhan Dress," *Antiquity* 90, no. 349 (February 2016).

9. I wish I could have got my hands on these textiles to analyze the techniques, but all these fantastic details are courtesy of Gillian Vogelsang-Eastwood, "Textiles," in *Ancient Egyptian Materials and Technology*, eds. Paul T. Nicholson and Ian Shaw (Cambridge University Press, 2000), 268–98. The detail about Pharaonic eschewing of mended clothes is in her *Tutankhamun's Wardrobe* (Barjesteh van Waalwijk van Doorn, 1999).

10. The remains of 111 prehistoric Alpine pile dwellings are a UNESCO World Heritage Site: http://whc.unesco.org/en/list/1363/.

11. Paul Einzig, *Primitive Money in Its Ethnological, Historical, and Economic Aspects* (Eyre and Spottiswoode, 1948), 253–58.

12. Wayland Barber, *Women's Work*, 200.

13. Elizabeth Coatsworth and Gale Owen-Crocker, *Clothing the Past: Surviving Garments from Early Medieval to Early Modern Western Europe* (Brill, 2018), 436 (see note 16).

14. It's the famous story of a teenager and a cup of tea. Empress (or goddess) Hsi Ling Shi (or Lei Zu), wife (or concubine) of Huang Ti (or the Yellow Emperor), sitting under a wild mulberry bush, had a cocoon fall into her hot drink, and unravel into a silk filament. She then invented weaving.

15. Though there is evidence of Bronze Age silk woven from wild filament-producing *Lepidoptera* in at least some of Europe. See E. Papagiotakopulu et al., "A *Lepidopterous* Cocoon from Thera and Evidence for Silk in the Aegean Bronze Age," *Antiquity* 71 (1997): 420–29.

16. I'm especially indebted to Elizabeth Coatsworth and Gale Owen-Crocker, whose magnificent new study, *Clothing the Past: Surviving Garments from Early Medieval to Early Modern Western Europe*, (Brill, 2018),

featuring one hundred extant medieval garments, includes a wealth of parenthetical information on mending.

17. Details of the underpants, their mends, construction, composition, and dating are from their discoverer, Beatrix Nutz, especially two publications, with Harald Stadler, *Gebrauchsgegenstand und Symbol. Die Unterhose (Bruoch) aus der Gewölbezwickelfüllung von Schloss Lengberg, Osttirol, in Neue alte Sachlichkeit,* ed. Jan Keupp (Ostfildern, 2015), 221–50, and, for medieval textile recycling practices, *"Ich brauch Hadern zu meiner Muel" Von Altschneidern, Lumpensammlern und Papiermachern—Wiederverwendung und Wiederverwertung von Textilien,* 2014. For the latter, also see Maren Clegg Hyer, "Reduce, Reuse, Recycle: Imagined and Reimagined Textiles in Anglo-Saxon England," in *Medieval Clothing and Textiles 8,* ed. Robin Netherton and Gale Owen-Crocker (Boydell & Brewer, 2012), 49–62.

18. Anyone with even a passing interest in the history of decorative stitchwork must read Rozsika Parker's *The Subversive Stitch: Embroidery and the Making of the Feminine* (The Women's Press Ltd., 1984). This quote is from the foreword, but I also draw on Chapter Three, "Fertility, Chastity, and Power," which has much rich detail about medieval embroidery practices.

19. Written into canonical law by the Benedictine monk Gratian in his 1140 *Decretum.*

20. Coatsworth and Owen-Crocker, *Clothing the Past,* 171.

21. For a comprehensive, fascinating discussion of medieval slash fashion and its implications, see Andrea Denny-Brown, "Rips and Slits: The Torn Garment and the Medieval Self," in *Clothing Culture, 1350–1650,* ed. Catherine Richardson (Routledge, 2017).

22. From the Old French *taill, taille,* "cut" or "cutting"— the first mention of tailor as clothes maker is not until 1599. Etymological data are from the University of Manchester's "The Lexis of Cloth and Clothing in Britain c. 700–1450: Origins, Identification, Contexts and Change," accessible at http://lexisproject .arts.manchester.ac.uk.

23. "Clo'"—a charming diminutive for clothes: James Grant, *Lights and Shadows of London Life,* vol. 1 (1842), 128.

24. Luca Molà, *The Silk Industry of Renaissance Venice* (Johns Hopkins University Press, 2000), 96; Liu, *Collegia Centonariorum,* 71; Carole Collier Frick, "The Florentine 'Rigattieri': Second Hand Clothing Dealers and the Circulation of Goods in the Renaissance," in *Old Clothes New Looks: Second Hand Fashion,* eds. Alexandra Palmer and Hazel Clark (Berg Publishers, 2005).

25. "Second-hand clothes were often re-cut and sewn by the local tailor," Françoise Piponnier and Perrine Mane, *Dress in the Middle Ages,* trans. Caroline Beamish (Yale University Press, 1998), 28. Details of medieval recycling in Nutz, *"Ich brauch,"* 2014, 26–32, and Hyer, "Reduce, Reuse, Recycle," 50, among others.

26. From Anglo-Saxon monk Eadmer of Canterbury's "Miracles of St. Dunstan," recounted in Hyer, "Reduce, Reuse, Recycle," 60.

27. Both these memoirs—Joseph Barker's *The History and Confessions of a Man as Put Forth by Himself* and *The Life and Remarkable Adventures of Israel R. Potter*—are cited by Tim Hitchcock in his excellent 2005 book, *Down and Out in Eighteenth-Century London* (Bloomsbury Academic), 102–3.

28. Santina Levey, writing Pamela Clabburn's obituary, in *Costume* 45, no. 1 (2011): 147–48.

29. This section draws on many sources, including Pamela Clabburn, *Samplers* (Shire Publications, 1977); Donald King, *Samplers* (Victoria and Albert Museum, 1960); Susan Burrows Swan, *Plain & Fancy* (Henry Holt and Company, 1977); Mrs. Archibald Christie, *Samplers and Stitches* (1921); Martha Genung Stearns, *Homespun and Blue* (Scribner, 1963), and Parker, *The Subversive Stitch.*

30. Marla R. Miller, *The Needle's Eye: Women and Work in the Age of Revolution,* (University of Massachusetts Press, 2006), 63.

31. Wonderful how the most notorious poet of all time plays a role in the stocking story, mere days before his outrageous worldwide fame struck. He delivered this barnstorming maiden speech in the House of Lords on February 27, 1812, https://api.parliament .uk/historic-hansard/lords/1812/feb/27/frame-work -bill; the first two cantos of "Childe Harold's Pilgrimage" were published on March 10, 1812.

32. "A Practical Side of It," *New York Tribune,* December 24, 1887, 4. This and hundreds more sources, some cited here, fed my MA thesis, "Evil in the Wardrobe: Stocking Darns and the Gilded Age Woman in New York." Yes, nineteenth-century stocking darning is a specialist subject of mine.

33. "Homely Topics—Saturday's Mending," April 1856, and "Everyday Economies," October 1856.

34. "Will It Pay?," *Harper's Bazar* 4, no. 22 (June 3, 1871): 343.

35. Extracts from *Godey's,* June 1, 1860, and *Michigan Farmer,* September 15, 1885, but many more exist.

36. "100,000,000 Needles a Month," *Scientific American*, 1871, 336.

37. Among dozens of accounts of such activities: Mary Graham, *The Four Girls' Saturday Morning Mending Club*, February 19, 1901; Edith Lawrence, "What Girls Are Doing," *Harper's Bazar* 31, no. 42 (October 15, 1898); "An Independent Girl," *Evening World*, May 15, 1894; "A Curious Sisterhood," *Evening World*, January 11, 1893; "Men, Women and Things," *Woman's Voice*, June 1, 1895; "Some Lenten Fun," *Woman's Voice*, April 10, 1892.

38. "Noblesse Oblige," *Vogue*, July 15, 1915, 78.

39. "Thousands Needed to Do War Mending," *New York Times*, November 21, 1918, 5.

40. Lauren Alex O' Hagan, "Book Inscriptions Reveal the Forgotten Stories of Female War Heroes," *Conversation*, November 8, 2017; "Toupie Lowther in the Well of Loneliness," Story 8069, *Lives of the First World War*, Imperial War Museum, London. Coat details: Norfolk Museum Service.

41. "The Odd Occupations Some Folks Follow in New York," *New York Times*, October 5, 1913, 7.

42. Many details were confirmed by or gleaned from the London Imperial War Museum's 2015 exhibition and its accompanying book, by Julie Summers (Profile Books, 2016), both called *Fashion on the Ration*.

43. "Women and the New Deal," Living New Deal, https://livingnewdeal.org/what-was-the-new-deal/new-deal-inclusion/women-and-the-new-deal/.

44. Donald S. Howard, *The WPA and Federal Relief Policy* (New York: Russel Sage Foundation, 1943), 134, 281.

45. "Salvage Fashion Fair Shows How to Make Wearable Clothes from Scraps," *Life* 12, no. 26 (June 29, 1942): 94–97.

46. "Patches Are Popular," *Life* 12, no. 15 (April 13, 1942): 106–11.

47. "Sunday Clothes," *Life* 20, no. 15 (April 15, 1946): 77–86.

48. Marilyn Bender, "Convention, Lack of It Meeting in Trend," *New York Times*, March 28, 1971, 2-F.

49. Carol Cooper Garey, "The Fabrics: Patchwork," *Women's Wear Daily*, January 29, 1969, 58. Cherie Hart-Green, "The Inner Fashions: A Quilting Be-In," *Women's Wear Daily*, June 5, 1969, 25; Angela Taylor, "Dressmaking for Those Who Are All Thumbs," *New York Times*, March 12, 1971, 47. "The Retail Scene," *Women's Wear Daily*, September 8, 1970, 48. Herbert Koshetz, "Embroidery Invades Even the Casual Fashions," *New York Times*, March 7, 1971, 225.

Chapter Four: **who**

1. Long story: Siegfried Sekules took his own life in 1938. Most—though not all—of the Engl siblings, spouses, and offspring escaped Vienna in various ways. My grandmother Rosa cofounded the London hat business with her brother. She died in 1966.

2. It wasn't hidden, just nobody said. I learned my father and aunt had escaped on the Kindertransport and about those who didn't escape, like the sixth child, Lili, who perished in Auschwitz; her husband, Hannes, in Theresienstadt. How had they got all these furs and linens out? Oskar, the only boy of the six, had reached London early with luggage, before the Anschluss; he paved the way for the others and established the hat business. PS: I know my being Jewish doesn't count because it's not the maternal line, but I'm counting it. PPS: I am antifur, but vintage fur is different—the poor creatures are long, long dead and there's nothing that will bring them back, so they ought to be honored, loved, and worn.

3. The final of the three incarnations of Barbara Hulanicki's beyond-influential store, the legendary Big Biba on Kensington High Street, became my other clothes playground and church, and I would love to go on and on about it, but it really has nothing to do with mending. If you've heard of it, you'll get the continuing obsession. I collect early Biba now.

4. Her mother, my grandmother, secret Hitler hater (it was very dangerous), committed suicide when her husband ran off with another woman and her son (drafted: Kriegsmarine U-boat engineer) was killed. It's another long story.

5. The Westway was completed in 1970, a new motorway section with a flyover bisecting Portobello Road under which old-clothes stalls clustered. Notting Hill was already seriously insalubrious (probably how Hugh Grant could afford that nice blue house), but for the rest of the decade, the Westway made it worse.

6. Father died, I went to Manchester University at height of Madchester (first version), joined band, formed other band, supported Joy Division, gigged, recorded two John Peel sessions (proudest moment) and some vinyl, moved back to London, band broke up.

7. John Galliano's "Pannier" coat from one of his first commercial collections, 1987, in Harrods' Young Designer department—I was copy editor at Condé Nast's *Harrods Magazine* at the time. At 80 percent off on sale, plus 17 percent employee discount, it still cost my entire month's salary.

8. The magazine accompanied *The Clothes Show*, a popular weekly program on the BBC presented at the time by the coeditor of *i-D*, the fabulous Caryn Franklin. The column was my side hustle: I was deputy editor of a travel magazine at the same publisher.

9. "You're the most nonlinear person I've ever met" was my favorite ever compliment—spoken by someone with the nonlinear career of moving to Africa to save elephants, found educational programs, and run safaris. Women's boxing is normal now but didn't exist then: I was one of five women at Gleason's Gym when I started; twenty years after I fought pro, there was women's boxing in the London Olympics. Result! I wrote a book about it: *The Boxer's Heart*. Before *C+T* I was ten years as travel editor of *Food & Wine*, then I was editor in chief of *Gourmet*! That is, *Gourmet LIVE*, the great magazine's sad afterlife as an app. Also, I wrote freelance a lot.

10. The name riffs on Tom of Finland, alias Touko Valio Laaksonen, the late twentieth-century artist whose distinctive work defined a lastingly influential homoerotic, hypermasculine subculture.

11. . . . and "that breaking is generative and productive . . ." Steven J. Jackson, "Rethinking Repair," in *Media Technologies: Essays on Communication, Materiality, and Society*, eds. Tarleton Gillespie et al. (MIT Press, 2014), 221–60. It's well worth reading the whole essay by Jackson, an associate professor in the Department of Information Science at Cornell University. He's writing primarily about technology and its repair, but it applies to everything we (over)produce.

12. In Tom's words, "Many artists use mending in their practice and started this before me. Celia Pym comes to mind straightaway for obvious reasons, but for instance [Italian Modernist artist] Enzo Mari repairs furniture in a very visible way." Celia Pym is a British artist who does extensive contrasting darns. She declined to be featured here, saying she was working on new projects and that her mending work had been widely shared already.

13. Anne worked at the Patagonia Reno center for three years, one of forty-five full-time mender-repairers, who together complete around forty thousand repairs annually. Unsurprisingly, it's the biggest clothes repair facility in North America.

14. Thomas Fuller, "Life on the Dirtiest Block in San Francisco," *New York Times*, October 8, 2018, https://www.nytimes.com//08/us/san-francisco-dirtiest-street-london-breed.html.

15. "The new Levi's® Tailor Shop will be the only one to feature Japanese-inspired techniques such as shibori dyeing and sashiko embroidery," claimed the company, hiring Brooklyn Beckham for the launch. "Brooklyn Beckham Launches New Levi's® Tailor Shop," *Off the Cuff*, June 6, 2018, https://www.levi.com/US/en_US/blog/article/brooklyn-beckham-launches-new-levis-tailor-shop/.

16. Glenn Adamson, *Fewer, Better Things: The Hidden Wisdom of Objects* (Bloomsbury, 2018), 209. This is a wonderful, thought-provoking, scholarly, yet personal and entertaining book about our relationship with the material world.

17. A little later than but not dissimilar to the Arts and Crafts movement in England, the folk craft movement mingei was founded and named by philosopher Soetsu Yanagi in 1925 to elevate everyday objects made in quantity by ordinary people to the status of artworks.

18. "By donating fabric to the Buddhist clergy, the lay community earned religious merit, and by stitching the fabric into a patchwork robe, the monks concentrated their attention on the creation of a devotional work of art, every stitch part of an act of meditation on the teachings of the Buddha." From Meher McArthur, "*Kesa*: Robes of Patched Perfection," *The Buddhist Door*, July 18, 2018, https://www.buddhistdoor.net/features/kesa-robes-of-patched-perfection.

19. The quote is from the label accompanying this kantha quilt in the October 2018 to June 2019 exhibition at RISD Museum called *Repair and Design Futures*. I do believe this was my favorite ever exhibition and I am grateful to chief curator Kate Irving, for not just staging it (it took a decade), but also welcoming me generously and warmly. Running visible mending workshops at the museum during the exhibition's run was a major 2019 highlight.

20. Alternate spellings abound, the most common being *pojagi* and *chogakbo*, or *chogak/jogak bo*.

21. The tokens aren't on display at the museum that now exists in the Foundling Hospital at Coram's Fields, but the 2010 exhibition and especially the accompanying book, *Threads of Feeling: The London Foundling Hospital's Textile Tokens, 1740–1770*, from which the data and photos are taken, tell the story beautifully. The author, John Styles, points out this collection of five thousand scraps also represents a treasure trove of rare information on eighteenth-century ordinary dress—on which he is one of the few experts, and probably the leading authority.

22. Between 1741 and 1760, 152 children were reclaimed out of the 16,282 left at the Foundling Hospital. Styles, *Threads of Feeling* 13.

23. Thank you to Ruth Battersby Tooke, textile curator at the Norfolk Museum Service, which owns the embroideries. Ruth, thanks to her own love for Lorina, has researched these pieces deeply, and transcribed them, including the quote here. And thanks, Ruth, for letting me meet them!

Chapter Five: **where**

1. Mercerization is the process of treating cotton with alkali under tension, increasing its strength, dye absorbtion, and luster. Patented by and named after English calico printer John Mercer in 1850.

2. Employing the Rolling Stones spelling.

3. The first patent for this curious clamp was granted in 1853 to Charles Waterman of Meridan, Connecticut, who registered a "feathered bird upon the wing, bearing a burden upon its back"—this burden being an emery ball. The pincushion lies between the tabletop and the bird's beak, which holds the fabric. Charming.

4. The set point of stuff theory is very like the set point theory of body weight, where your metabolism adjusts to maintain the same weight no matter what you eat—only it's stuff instead. Somehow you will regain the comfortable level of possessions, no matter what you get rid of. I made it up.

5. As in Marie Kondo, the Japanese *Life-Changing Magic*, "does it spark joy," decluttering guru.

6. Leaving aside underpinnings, for now. A different method applies.

7. This can be a challenge, but if you're not blessed with basement or garage, can you overflow into your parents' place? Could you spring for a small storage unit? Find a high-up shelf, a chest, a large suitcase, underbed drawers? Or even consider investing in a new wave, full-service storage space (they bring anything back on demand) from the likes of MakeSpace or Clutter.

8. One good newspaper report on the beginnings of this practice is Kimiko de Freytas-Tamura, "For Dignity and Development, East Africa Curbs Used Clothes Imports," *New York Times*, October 12, 2017.

Chapter Six: **how**

1. Thank you, Avery Hays, no longer sixth grade! You slightly changed my life.

2. A sashiko thimble resembles a ring worn at the base of the middle finger of the dominant hand, often with a dimpled disk below it over the palm. The hand is held in a clawlike position with the needle's eye pressing against the disk. This definitely takes practice.

3. The official method is the reverse of this, bringing the needle up through the previous stitch rather than downward. This method is easier.

4. For the related slip stitch, often used for hemming, you take tiny catch stitches between sliding the needle along inside the fold. It gives maximum invisibility so belongs in the endnotes.

5. *Diaper* pertains not to baby knickers but derives from the Greek *diaspron*, Latin *diasper*, "I separate," describing the separation of the woven pattern from the ground. They're complex designs woven by needle, of the sort found in darning samplers like the one on pages 34–37, and were used for darning linens and, as stated, rarely for practical mends, but just for show. So were the similar, even more complex damask darns that replicate any number of weave structures from damask and brocade to herringbones and twills.

6. If shopping for new clothes, a vegan dresser might seek ahimsa or peace silk, which allows the moth to hatch naturally before harvesting. Also, the rare and costly tussah—wild silk. Experiments with spider silk, including splicing arachnid with goat to produce silk-spiked milk, have yet to be perfected.

7. "Nylon." *Fortune* 22, no. 1 (July 1940): 56.

8. Unreliable statistic that I made up. This is an experiment in misinformation. Because nobody's done this math, I wonder if the figure I just invented will get quoted and thereby eventually become true?

9. No, really, *perma-stink* was coined by human ecology professor Rachel McQueen et al., "Odor Intensity in Apparel Fabrics and the Link with Bacterial Populations," *Textile Research Journal 77, no. 7* (2007): 449–56.

10. The no wash and the dry (or raw) denim movements are ecologically motivated but are also having the effect of bringing more natural fibers and finishes to market. They sell at a high price point for the most part, but this is beginning to trickle down—though such clothes can't and shouldn't be sold too cheap; they're investments. Also, PS, infusing with peppermint oil or whatever does nothing long term to decrease the need for washing: all natural, untreated fibers are resistant to microbes.

11. Ulterior motive: as a lifelong devotee of pure cotton sweats, I prefer its wicking, slightly baggy, nonstinking qualities, and wish it would catch on.

12. I could go on and on about detergents, which are often foul in so many ways. For an up-to-date and reliable breakdown of their relative merits, see the rated reviews by the 501(c)(3) nonprofit Environmental Working Group, https://www.ewg.org/guides/categories/9-Laundry/. You may find your go-to wash solution has earned a solid "F" grade.

13. Extra credit: invest in a horizontal drying rack or make one out of window screen gauze.

14. A steamer is a wise investment—they're effective, gentle, and far more fun than ironing.

15. Hates sunlight, but enjoys some light frequencies, e.g., TV, which may attract a clothes moth flutterby.

16. Ask a museum conservator and -20°C is the absolute law, but a handy chart in "Controlling Insect Pests with Low Temperature" (Canadian Conservation Institute Note , 1997, updated 2008) by Tom Strang, the guru of modern antipest conservation science, clearly shows the continuum is much more lax. Even 20°F (-6°C) will kill infestations if you freeze for long enough, say, seventy days. As a reference point, the Food and Drug Administration advises setting your freezer at 0°F (-18°C), but the rule is: when in doubt, freeze longer. Conversely, if you have access to a commercial freezer, death can be inflicted in under a week.

17. It's okay, low density polyethylene, as in Ziploc bags, only starts to soften at 195°F—still, oven bags are actually designed for high-heat roasting. Cooking parchment works fine, too. If you're nifty with the culinary origami and can rustle up *tricot en papillote,* that is more sustainable.

18. Solar bagging is surprisingly recent tech. It was developed by Tom Strang—see note 16—who first presented it at the Third Biodeterioration of Cultural Property conference in Bangkok, 1995. See Newsletter #23 of the Western Association for Art Conservation, May 2001, for Bonnie Baskin's great account of a comprehensive bagging at Luang Prabang Museum, Laos: "Solar Bagging: Putting Sunlight to Work to Eliminate Insect Infestations in Mere Hours."

19. In the early days of the internet, software or word processing was quite fancy if it was WYSIWYG, pronounced "whizzy wig," acronym for "what you see is what you get"—because then the formatting didn't change from composing a document to the final printout. I remember this not fondly.

20. I believe this is more or less what Marie Kondo prescribed, but she didn't invent it. Much of her advice was not useful. For example to "discard things that are out of date, such as clothes that are no longer in fashion," or to purge clothes as your first category because "they carry the least emotional attachment." I mean! Most worryingly, she never mentions how and where to discard your nonjoyful stuff.

21. The adoption of what we unquestioningly take as real time is a fascinating story, and sobering thought exercise. The existence of countless local times set by continents, countries, states, towns, even neighborhoods, wasn't such a problem until telegraphy and railways and steamships and the metastasizing of the import-export trade—in other words, when time became money, at least for the few. North American railways started it, in a way. Seventy-five different local times were causing timetable havoc, leading American (or Scottish-Canadian) railway engineer Sandford Fleming to publish "Time-Reckoning and the Selection of a Prime Meridian to Be Common to All Nations" in 1879. This paved the way for the International Meridian Conference of 1884 in Washington, DC, and the eventual adoption of Greenwich as the prime meridian. A good, concise version of the history is available at www.thegreenwichmeridian.org.

Chapter Seven: **which**

1. It does work, and I had nothing special around the house, just an old sheet and a can of spray glue. I glued the sheet to a piece of regular printer paper; completely smoothing out all wrinkles; trimmed it precisely (with a rotary blade, though scissors would have done); ensured no fraying edges; set my inkjet printer to normal; inserted paper, fabric side up; and used black ink only. After printing, I peeled off the paper and set the print with a hot iron, a bath in vinegar solution, and another pressing. That one is a bit faded seven years on, but still alive. Still, do invest in the printable fabric; at about one dollar a sheet, it is very much easier and less fadey.

2. Please don't hate. I know this stuff is life itself for real dressmakers.

Postscript: **whether**

1. I contributed a mending tutorial to *The Conscious Closet,* and Elizabeth and I are friends—I did tell you this is not even slightly objective.

2. Kate Raworth, *Doughnut Economics: Seven Ways to Think Like a 21st Century Economist* (Chelsea Green Publishing, 2017), 9. The way Raworth makes the doughnut shape stand for the entire future of economic thought is beyond the scope of this chapter, but it's probably caught on enough by now that you know all about it. In brief, the inside of the doughnut's hole represents "a social foundation of well-being that no one should fall below," while outside the doughnut lies "an ecological ceiling of planetary pressure that we should not go beyond." The cake part is where we need to concentrate our economic efforts: "Between the two lies a safe and just place for all."

credits

Composite image by Kate Sekules: Stockings, 1875–1905 Metropolitan Museum of Art Costume Institute, Museum of Fine Arts, Boston, Arthur Warren Rayner Collection; Victoria & Albert Museum (title page, pp. 42–43). Courtesy of Cathy Crawford: The Opposite of Hate Is Mending sweater (p. 4); Meiji era Boro fragment (p. 80); vintage men's mending kit (p. 90); microscopic sewing kits, used mending silks kit (p. 92); traveling kits, basket kit (p. 93); vintage needle books (p. 97); antique needle packets (p. 99); Threads (pp. 102–3); Threadscape (pp. 104–5); darning and mending aids: holders, defunct mending aids (p. 109); underpatch gray linen sweater (p. 163), eye eyelet (p. 165); Cheatos wool & lace, Cheatos 40s jacket (p. 176); Heart on Sleeve (p. 177); The Opposite of Hate (p. 178); Underarm underground, Oops America (p. 179); Embellishment Couching Anglomania, Faith tee (p. 180); The Opposite of Hate (p. 181); Fine darns brown cardi, More is more sweater, Darns on pink (p. 184); Multidarn cardi (p. 186); Porthole sweater, CDG scarf, Green CDG jumper (p. 189); The first Greasytee, Greasytee two winged tees (p. 190); Frankenstein sheepskin coat (p. 191); Sprinkles pinstripe jacket (p. 194); Cardiganized (p. 203); Thread palettes/fridge magnet needles (p. 212). Courtesy of Fashion Revolution: "I made your clothes" (pp. 6–7). Courtesy of Kheel Center, Cornell University: 1911 Triangle Shirtwaist Fire editorial cartoon (p. 11). Courtesy of Sajid Hossain/Reuters: Rana Plaza factory collapse aftermath (p. 12). Courtesy of Colourpicture Publishers, Inc. Darn It I Plum Forgot, ca. 1932, Asheville Postcard Co. (p. 18). Courtesy of Art Institute of Chicago/Gift of Mrs. Leigh B. Block: Woman Mending, 1885, Camille Pissarro, 1959 (p. 18). Courtesy of Five Colleges and Historic Deerfield Museum Consortium: Domestick Amusement. The Fair Seamstress, James Watson, ca. 1764 (p. 18). Courtesy of Indianapolis Museum of Art Gift of Mrs. Joseph E. Cain: A Girl Sewing, Nicolaes Maes, ca. 1650 (p. 18). Courtesy of Knute O. Munson: Mending the Jeans, ca. 1955 (pp. 18, 120). Courtesy of La Vie Parisienne: De Fil en Auguille, Arman Vallee, 1921 (p. 18). Courtesy of Metropolitan Museum of Art: Augusta Sewing Before a Window Mary Cassatt, 1905 (p. 18); Tutankhamun's mended kerchief (detail), Gift of Theodore M. Davis, 1909 (p. 22); Beggar Man and Beggar Woman Conversing, Rembrandt, 1630 (p. 32). Meiji era shippô-tsunagi sashiko jacket, Detail (p. 81). Courtesy of Rijksmuseu Amsterdam: Interieur Met Een Slapende Man en Een Vrouw Die Sokken Stopt, Wybrand Hendriks, ca. 1825 (p. 18). Courtesy of Rothschild Collections, Waddeston Manor, National Trust: Madonna Sewing with Saint Catherine of Siena and the Christ Child, Master o Osma (attrib.), ca. 1520 (p. 18). Courtesy of Nationalmuseet i København: The Egtved Girls costume (p. 21). Courtesy of South Tyrol Museum of Archaeology: Ötzi's back, reconstruction. Flip Flop Collective (p. 21). Copyright © Beatrix Nutz: The Lengburg Underpants, Beatrix Nutz; The Lengburg Bra, Beatrix Nutz (p. 25). Courtesy of Metropolitan Museum of Art, Fletcher Fund: Chichester-Constable Chasuble, detail (p. 26). Courtesy of Abegg-Stiftung, Riggisberg, Switzerland: Cowl of St. Francis of Assisi (p. 27). Courtesy of Info Bretagne: Pourpoint of Charles de Blois, interior (p. 29). Courtesy of Musée de Tissus, Lyon: The Pourpoint of Charles de Blois, The Pourpoint of Charles VI of France, Detail (p. 29). Courtesy of Musée des Beaux-Arts, Chartes: The Pourpoint of Charles VI of France (p. 29). Courtesy of Bibliothèque nationale de France: Observations sur la nature et les propriétés de divers produits alimentaires... Albucasis. NAL 1673; Poésies: Jugement du roi de Bohème, Remède de Fortune, folio 40v, Guillaume de Machaut (p. 30). Courtesy of The Royal Collection Trust: Rag Fair, Thomas Rowlandson, ca. 1799 (p. 31). Courtesy of Morphew Vintage: French work pant (p. 33). Courtesy of Norfolk Museums Service: Eighteenth-century work trousers, Gressenhall Farm and Workhouse (p. 33). Courtesy of Cooper Hewitt: Bequest of Gertrude M. Oppenheimer: Sampler, Netherlands, 1769, silk embroidery on cotton foundation, Rindeltje Brougers (p. 34); Bequest of Mrs. Henry E. Coe: Sampler,

American 1831; cotton and silk embroidery on cotton foundation; Margaret Barnholt (p. 36); Sampler, American 1831, silk embroidery on linen foundation, Ellen Caulfield (p. 37). Public domain: Song of the Shirt, John T. Peele, 1849 (p. 38); Tide advert, 1954 (p. 147). Courtesy of Harper's Weekly: "Cheap Clothing: The Slaves of the Sweaters," W. A. Rogers, April 26, 1890 (p. 39). Courtesy of Schlesinger Library on the History of Women in America, Radcliffe Institute: Annie Ware Winsor Allen darning a stocking, 1884 (p. 40). Courtesy of Vogue archive: "Noblesse Oblige" The Mind Your Mending Shop, 46, 2, Jul 15, 1915, 78 (p. 40). Courtesy of William A. Webster: Waverly School for the Feeble-Minded: Darning Class, 1902, Harvard Art Museums/Fogg Museum (p. 41). Courtesy of Mel Sweetnam: Mamie Sweetnam and siblings, ca. 1942 (p. 46). Courtesy of British Board of Trade: Deft Darns: Mrs Sew-and-Sew (p. 47). Courtesy of Life: "Patches are Popular," 12, no. 15, April 13, 1942 (p. 48). Courtesy of Associated Press: Hippies decorate each other with flowers on August 26, 1967 at Woburn Abbey, stately home of the Duke of Bedford at Woburn, England (p. 48). Courtesy of American Crafts Council Library and Archives: "Levi's Denim Art Contest Catalogue of Winners." Museum of Contemporary Crafts, 1974, Anne Meshe; "Levi's Denim Art Contest Catalogue of Winners." Museum of Contemporary Crafts, 1974, Bill Shire; "Levi's Denim Art Contest Catalogue of Winners." Museum of Contemporary Crafts, 1974, Wende Stitt; "Levi's Denim Art Contest Catalogue of Winners." Museum of Contemporary Crafts, 1974, Peggy Moulton (p. 50). Courtesy of Sunset Hobby & Craft Books: "Clothing Decoration" 1973 (p. 51). Courtesy of Eva Sekules: Siegfried Engl Fabrik (p. 54). Courtesy of Hazel Inskip: Marianne Sekules (p. 54). Courtesy of Siegfried Engle: Rosa Sekules (p. 54). Courtesy of Penguin: Friends of the Earth Cookbook, Penguin, 1980, Veronica Sekules, illustrations Donna Mueir; Ibid 18–19 (p. 55). Courtesy of Historic England Archive: Rag and Bone man's cart, St Alban's Grove, W8, John Gay, 1965 (p. 56). Courtesy of Victoria and Albert Museum: Comme des Garçons Jumper, 1982 (p. 58). Courtesy of A Magazine curated by Maison Martin Margiela November 2004: Curated by Maison Martin Margiela, June 2004 (p. 59). Courtesy of Redwood Publishing: Clothes Show magazine, "The Dilemma of Dressing Green" (p. 60); Clothes Show magazine, "Resolutions for 1993"; Clothes Show magazine, "Kate Sekules Shops with the Superrich"; Clothes Show cover April 1992 (p. 61). Courtesy of Louise Blouin Media: Culture+Travel magazine, May/June 2008, Balint Zsako (p. 61). Courtesy of Observer Sport Monthly: "Just Give Her a Ring," James Rexroad, 1999 (p. 61). Courtesy of Zoe Adlersberg: Refashioner v3.0 homepage, 2019 (p. 62). Courtesy of Anna Maltz: Tom of Holland Six Year Sweater (p. 64). Courtesy of Felicity Ford: Aleotoric Fair Isle Swatch 1, Tom van Deijnen, Felicity Ford (p. 64). Courtesy of Tom van Deijnen: Tom of Holland Amazing Jumper (p. 64). Courtesy of Bridget Harvey: MEND MORE Jumper (p. 65); Bridget Harvey portrait photographed by David Stelfox (p. 66); MEND MORE Jumper on London climate march photographed by David Stelfox (p. 67). Courtesy of Amy Twigger Holroyd: Reknit Sampler (p. 68); Reknit spectrum (p. 136). Courtesy of Jonathan Hamilton: Amy Twigger Holroyd (p. 68). Courtesy of Karen Nichol: Javelina embroidery; Woven darn (p. 69). Courtesy of Margrett Sweerts / growing Golden Joinery "collection" is visible at www.goldenjoinery.com: Sweerts and van Drimmelen at Droog Design photographed by Fan Liao; Saskia van Drimmelen and Margreet Sweerts photographed by Peer Johnson (p. 71). Courtesy of Nick McFadden: Ruth Katzenstein Souza mending (p. 72). Courtesy of Ruth Katzenstein Souza: Ruth Katzenstein Souza face mend (p. 72). Courtesy of John Souza: Ruth Katzenstein Souza Mending Circle (p. 73). Courtesy of Jessica Marquez: Jessica Marquez denim jacket, Jessica Marquez jeans and dogs, Jessica Marquez stripe patch (p. 74); Jessica Marquez mending (p. 75). Courtesy of Miriam Dym: Logos removed; Miriam Dye removing logos, Oakland Museum of California, photographed by Sean Olson (p. 76). Courtesy of Ymy Sfumato: Logo Removal Service (p. 76). Courtesy of Anne Graham: Anne Graham with sewing machines, Anne Graham in Patagonia truck (p. 77). Courtesy of Daniel Gorrell: Swaine, mending (p. 78). Courtesy of Darryl Bush: Swaine, mending (p. 78). Courtesy of Gil Riego Jr.: Michael Swaine, mendinglibrary (p. 78). Courtesy of Michael Swaine: The Roving Tailor Returns photographed by Patrick Kavanagh (p. 79). Courtesy of Coram: Foundling Hospital Token 1758 (p. 85); Foundling Hospital Token 1748, Foundling Hospital Token 1765 (p. 86). Courtesy of Prinzhorn Collection: Agnes Richter's Jacket (p. 87). Courtesy of Koichi Nishimura: Nui Project shirt, Keisuke Nomaguchi (p. 89). Courtesy of Naho Kubot: Sara Berman's Closet at Mmuseumm, NYC 2015 (p. 115). Courtesy of Olaf Leillinger: Clothes moth, tineola bisselliella (p. 149). Courtesy of Kerry Taylor Auctions: 1920s, 1930s, 1940s, 1950s (p. 154); 1960s, 1970s, 1980s (p. 155). Courtesy of Marc Jacobs, Inc.: 1990s (p. 155).

 penguin books

mend!

kate sekules

is a writer, clothes historian, mender and mending educator. A leading light in the visible mending movement, she has shown her work and taught the techniques and history of repair in universities, museums, and symposia, including New York University, Parsons, the Fashion Institute of Technology, the Textile Arts Center, RISD Museum, Columbia University Chicago, the Costume Society of America, the Textile Society of America, and the UK Association of Dress Historians. Her writing has appeared in publications such as *Vogue*, *Harper's Bazaar*, *The New Yorker*, *The Guardian*, *The New York Times*, and academic journals. She is a PhD candidate in material culture at the Bard Graduate Center, New York; holds a masters degree in Costume Studies from NYU, and runs the Menders Directory on her website visiblemending.com. She lives in Brooklyn with her husband and daughter.